THE 1980s AND BEYOND

THE CHANGING SCENE OF YOUTH AND COMMUNITY WORK

frank booton

alan dearling

Design by Alan Dearling and Frank Booton
Line Drawings by Alan Dearling
Layout by Dominic Mackintosh
Texts transcribed for publication by Paul Cousins
Typeset and Printed by Salvotype
Berrington Road, Sydenham Industrial Estate, Leamington Spa
Warwickshire CV31 1YA

ISBN 0 86155 018 8
January 1980   Price £2.95

Contents

Introduction

Given a club or classroom bubbling with kids, or perhaps a heavy social work case-load and a seemingly endless day, some workers might justifiably groan at the sight of yet another book. We make no particular claims for your attention to this one outside of the fact that its subject, the changing nature of services to young people in the community, is now somewhat overdue for examination.

For the first time, in 30 years youth and community work in this country has come to the end of a decade without an official report on its recent past, or a policy for its immediate future, being available to us. Few people involved in the work will fail to note the significance of that fact, and perhaps even fewer will not regret it. Some will regard it inevitably as a further, typical confirmation of the 'unwritten policy' of the 1970s, an haphazard, 'stop-go' affair in which increasing confusion in the field reflected the apparent basic indifference — outside of certain token gestures — of successive governments. Others, more cynically, will point to the history of Youth Service and ask if it was ever really any different. Whatever the view, it can safely be asserted that the absence of a formal statement of intention can only add to the doubt and pessimism presently widespread throughout the Service.

This collection of readings is not intended to fill that gap, but rather to emphasise it by reviewing certain developments which have occurred, and by making reference to the social trends to which they are a response. We are confident that in this manner the perpetual question surrounding the work will at least have been posed again — whether it is prudent any longer to leave the development of important elements of education and welfare provision on the fringe of social policy without the thought, coordination and accountability that are applicable elsewhere in the public services.

The original idea for the collection came from various sections of the field, some of whom pointed to the recent erosion of the concept of Youth and Community **Service,** that (arguably) it no longer exists as such at all, but currently takes the form of an increasing proliferation of **services.** The 'specialist' practitioners with formal responsibilities for young people in the community are now often located in several different departments of a single local authority. In addition, there are the 'traditional' voluntary organisations, now more complex in structure and varied in operation than ever before. Beyond these there has developed in the past few years yet another element, a

1

rapidly growing number of full-time youth work and/or community work/action projects, initially established under the various programmes of urban renewal and sometimes referred to as the 'alternative field'. One effect of this diversification has been to leave the practitioner and the student alike dismayed by the problem experienced in grasping the coherence of a structure which was always disparate, but, devoid of clear and consistent guidelines for national development during the last ten years, has further fragmented at an alarming rate. This is the consequence of localised, largely ad hoc and, to some extent, opportunistic initiatives. The rapid rate of sub-specialism to which these 'services' are currently subjected seems to deny the possibility of describing the present state of the **national** system of provision other than by a collection of individually written papers. In turn, this creates difficulties in the selection of priorities. Some readers will certainly not agree with us in what constitutes the significant developments of recent years, nor perhaps on the contemporary direction of the work in general. Agreement is even less likely on the social and political stance adopted by some of the contributors. Examples of good and bad modern practice abound in this collection, though it may be that the work described is somewhat removed from the conventional wisdom of the present time. Certainly some of the ideas here are hardly in accordance with those currently aired at professional conferences, lectured on in the training agencies or talked about in the area Youth and Community offices in certain parts of the country. We make no apologies for that.

In determining the format for the collection the subject areas suggested to us were adopted: 'Youth', 'Community' and 'School'. The margin of overlap and duplication between these has been the source of frustration to policy-makers and professionals alike since the 1950s. Within this separation of interests the approach that appeared appropriate was conceptual rather than prescriptive. Inevitably, certain modes of current practice had to be left out. In respect of community work our responsibilities were restricted to work with youth as a single — and admittedly confined — aspect of it. Youth work perhaps suffered in our selection in respect of certain recent projects such as those with black youth, the unemployed, the debates on sexism and political education, not least the interesting current trends within the voluntary organisations and emergent inner-city initiatives. To balance this, we feel that the inclusions on community work approaches to working with youth, youth social work and a case-study of a radical voluntary organisation, coupled with the thematic link of social change and social control, do give a fair indication of the direction in which youth and community work has drifted during the 1970s. Similarly, in terms of 'School', our concern has been with those aspects of secondary and further education in which the techniques of youth and community work are customarily applied, or specific 'problem' issues of modern schooling such as 'pastoral' developments in which they are likely to be. To some extent these omissions are, in part, compensated for by published material available elsewhere. Most regrettably, we could not include analyses of other topical 'open questions' such as the implications of 'professionalism' and what has been called the *problematic of youth leisure provision*. This catalogue of omissions could doubtless be extended: no such collection could now hope to be comprehensively relevant. We have tried to be representative within the general theme of **change**, and we feel that most people engaged in the work will find some aspects here to identify with.

Individual contributors were not given specific instructions, but were simply invited to submit papers in the area of their own acknowledged specialism. In view of this, and the fact that none read anyone else's material prior to the circulation of the finished manuscript, it is interesting to note the focus of criticism that the collection as a whole brings to bear on the present state of youth and community work. Moreover, whilst we hope that this is both responsible and constructive, we cannot claim that the overall tone is optimistic. The frustrations of the last few years are likely to remain for some time to come as the general situation of young people in society deteriorates, and work with them in many areas of the country loses its traditionally unique identity between the functions of education and social welfare, and is reduced to its lowest common denominator — mere diversionary recreation. This is perhaps the logical outcome of a paradox inherent in the 'Service'; that whilst youth and its relation to the community is a subject of ever increasing public discussion, the services for it remain the victim of ever diminishing governmental concern.

Frank Booton
Alan Dearling

Acknowledgements

This collection was put together in response to suggestions from colleagues in the field. The contributors would like to thank them, in particular those youth and community workers and officers who read and commented upon various sections of the manuscript. Our thanks also to the National Youth Bureau for permission to reproduce chapter two; to 'Hard Cheese', the journal of radical education, for chapters five and six, and to Schoolmaster Publications for chapter thirteen, which first appeared in 'Youth Review'. Our special thanks are due to Glynis Johnstone who typed the manuscripts, and Ric Rogers and Carla Schiannini for editorial assistance.

Frank Booton
Alan Dearling

Chapter 1

Policies and Priorities in Youth and Community Work: a Review of Two Decades

BERNARD DAVIES

Bernard Davies has been involved in youth work, both as practitioner and trainer, since the late 1950s. He writes regularly on youth and community work and youth policies for *New Society,* and is the author of a recent occasional paper published by the National Youth Bureau, *'Part-time Youth Work in an Industrial Community'.* He is currently Senior Lecturer in Applied Social Studies at the University of Warwick.

Introduction: Out of the Doldrums of the 50s

For many of us involved in the Youth Service when the Albemarle Report[1] was published its main problems seemed clear, and possible solutions not too complicated. It was weak, we felt, primarily because as the 'Cinderella Service' it was underfinanced and overstretched.

Even in 1960 this was, of course, an oversimplification. Some local authorities had built up a comprehensive Service, though even in these areas tightly tied strings were often attached to what was done. The riches of Glamorgan and Essex, for example, were considerable, but to share in them you had to be prepared to operate 'evening institute style' in school buildings. Here, and in places like Derbyshire, policies were monolithically statutory and had often no time or money for voluntary activity.

In itself this did not necessarily mean loss, since few of the traditional 'voluntary' organisations or the volunteers they used were strikingly pioneering. However, where it existed, this public dominance did seriously curtail spontaneous responses and small scale experiment.

On the whole, however, the problem was not that facilities were large scale and stereotyped, but that over most of the country development was haphazard or non-existent — that the Service was *in a critical condition*[2]. It had no building programme, no corps of professional practitioners and no coherent philosophy which spoke to the conditions of the time.

Philosophies there undoubtedly were — in plenty. But they were sectarian and highly traditional. They were too often presented in a language which was either negative, or moralising, or both — 'For God's sake, keep those kids off the street!'

Thus, though there was some criticism of **Albemarle**, especially from those with sectional interests or conservative philosophies to defend, the broad policies it laid down were hardly challenged. In fact, they were invariably endorsed without comment as promising an inevitable improvement on what had gone before[3]. Decisions were taken in a reactive and often intuitive way — decisions on how money should be spent, on how and in what staff should be trained, even on how youth work should actually be carried out.

This is, of course, how social policies are often determined. Yet, precisely because **Albemarle and post-Albemarle policies rested on** such taken-for-granted principles, it seems important now to strip away some of the 'naturalness' and inevitability which overlay them. This means raising questions like:

• What assumptions were embedded in Youth Service policies because they emerged out of a particular historical period?

• What priorities did these policies set — that is, what did they establish as essential, what as non-essential but important, and what as unimportant?

• What criteria were used to decide these priorities, who decided them, and in whose interest?

This paper will hopefully illuminate possible answers to such questions, though without necessarily addressing them directly. Nor will the analysis be particularly profound or conclusive. However, a focus will be maintained on the **policy** contexts within which youth work **practice** has developed over the past two decades, with the aim of examining under-explored features of the Service in that period.

The Assumptions and Solutions of the '60s

The Youth and Community Service (YCS) policies we have today still rest to a significant degree on the assumptions which dominated the 'affluent' 1960s. Ushered in by Macmillan's assurance *'You've never had it so good'*, here was a period in which, it was widely assumed, poverty had virtually been eradicated, continuing economic growth and rising material prosperity were assured, and therefore basic conflicts of interest and values within British society had finally been resolved[4].

Thus, any social problems which remained — like, say, juvenile delinquency — were viewed not as evidence of fundamental defects in the structure of society, but as little, local, **residual** difficulties. A few communities might have remained under-privileged because the techniques and organisation needed to reform their deviant sub-cultures had still to be refined. Most commonly, however, social problems, including adolescent problems, were seen as originating in a small number of 'problem families' and in the poor socialisation that children received in them[5].

Youth work was not of course the only, or even the main area of social policy to be influenced by these ideas. Social work was dominated by pathological explanations of social problems which invariably *'blamed the victim'*[6]. Early government statements on the purposes of the community development projects suggest that community work cut its teeth on such explanations[7]. And education, too, depended on them[8].

But youth work was certainly not immune. For one thing, it became increasingly 'person-centred'. Family and peers might be acknowledged as helping to shape and channel behaviour, but its mainspring was seen as the individual and his or her personality. Adolescent behaviour especially was assumed to have these individualised roots. Despite the gloss on conventional wisdoms provided by anthropologists like Margaret Mead[9], by 'new' psychologists like Erik Erikson[10] and a growing interest in 'youth culture'[11], traditional psychological and physiological perspectives continued to dominate. Above all, they 'proved' that young people needed help to negotiate the natural traumas of adolescence resulting from changes within their bodies and emotions, and to tackle society's required *'developmental tasks'*[12].

Inevitably, therefore, the primary youth work focus was on 'face-to-face' practice — on direct work with individuals, whether separately or in group situations. Young people were encouraged and enabled to use the opportunities which, it was now believed, had been provided for everyone in order to realise their potential, and thereby also to contribute to the common good. Person-centred practice was seen as having its own inherent validity and inevitable benefits. No attention was paid to the constraints placed on it, not just by the resources made available to it directly, but also by the broader economic and political processes which set its parameters. Nor were questions asked about its implicit (societal) goals or about why certain interest groups, often with conflicting motives, gave it their support[13].

Great attention **was** paid however to the special 'skills' required for such person-centred practice and how best these might be acquired. In youth work this was best illustrated by the fascination initially with group work and later with 'counselling' and 'management'. It was backed up by an interest in 'supervision' and 'training' which conveyed powerful messages about the importance of person-centred approaches, not only in their content but also in the way they were carried out[14].

This stress on technical competence also contributed significantly to the emergence of a concept of professionalism in youth work. Central to this very complex notion is the assumption that 'the practitioner' is clearly distinguishable from 'the layperson', because she or he has acquired, mainly by training, a range of specialist occupational skills. These were precisely what in the '60s youth workers said they were developing.

However, such professionalism has an additional usefulness for the practitioners concerned: it justifies their claim to higher status, higher rewards and greater autonomy in the management and conduct of day-to-day practice. Thus it encourages them to develop as a self-protective interest group which can have unintended but important consequences for that practice. For one thing, it can distance workers from clients by emphasising the power and competence of the former and the dependency and lack of competence of the latter. And secondly, it can imply that workers can solve social problems merely by, in this case, refining their interpersonal skills, that 'therapy is all'. Policies and politics are thus here, too, treated as of no great significance[15].

Within the youth work of the 60s, this primary concern with means and techniques and the consequent indifference to longer-term ends and underlying values was perhaps demonstrated most vividly by the growth of detached work. This was intended to be the Youth Service's great breakthrough into alternative, progressive practice. And in method, at least initially, it was indeed often innovatory if only because it involved work outside premises or the use of unpretentious buildings in flexible and imaginative ways. Yet the deeper purposes of detached work schemes were little different from most other youth work of the period. They too, for example, took it for granted that young people must at all costs be kept in school, or in work, or at home, regardless, it often seemed, of how uncomfortable and even oppressive the young themselves found these institutions[16]. Rarely did even the most radical of detached youth workers offer any sustained critique of the institutions themselves. Certainly they seemed never to explore systematically with young people such questions as: Do you need just to accept the school's often humiliating treatment of you?; or: Could you get involved in any collective action to challenge such destructive working conditions?; or: How far does your personal growth (perhaps especially as a girl) depend on your leaving home, at least for a time?

In any form of youth work these can never be popular questions, since they cannot lead to easy forms of practice. But the fact that they were so rarely ever posed, even by 'progressive' detached workers, illustrates how completely in the '60s person-centredness could blinker youth workers. It also shows how, well into the '70s, it constrained the whole Service from looking beyond individual personality and motives to family relationships and peer group networks and the depoliticised 'skills' needed for influencing these. This, of course, is not to suggest that the youth work of the '60s was based entirely on false principles. Its stress on the person was, in fact, for the times often extremely progressive and, what is more, this has left behind a commitment to individual caring and to humane and sensitised approaches which, today especially, need uncompromising defence.

However, this commitment was often overlaid by the contradictory pressures to refine technique almost as an end in itself, and to achieve a superior professional standing. It was also increasingly undermined, too, by organisational developments which again, in common with other forms of helping practice, imposed new and often restrictive structures and procedures on day-to-day practice.

In youth work much of the post-Albemarle expansion — the new buildings, the extra full-time and part-time posts, the part-time worker training courses, even the detached work schemes — relied heavily on **statutory** money or at least backing. Accompanying this was a greater stress on accountability — not just for money but also for philosophies, purposes and methods[17].

Much of the provision made was, as a result, cautious and even stereotyped. Many authorities built their youth centres to a standard design and later began to place them all on school campuses. Many made financial support to voluntary organisations dependent on a number of restrictive conditions. Most continued to insist that only young people who 'joined' could use Youth Service facilities. Increasingly, in fact, the Youth Service was being bureaucratised and its staff were being cast in the role of local authority officials.

Reappraisal and Organisational Adjustment: the Policies and Priorities of the '70s

Eventually, the full effects of all this could no longer be ignored, especially since by the end of the '60s youth seemed even more of a problem than it had earlier in the decade. Though the results of Bone and Ross' investigation into Youth Service usage[18] were not actually published until 1972, their field work was carried out in 1969. Indeed, the study was instituted in the first place precisely because politicians like Denis Howell, the Youth Service Development Council and youth workers themselves were expressing increasing disquiet at young people's low 'take-up' of the Service.

Bone and Ross confirmed that only just over a quarter of all 14-20 year olds were at any one time attending a youth club. As they grew older, even fewer used Youth Service facilities — only 15% of the 18 year olds, for example. For 18 year old girls, there was only a one in 12 chance of their participating.

The official response to the problem was the Milson-Fairbairn Report, published in 1969[19]. Though to some extent it did consider purpose and philosophy, and though its policy recommendations, such as they were, were often implemented in unintended ways, its primary concern was to achieve limited forms of institutional change as the primary means of combatting young people's often deep political and social alienation. Like the Plowden Report[20], which appeared in 1966, and the Seebohm Report[21], published in 1968, the Milson-Fairbairn Report implied that such oiling of wheels and adjusting of mechanisms — especially if they were designed to integrate the Service more fully into the community — would enable it to win the hearts and minds of its clientele and, almost it seems as an inevitable consequence, to solve their and society's worst problems.

The main results of the Report were thus **organisational.** On the one hand, youth work became linked much more closely with the schools, in part, it would seem, because these would supply not only additional facilities, but also a more coherent and controlling structure for practice with this fractious age group[22].

On the other hand, the Report led to a strengthening of the administrative links between youth work and more formal kinds of adult education. In part this had a similar rationale to that offered for the link-up with schooling. But it occurred, too, because a closer and earlier contact between young people and their elders would, it was believed, help close the so-called 'generation gap'[23].

However, the main effect of all this, especially after local government reorganisation in 1974, was to incorporate youth work even more tightly into the burgeoning local government structures. In other words, the new Youth and Community Services, far from releasing youth work's imagination, flair and dynamism, ensured that it was even more subject to the often stifling controls of local bureaucracy and corporate management.

At first sight it might have been expected that these powerful new bureaucracies and the self-conscious welfare professionalisms which were emerging would come into conflict. The 'youth work profession' however was still far too weak and internally divided to attempt such a confrontation. Moreover, 'professionalism' and 'bureaucracy' were now in many ways mutually reinforcing. For the lengthening agency hierarchies provided youth workers with many more opportunities for acquiring the status and positions of administrative influence which the more self-protective forms of professionalism sought; while the de-politicised, person-centred 'skills' of these professionals, far from threatening the new bureaucracies, promised them considerable help in containing an increasingly turbulent and dissatisfied adolescent generation[24].

Despite the extra resources provided during the '60s, and the efforts at institutional restructuring in the early '70s, the priorities of the new Youth and Community Services remained largely unaltered. That they still lacked variety and flexibility was revealed by an *'Education'* survey published in September 1976[25], which showed, for example, that of the 86 LEAs which responded:

• 85 were running the Duke of Edinburgh Award Scheme but only 15 sponsored a Community Industry Scheme.
• 83 ran activity competitions but only 43 undertook detached work.
• 81 grant-aided activity courses but only 12 ran schemes for homeless young people.

In other words, the YCS of the '70s was set in a rigid pattern of quite formalised programmes and of, usually, expensive buildings requiring maintenance, protection and heating as well as staffing — all of which, especially in a period of severe economic cut-back, absorbed high proportions of recurrent expenditures. Moreover, most of the buildings were designed, and the staff running them recruited and trained, to provide **recreational** activities on the assumption that **leisure** was such an influential feature of people's lives that through it major personal and collective change could be achieved[26].

Furthermore, as a result of post-Milson-Fairbairn policy choices, the YCS during the '70s increasingly deserted what had traditionally been, and what contemporary developments suggested should have remained, its priority clientele — adolescents. In part this resulted from the growing stress on 'community', which more and more local authorities chose to interpret as meaning work with adults or, even more narrowly, as adult education classes. But as the swing to school-based work gathered momentum and as the problems of older adolescents became more intractable, youth work agencies also increasingly emphasised children's work.

11

Thus, 80 out of the 86 LEAs surveyed by *'Education'* sponsored youth work with the under-14s; while in 1978 the Scouts, after investigating the needs of eight to 14 year old Asians in Slough (half of whom were under ten), initiated a project for this group which they also described as youth work[27].

Into the '80s: Problems, Policies and Priorities

By the end of the '70s, policies of this kind had come to seem less and less appropriate. For, in sharp contrast to the assumed affluence and continuing economic growth of the '60s, the new decade — especially from the oil crisis on — had brought massive and long-term unemployment, accelerated inner-city decay and economic decline, and therefore increased poverty. The almost daily evidence was not of a consensus of values, but of a deep-seated clash of interests. Moreover, these conflicts were clearly based less on the comparatively transitional generational differences which the '60s had feared than on much more persistent and fundamental economic, class and racial differences. On adolescents in particular — especially those between 15 and 19 — the effect of all this was often catastrophic.

No doubt, some of the problems did indeed stem from individual inadequacies, family breakdown or peer group influences. Certainly they were as always experienced, often painfully, in **personal** ways. Nonetheless, by the later '70s it was no longer possible to miss, as the '60s had done, how far those problems emanated from faults structured deeply into key economic and political institutions in our society.

Hence, youth unemployment could no longer be explained simply as the poor adjustment to working life of a few lazy and disorganised individuals; nor homelessness as the bad judgement of a few footloose and irresponsible tearaways; nor even truancy as a series of silly escapades by a handful of silly children disillusioned with a particular day's timetable. Even racism — which, as racial prejudice, had long masqueraded simply as an accumulation of irrational attitudes amongst a few 'pathological' individuals — had increasingly to be recognised as something deeply embedded in the structures of our society, and even as highly functional to its operation.

In other words, approaching the '80s, it became more and more difficult to deny that the most severe problems, and perhaps especially the problems facing the young, were basically **political,** and that their roots lay deep in the economic and social conditions of the time. Clearly a tiny, underfinanced and loosely-organised Youth and Community Service could on its own do little to solve such problems. It could not supply the jobs which the economy as a whole was too frail to generate; or the education which over-controlling and overburdened schools were unable to supply in an appropriate form; or the accommodation needed by young people impelled to move to the large cities by boredom, unemployment, poverty and the sense of a hopeless future in their own localities. The YCS on its own certainly could not root out the racism — or indeed the sexism — within a social structure and an economy often requiring ruthless mechanisms for allocating people occupationally and socially. It could not give the political power which, in spite of the vote at 18, young people still lacked but had to have if they were to make their special interests count.

However, into the '80s, what the YCS can and will need to do, is to look again at its own basic assumptions and the priorities which were inherited almost by absence of mind from an era which already seems a millenium away. That is, it will have to ask questions like:

• How best can more varied, adaptable and less expensive forms of accommodation be provided for youth work programmes?

• How best can the Service's so-called 'neutral' and 'detached' technical 'skills', focused on intra- and inter-personal growth, be applied to the demonstrably **political** problems now facing young people?

• How best can the Service's reliance on distancing 'professional' ideologies and approaches be converted into the deep personal and, again, political engagement required to tackle those problems?

That is, how best can the undoubted advanced of the past two decades be used for political as well as personal and inter-personal ends — by, for example, seeking to influence and mobilise other organisations, such as trade unions, which have greater clout and at least some shared or parallel commitments?

If the YCS is not just to atrophy — as over a decade ago some members of the Milson-Fairbairn Committee wanted it to do[28] — and if young people are to continue to receive some service which is about **their** needs and demands, then some answer to these questions is urgently required.

For even before the end of the '70s, attempts had been made (some successful) to shift resources away from the YCS towards other kinds of youth-serving agencies. As early as 1970-71, the separate Youth Service building programme was abolished and innovatory youth work schemes had to look increasingly to the Urban Aid programme for support. By 1975, the DES was issuing a discussion paper which clearly implied a retrenchment in the role of the Youth Service, with other government departments being sharply reminded of their responsibility for 'the disadvantaged', and youth workers being firmly told to return to providing straight leisure activities[29]. The local authority cut-backs of the mid-'70s hit the YCS disproportionately, as always, while in 1977 the DES was only just prevented from giving up all its obligations for supporting voluntary organisation building projects.

At the same time other state agencies began to develop youth work programmes of their own. Indeed, the Manpower Services Commission, with its massive budgets and apparently even more massive ambitions, seemed determined from very early on in its existence to build up training schemes which would, in effect, keep all those without 'real' jobs in forms of compulsory, informal as well as formal, education until the end of their teens. Welfaring agencies, especially via an expanding application of intermediate treatment, have also been hard at work carving out a youth work role for themselves.

Yet none of these agencies can claim an approach to young people which is either non-stigmatising or motivated by the more personalised educational concerns of the traditional Youth Service. They would also seem to have fewer opportunities and even less will deliberately to nurture young people's collective identity and strength by using group work skills for political as well as therapeutic and recreational ends.

Indeed, the specialist youth work done increasingly with the unemployed and delinquents throughout the later '70s seems to have had as its primary focus **societal** needs; that is, channelling the young as quickly and as effectively as possible into their roles of 'compliant labourer' and 'law-abiding citizen'. Anything these young people may have gained personally is usually an accidental bonus — while their development of a collective identity, through say, trade union membership, has in fact been actively discouraged, especially by the MSC. Infiltration of these agencies by YCS-oriented staff will no doubt repay valuable dividends, perhaps by pushing them out of their very narrow 'policing' and 'welfaring' functions. It might, for example, help to extend the MSC's conception of the social and life skills[30] needed by young people beyond what is required merely for an uncomplaining adjustment to often very oppressive work situations.

However, the YCS can seek to do even more than that. It will also have to make its contribution, as it has throughout its history, to the disciplining processes through which the young have to pass. But given the room for manoeuvre which YCS staff have traditionally had and which, even within the new bureaucracies, they have often managed to some degree to preserve, the Service can certainly respond to young people's own individual and collective perceptions of their situation and needs more wholeheartedly than the MSC or a social services department.

In particular the YCS must avoid becoming too conditioned by the stigmatising labels and approaches of the new youth work agencies, since this could mean abandoning its traditional commitment to a wide cross-section of **self-selected** young people. In the '80s this will be particularly important, since confronting the main youth issues cannot just mean dealing head-on with unemployment, truancy and the rest. It must mean, too, developing the social education and political education roles to which the YCS is committed, so that the consciousness of more and more young people is raised regarding the nature and origins of poverty, unemployment, racism, sexism and the major imbalances of political power in our society. This in turn must mean deepening young people's understanding of how each of these creates the material and psychological conditions of life for **everyone**, and of how therefore they mould young people's views of themselves and of others in crucial ways.

To illustrate, such an adjustment of YCS policies and priorities would mean treating youth unemployment as a key issue only partly because approximately a quarter of a million 17-19 year olds have remained unemployed throughout the late '70s. After all, however appalling that figure, it has constituted only a small percentage of the total adolescent age-group. Youth unemployment needs also to be a central educational concern because the unemployment of even one young person in a self-proclaimed democratic and egalitarian society impoverishes all young people — indeed, all people. Moreover, it must be recognised as impoverishment if society is to justify its democratic and egalitarian pretensions and if stigmatisation by the persistent selection of special category 'clients' is not to compound the problem still further.

Changing policies in these directions will not of course be easy. As I suggested earlier, the processes for determining policies in state agencies like the YCS are usually complex, diffuse and unplanned. Moreover, the increasing bureaucratisation of the Service has concentrated more and more of the power of decision-making in the upper reaches of the organisational structures[31].

Thus, the day of the free-wheeling, even maverick innovator — the Baden-Powell, the Charles Russell, the Lloyd Turner[32], the Joe Benjamin[33] — has largely gone. Innovation, where it occurs at all, is more and more institutionalised and so constrained and limited. Decisions, even about everyday matters, are taken further and further from where the action is, so that, for the field worker, practice is in danger of becoming more and more routine. Moreover, these decisions are determined increasingly by managerial criteria — is it cost effective?; can workers be made to account for what they do?; does it faithfully represent agency policy?; and so on. The perceptions and priorities of field staff — and, of course, of clients — are thus influencing policy-making less and less. This in a sense places the YCS — again like other services — in a Catch 22 situation. For how can not only its actual priorities, but also the processes for determining these, be altered when the priorities and processes we have apparently well suit its most powerful decision-makers?

The only possible, though very partial, answer must be: via much more concerted action from below, through the organisation of 'low-level' practitioners and, where feasible, consumers in professional associations, trade unions, consumer action groups and the like. Such developments might just, in the longer term, alter the balance of power in the way priorities are determined. However, that too would demand a much more systematic and determined effort to apply the professionalised 'skills' developed in the '60s and '70s to the political as well as personal groups which in the '80s confront YCS consumers — especially those in their middle and later teens.

15

References

1 *The Youth Service in England and Wales,* Ministry of Education, HMSO, 1960.
2 Ibid., para 2. See also paras 35-45.
3 *The Youth Leader,* Vol. 8, No. 2, Autumn/Winter, 1960, indicates fairly accurately the level of the debate on Albemarle at the time. See also *A Pattern for the New Youth Service,* National Association for LEA Youth Leaders, 1960.
4 See for example **F Zweig**, *The Worker in an Affluent Society,* Heinemann, 1961, pp.205-222.
5 See for example **J B Mays**, *On the Threshold of Delinquency,* Liverpool UP, 1959, which describes one of the first British youth work projects to employ 'group work methods' to combat juvenile delinquency.
6 See **R Holman**, 'Social Workers and the 'Inadequates'', in *New Society,* 5th September 1974.
7 See **J Benington**, *Strategies for Change at the Local Level: Some Reflections,* in **D Jones** and **M Mayo** (Eds.), *Community Work One,* RKP, 1974, p.260.
8 See **B Bernstein**, 'Education Cannot Compensate for Society', in *New Society,* 26th February 1970.
9 **M Mead**, *Coming of Age in Samoa,* Penguin, 1928, and *Growing up in New Guinea,* Penguin, 1930.
10 **E Erikson**, *Childhood and Society,* Norton and Co., 1963, and *Youth: Fidelity and Diversity* in **E Erikson** (Ed.), *The Challenge of Youth* Doubleday Anchor, 1965.
11 See **B R Wilson**, *The Social Context of the Youth Problem,* 13th Charles Russell Memorial Lecture, 1965.
12 See for example **J Klein**, *Human Behaviour and Personal Relations,* National Association of Youth Clubs, 1963, chapters VI and VII, and **J Hemmings**, *Adolescents and Society,* Arthur Mellows Memorial Lecture, 1962.
13 See for example **B Davies** and **A Gibson**, *The Social Education of the Adolescent,* University of London Press, 1967, pp.86-95 and 150-161. Also, **H E Higgins**, *The Essentials of Boys' Club Leadership,* National Association of Boys' Clubs, 1967, p.8, and *The Schools and the Youth Service,* National Association of Youth Service Officers, 1969, p.7.
14 See for example **Davies** and **Gibson**, op cit, pp.214-215 and chapter 10; **J Matthews**, *Working with Youth Groups,* University of London Press, 1966; **A Alcock**, 'Aspects of Counselling' in *Youth Review,* No. 10, Autumn 1967; **J Tash**, *Supervision in Youth Work,* National Council of Social Service, 1967.
15 See also **B J Heraud**, *Sociology in Social Work,* Pergamon, 1970, chapter 10, and **J Galper**, *The Politics of Social Services,* Prentice Hall, 1975, pp.89-100.
16 See, amongst many others, **G Goetschius** and **J Tash**, *Working with Unattached Youth,* RKP, 1967, chapter 5, and **D Ince**, *Contact,* Youth Service Information Centre, 1971, chapter 7.

17 For some indication of the development of this trend, and of the views emerging amongst senior youth service administrators, see **E Bourne**, *'The Unprofessional Youth Service'* in *New Society*, 7th December 1967.
18 **M Bone** and **E Ross**, *The Youth Service and Similar Provision for Young People*, HMSO, 1972.
19 *Youth and Community Work in the 70s*, HMSO, 1969
20 *Children and their Primary Schools*, HMSO, 1966.
21 *Report of the Committee on Local Authority and Allied Personal Social Services*, HMSO, 1968.
22 See *Youth and Community Work in the 70s*, op cit., paras. 185-188.
23 Ibid., para. 49.
24 See also **G Pearson**, *The Deviant Imagination*, Macmillan, 1975, pp.127-132.
25 *'Service of Youth: an 'Education' Survey of LEA Provision'* in *Education*, 17th September 1976.
26 See for example *Youth and Community Work in the 70s*, op cit., paras. 287-329.
27 **P Livingstone**, *The Leisure Needs of Asian Boys Aged 8-14, in Slough, Bucks.*, Scout Association, 1977.
28 *The Relationship of the Youth Service with the Schools and Further Education*, Report of Youth Service Development Council Sub-committee under the Chairmanship of **A N Fairbairn**, unpublished, 1968, para. 301, p.53.
29 See *Youth Service*, Autumn 1975.
30 See *Instructional Guide to Social and Life Skills*, Manpower Services Commission, undated.
31 For a discussion of these developments within local government generally, see **J Benington**, *Local Government Becomes Big Business*, CDP Information and Intelligence Unit, 1976. For the way they can be used to subvert 'community' approaches within the 'helping' services, see **C Cockburn**, *The Local State*, Pluto Press, 1977.
32 **M Lloyd Turner**, *Ship Without Sails*, University of London Press, 1953.
33 **J Benjamin**, *In Search of Adventure*, National Council of Social Service, 1961.

Chapter 2

The Young People we Deserve
MICHAEL WINWOOD

Michael Winwood was a full-
time youth worker between
1965 and 1970, working in
South London, Bromley and
Southampton. He is now a
lecturer in Social
Administration and Social
Work at the University of
Bristol, where he specialises in
the political economy of social
policy and community
organisations. His current
research interests include
community work training, and
a practical involvement in a
young adults' project.

2

In his recent article entitled 'The Theory and Practice of Youth Work in One Large Youth Centre', Alan Dearling seeks to show that much of the work that is done there amounts to little more than policing[1]. He argues that the ideologies and orientations of (some) youth workers are geared more towards controlling young people than they are towards enabling youth people to become what Fred Milson would call 'critical participants' in their community[2]. Many of us who work in schools, youth clubs, neighbourhoods, social work settings and the like would want to claim that our work is designed to help young people grow up as 'good citizens', taking their place in the worlds of home, work and leisure and making there a contribution to the collective life as well as deriving satisfactions for themselves. Many of us, however, fail to see that the worlds of home, work and leisure are very different for different groups of people, and what constitutes good citizenship, or a contribution to the collective life, or even personal satisfactions differs widely between these groups and their social contexts. We often fail to see that this is so, let alone what our role might appropriately be. Even if we recognise the differential distributions (of wealth, income, influence, education, prestige and opportunity) that lead to structured differences and inequalities, we are likely to ignore our analysis in our everyday work with young people, since to make the necessary connections between our taken-for-granted assumptions about the social world of everyday relationships and our assumptions about the social structure and context of those relations requires a disciplined rigour that most of us do not manage.

It is, by now, well established by research that poverty has not been significantly reduced by the introduction and development of the 'Welfare State', let alone banished as was claimed in the early 1960s. Several recent publications confirm previous findings: that the very poor or severely disadvantaged groups in our society experience a situation which is virtually impossible to change by individual (or even minority group) action. Wedge and Prosser[3] demonstrate con-clusively that some children (estimated two million) 'suffered adversity after adversity, heaped upon them from before birth; their health was poorer, their school attainment lower and their physical environment worse in almost every way than that of ordinary children'. Michael Young's 'Poverty Report 1974', George Clark's research notes and the Child Poverty Action Group's conference document, 'Unequal Britain', all show (again) that inequalities in terms of income, housing, educational experience, job opportunities, leisure facilities, environ-mental circumstances etc persist in our society[4]. Using a very low definition of poverty, Abel-Smith and Townsend estimated that over seven million people were living at or below the poverty line in 1965[5]. There is no reason to believe that this number has been reduced, since more recent estimates (using the Government's own figures) suggest that, if anything, the number of people thus affected is increasing[6]. But we can easily be lulled into a false sense of security, believing that such inequalities only affect a residual minority whilst the rest of us need not worry unduly. Whilst it is true to say that industrialisation and later developments have improved the lot of many (especially with the rapid development of the service sector of the economy improving the circumstances of the middle classes), we are now rapidly moving into an era where disaffection and alienation are being experienced by the middle classes as well as industrial workers. Witness the current frustrations over planning decisions and the increasing militancy of public employees and other quasi-professional groupings. But whilst the poor have remained poor and the middle classes have grown marginally richer, the rich have remained virtually untouched by the so-called rapid social change that has been evident since the 1920s until only the last few years when the crises of international trade have begun to impinge upon them. Titmuss, Blackburn, Webb and Sieve and others have shown that the wealth of this nation is owned by a very small proportion of people (seven per cent of the population owning 84% of all private wealth[7]). This proportion has not altered significantly, in spite of the growth of the gross national product, over the last 40 or more years. Since this is the case, inequalities are likely not only to persist but to deepen as economic recessions continue on an international scale. We live in a world characterised by an increasingly complex web of multi-national and international economic exchanges, where poverties and inequalities, exploitations and plunderings (not only of natural resources but of whole cultures and ways of life) are rampant; where the rich live not only off the backs of the poor in their own lands but from the sweat of peasants and workers in the third world. The comparative wealth of the poorest in the West represents to the peoples of the third world the very threat of domination and subjection[8].

Such a national and international pattern in the distribution of wealth can also be related to other elements of the structure of social reality. The distribution of annual income follows a similar pattern, with a mere four per cent of the population gaining any income from company shares (one per cent of the population owning 81% of all private company shares in 1966). At the other end of the scale, 38% of all households in Britain have incomes less than the national average (21% having a total household income of less than £30[9]). There is, then, an enormous gap between the highest and the lowest income groups, and as we look higher up the income level we find curious anomalies that favour the better off (child tax allowance, purchase or value added tax, tax allowances on mortages, expense accounts, insurances, house-ownership schemes sponsored by employers, cars and car allowances and many other perks[10]). But a closer analysis reveals not only significant

21

differences between groups on the basis of structured inequalities of income and wealth but, in almost all dimensions of life, we find that some groups are consistently denied access to opportunity and so-called public resources.

Much research in education over the last 15 years or more has shown that the structures of educational opportunity and the practices of educational institutions consistently favour the middle and upper classes to the detriment of manual and non-manual working class children. The Plowden Report demonstrated beyond doubt that environmental and parental influences (not to mention the emphasis on health and school standards) are amongst the most severe in affecting a child's educational performance[11]. A whole host of researchers have argued that the structure of educational opportunity merely reflects the prevailing structure of the wider society[12]. Is it any accident that approximately eight per cent of the school-age population attends private school and a similar proportion of the whole population owns by far the largest share of all private wealth? Is it an accident that over 30% of the secondary age population attends secondary modern or the lower streams of comprehensive school, and a similar proportion of the occupied adult population is employed in the poorest paid jobs or is outside the labour force altogether? And what about the consistent under-representation of women in academic courses and higher education? Michael Duane says that *'post war research has confirmed the common-sense view that the public schools are populated by children of the upper-middle class and of the landed aristocracy; grammar schools by the middle class and a dispropor-tionately small number from the children of manual workers; and secondary modern schools by the children of the working class'*[13]. Similarly, it seems to be no accident that state expenditure on young people who leave school at 16, compared with expenditure on those still at school or in further or higher education, is grossly inadequate, disproportionately small and extremely difficult to prioritise and increase. The Milson-Fairbairn Report demonstrated the abysmally low expenditure on Youth Service and the relatively unimaginative work that Youth Service often promotes; the Russell Report recently called for resources to be channelled into further education, particularly with the training and retraining of young people in mind, and the Youth Employment Service has, until only the last year or two, been left to stagnate, whilst the effects of post-Robbins expansion of higher education has increased still further the social, economic and political advantage of the new elites through the educational system[14]. It is no accident that when we think of young people as 'a problem', on the whole we are not referring to students of universities, to young graduate trainees or to the post-A level entrants to the banks, big business or other white collar jobs. With notable exceptions, we are on the whole referring to the so-called 'less-able', the 'deviants', those who have left school since it offered them little; those for whom our society has denied its cherished opportunities and advantages. These are the same young people — be they black or white — who are often excluded from the work-force due to structural unemployment or who occupy the menial, dead-end or unskilled manual occupations in industry or commerce.

We cannot, of course, ignore what efforts have been made to change the structure of educational opportunity: the developing debate over the comprehensivisation of secondary schools; the emergence of the 'philosophy' of positive discrimination in favour of the 'disadvantaged' at primary and pre-school levels; and the proposed expansion of nursery education. But the political and financial commitment devoted to these developments, in spite of all the talk during the 1960s, has been pitifully low. A. H. Halsey concluded that *'the essential fact of twentieth century educational history is that egalitarian policies have failed'*[15]. Even the attempts of the EPA action programme that Halsey's report describes have had only limited effects and made only marginal in-roads into the inequalities of which its rhetoric spoke. Similarly, in the United States where a much wider and better financed series of attempts was made at compensatory education, only very modest achievements have been evident. Jencks concluded a review of much of the research associated with these innovatory programmes in the US, implying that, as Bernstein has said, *'education cannot compensate for society'*[16]. That is to say, that whilst the structure of job opportunities, income, wealth, prestige, urban environment, leisure facilities, housing and all the rest remain as they are, attempts to innovate significantly in education, with the aim of enhancing the opportunities open to children who hitherto have been ignored, will be frustrated and ineffective.

We must not suppose, however, that the prevalence of inequalities of physical resources or the relationship between a number of such structural elements of social reality are all that concern us. So far I have attempted to support the view that the distribution of wealth, income (and therefore job opportunities) and education are not only inter-related but serve to perpetuate the existing inequalities. What changes have occurred have been those which the powerful have deemed necessary and permissible in relation to their interests. The social institutions which serve the state and the existing structure of society are both pervasive and inter-related. Although similar relationships have been suggested and demonstrated between, say, housing distribution and wealth or health care and income, we are not dealing with the correlations between such hard 'variables' alone[17]. We are dealing also with the distribution of knowledge, social power, values and ideas; even language forms and patterns of cultural life differ significantly from group to group, class to class and area to area, as Bernstein's and Klein's works conclusively show[18]. Bernstein has demonstrated the culture-clash that occurs in many of our schools, where children and parents alike are asked *'to drop their social identity, their way of life and its symbolic representations at the school gate. For, by definition, their culture is deprived'*[19]. Such are the value assumptions of teachers, educational administrators, policy-makers, academics, politicians and others who would have us believe that compensatory educational programmes are essential. Such programmes are 'global' in nature; they are designed to deal with what are naïvely considered to be 'global' problems, but when we carefully analyse what is at stake in the implementation of such policies we begin to see that educational institutions (as well as social welfare, economic, penal, judicial and other institutions) are, in the main, perpetuating and developing scientific or quasi-scientific (so called rational) modes of thought which are impregnated with middle class values and which consistently understate the dimensions of human experience.

These value systems deny the existence of alternative ones, tend to deny or ignore the inequalities of which we have spoken, and leave unexplicated or only partially thought-out the bases and consequences of the framework they employ. In addition, the holders of such value systems are caught up in a series of contradictions which, for the most part, remain implicit. When we say, for example, that there is a 'culture clash' between the values, ideas and life-styles of a working class neighbourhood and those of a school, we are talking essentially about a clash of interests. The school staff (their ideas, methods of work, attitudes to children, parents and environment) and the rest of the educational hierarchy are predominantly middle class, either by origin or by training and socialisation into the roles of being a teacher. By far a larger proportion of these people will never have experienced any other situation. Many will never have worked outside of a school. Most will not live in the area in which their school is situated. Their orientations, the pattern of their social relations, their religious affiliations, their housing experience and their leisure pursuits will all differ significantly from that to which working class children are accustomed. But it does not end there. The internal organisation of the school, its aims and its methods of work, the structure of the timetable and the subject divisions within the curricula will also reflect the predominant values of the division of labour, the work ethic and the acquisitive materialism of advanced capitalism. The children, on the other hand, will probably be part of a more or less close-knit network of kin and group affiliations (not necessarily confined within the immediate geographical boundaries of the neighbourhood) where the taken-for-granted assumptions of everyday life and experience will revolve around very different institutions. The trade union club, the local pub, the hardships of large families perhaps, the experience of the irregularity of work, a physical environment which offers little scope for people to make it their own, long hours of work at jobs which offer perhaps little personal satisfaction, little space to call their own within the home as well as outside of it, few outlets for the energy of the young — the quality of all these experiences will be very different from those of the school teacher (or youth worker, social worker, probation officer and the like). The experiences of home and neighbourhood life, the language these children speak, their ideas, responses and skills not only will differ but may be unintelligible to the teacher, yet he will be in a position of domination and authority, since the child is required by law to be at school and is required by tradition, emphasis, overt and covert patterns of rewards and sanctions, to conform to the values of the school.

A possible consequence of this conflict may be that the child or the neighbourhood is subsequently labelled disadvantaged, deprived, less-able, backward, sub-normal or as disinterested, apathetic, in-attentive and the like. Seldom will it occur to a teacher that such children may be making quite 'normal' responses in terms of their own experiences of life. It may simply be that the teacher himself has not acquired the appropriate insights in order to make sense of such responses. Seldom will it occur to us that what we have been doing is inappropriate to the everyday worlds of the young people we confront. It could not possibly be our activities that are 'at fault', since our training, status, prestige, income and general life experiences confirm the legitimation of our role and our own view of ourselves as more or less effective practitioners of certain codes, ideas, methods and objectives acquired during our lavish socialisation into those present roles! We have acquired a sense of security in knowing what it is to be a teacher, and although sometimes we cannot escape some difficulties, these do not precipitate us into too close an examination of ourselves. Rather, we ask even more questions as to what is wrong with the child, the family, the neighbourhood, the school or the educational system, whilst assuming that our own role does not need to be considered too far, or that the system requires only marginal adaptations to ensure smooth running. In inner-London, and perhaps other inner-city areas, we are beginning to see this myth crack apart — but that is no reason for optimism. Similar codes, practices, ideas and orientations underpin an increasingly wide variety of occupations in very different settings, apparently, to that of the school room. In these settings the concrete circumstances that unmask the realities are far less advanced than in some educational institutions. But there is a common identity here. These occupations, and the people who get uncritically caught up in them, are the instruments of an amazingly complex and ever increasing system of state intervention, which is designed (sometimes with the best will in the world in pragmatic and ill-examined response to particular needs, crises or pressures) in the last analysis to further the interests of the few in the name of the many. We are required in these occupations (planning, management and administration of public services, social work, youth work, probation, medical care, social research, psychiatric services and the rest) to contribute to a process of helping people to adapt, change, develop, by using the alienated methods of control, mani-pulation, inducement, inculcation and coercion in the name of the public good, the social good or the individual good. Yet such ideas or ideals have nowhere adequately been defined, and there is certainly no consensus about them. These are the very ideas which, above all, will differ according to the life experiences of the various groupings in society, yet the ideas of the most powerful of these groupings so far still prevail as the legitimate ones, as the appropriate ones, as the morally right ideas.

There is an increasing amount of support for the view that linguistic forms, contents and expressions are context-bound. Only certain kinds of linguistic expressions facilitate conceptual thinking and the development of conceptual skills. Consequently, only certain kinds of social context will facilitate such a development[22]. There can be little doubt that we live in a world where the language forms and conceptualisations of so-called rationality predominate. But it is arguable that such forms of expression and thought have only developed in service to a particular class of persons. That is to say, the language forms and modes of thought, and even the meanings we attach to words that predominate, are those of the powerful classes, the elites. Rarely do we find in business, politics, commerce or administration, people who cannot express themselves, orally or in writing, with both lucidity and finesse. The products of our twentieth century educational and social system who will 'succeed' (in the system's terms) are the articulate and the self-assertive. These people will often be members of the new diploma elites and they will be increasingly drawn into the policy-making circles of state institutions as they expand their influence and modify their attitudes towards people they 'know they can trust'. Yet these institutions are caught up in the processes of maintaining and developing the interests of a minority class; attempting by every means in the book to ensure the continuance of the existing order of things regardless of the cost in terms of natural resources or human potential. The worlds of the social and public services are becoming increasingly dominated by the ideologies and practices of big business: management efficiency and cost-benefit criteria dominating first the re-organisation of social services and now of the National Health Service and Local Authorities. Corporate planning and cost-effectiveness techniques (the so-called neutral techniques to emerge through the sustained application of quantitative social science) have, for some time, been dominant technologies in educational and welfare policy-making, and they are now being extended by the 'new mandarins' into ever-increasing areas of social and public life. If we add to this the effects of an ever-increasing division of labour that has accompanied bureaucratisation and professionalisation during the last 50 years, we are left with a picture of mystification in a meritocracy, where only those who have been sifted out early enough will succeed. Behind this facade of neutrality lie the powerful and over-riding interests, not of human potential and cultural need, but the interests of capital, pushed forward by multi-national companies and international political and trade alliances mirrored, at the local level, by monolithic enterprises in public and private sphere alike. The young people to whom we refer when we speak about anti-social behaviour, aggression or violence are totally barred from the rewards of the world we have just described, and it, as it were by chance, they receive some of the so-called benefits, there is precious little opportunity to exert any influence or to have any personal impact. Those of us who work with them (or rather for the state to contribute to their suppression) are already on the lower rungs of the ladder, which may bring us influence and prestige if we are young and ambitious enough; those young people can often sense that that is so! We have already taken our place among the new 'professionals', the new 'experts'; we are amongst the chosen few who help to dictate the policies and whose perceptions give weight and support in the social processes whereby 'problems' are created, defined and determined[23].

It is little wonder then that so-called discipline problems arise in schools, clubs, and sometimes, whole neighbourhoods. It is little wonder that many kids prefer to stay away from school, thus avoiding the pressures which experience at school confirms. It is little wonder that children and young people find other responses (maybe dropping out, but there are other alternatives as well) towards a system which holds up its rewards as being easily obtainable, thrusting all the elements of 'the good life' at us through the media, through the values of state institutions, and through the everyday experience of school, club, remand home, prison, hospital or social worker's office. These children are caught in a double-bind situation[20]. Officialdom tells us that material well-being, fashionable clothes, jobs with opportunity for advancement, expensive holidays, fast cars, beautiful sexual relations and the rest are easily available. All we have to do is to smoke the right brand of tobacco in our pipes and women will flock around us necessitating a burly, bald-headed bodyguard to look after us! At the same time the working class youngsters' experiences of school, home life, leisure and first job are quite contrary to this illusion. But these are the same youngsters who, in all probability, have not developed the wherewithal to negotiate this contradictory world, either socially or economically. But in the later twentieth century it is also part of the experience of these young people that such material rewards as our society offers are acquired, if not by them, then by those who were 'lucky enough' to be picked out earlier down the line. It is quite likely that someone known to them (perhaps held up to them as an 'example') will, shortly after leaving grammar school or technical college, or even university, be sporting trendy gear or fast cars and may, before too long, be evidencing many of the material 'advantages' of which most working men know nothing throughout their lives. It is as though these alienated products had some intrinsic value, as though these material possessions were something other than a rather shallow manifestation of a shallow world. But it is little wonder that some young people start kicking over the traces in the locality when caught in this double-bind. And it is little wonder that schools and other state property soon become the object of petty damage. Such buildings represent the very institutions and processes whereby these youngsters are being excluded from all the 'good life' advantages and from the training in conceptual thinking whereby they might see such 'advantages' for what they are. Could it be that aggressive, violent or difficult responses towards these institutions (and even the persons who represent these institutions by their acquiescence) are quite intelligible reactions to disadvantage, inequality and deprivation when such structural circumstances are compounded by the clash of interests, values and ideas? It is possible that the phenomena we call 'problems' are themselves socially created, sustained and transmitted through quite specific kinds of stages and contexts[21]. Indeed, it has been argued that before a personal experience can be transformed into a group problem or public issue it goes through a number of socially-created processes to ensure that it is not too explosive or too threatening. These processes are situated themselves within particular kinds of social context, and even the experience of such a transformation will be very different for different groups. Consider; with the advent of monolithic local authority social services departments and the extensive development of casework practice over the last few years, the term 'problem family' has become common parlance. At a quite recent public meeting in South London, women rose to their feet in rage and demanded an explanation of the term when it was used in passing. To be called a 'problem family' is a very different experience from calling a family such, especially when the use of such a term is legitimised in common usage amongst one's colleagues.

We are often unaware of the fact that it is we who, by referring to our own difficulties (and the difficulties encountered organisationally or ideologically, or in terms of our methods in the agencies in which we are employed), at best contribute to the social creation of stigmatising conceptualisations of what constitutes social problems, and at worst project our own difficulties onto the young people whom we are employed to serve. Truancy, for example, is not a child's problem; it simply reflects the inability of most of our schools in inner-urban areas to attract, interest, stimulate or fire the imagination of the young people concerned. Yet when a local authority attempts to deal with truancy it will most often resort to the appointment of education welfare officers or home visitors, thus shifting the emphasis away from the practices of the school. It is only very recently that teachers themselves have begun to be really concerned about their own work, since the difficulties that they are encountering can no longer be ignored; they have grown to such proportions that in some areas there is an almost total breakdown of the schooling being offered. But with such a shift of emphasis (onto the child, the home and the locality) these youngsters may feel themselves increasingly to be failures or rejects, second class citizens shunned from the rewards of a school system that not only favours the conformists, but which creates and sustains a pattern of advantage that accumulates over time for those whose needs are least. Such a perception of self will not only be psychologically damaging, it will also further contribute to social, cultural and political barriers in our society and foster resentments and frustrations, since such experiences of self are likely to extend beyond the school into workplace and neighbourhood, where a continuing alienation will be deepened. If often seems to me a wonder that the incidents on the beaches of Brighton or Margate, the muggings in the East End or the gang conflicts in Liverpool are not more commonly prevalent rather than less. It seems amazing that there isn't much more violence and aggression in response to such a violent and contradictory society as ours[24].

If, in spite of the handicaps of our position as instruments of the state bound up in oppressive institutions, we are to relate to the experiences of young people in their everyday lives, where can we most appropriately begin? Firstly, we may be unaware of much that, if we can grasp, will severely affect our perceptions of the situation that confronts us[25]. It seems that we start with ourselves and attempt to understand the biases in the assumptions we make about the social world. What are the questions that we ask ourselves? Do those questions reflect a wide enough range of information needs? For example, do we consistently ask questions about the history of the neighbourhood, who the landlords are, what incomes the families have, what kinds of job they are in, what is their experience of work, what the local structure of political and social power looks like, whose interests are being served by this or that institution? We need to know something about the totality of the experience of the young people and the probabilities in their future situation. Only if we have such a picture will we begin to enter into the worlds of adolescents with whom we are anxious to work. If we do not or cannot relate closely with them then that is our problem, deriving from our inabilities to comprehend their situation. In the long run it will be futile for us simply to make our prognostications about their situation — since what matters is their experiences and the ways in which they might for **themselves** begin to create new experiences.

Secondly, we have to ask questions about our own situation and the extent to which it is realistic for us to imagine that we might be able to contribute something to the precipitation of adolescents into new learning experiences. We need to build up our understanding of the differences between our biographies and current situation and those of the young people in question. We need to attempt to assess what our responses would be if we were subjected to the kinds of situation in which many young people find themselves. How would we react to living in high flats, to menial work, to low incomes, to disproportionately poor health, to frustrations that were so much part of ourselves that we could no longer adequately express them?

Having asked ourselves these sorts of questions in our day-to-day work (not as something we do at the odd conference we attend when we get high on 'soul searching'), we will need to begin to record or note down our answers. We will need to be developing a reflexive attitude through which we might more effectively make the necessary connections between our awareness of ourselves and our awareness of others. Within such a framework of thinking we might then, and only then, begin to consider the appropriateness or otherwise of our present role with adolescents, and at the same time begin to re-align ourselves and redirect our work. If our role is not to be explicitly directed towards social change, we must accept that implicitly we will be accepting all the dilemmas and contradictions that have been outlined above, and that thereby we will be perpetuating an elitist and discriminatory social order.

When we talk about 'working with difficult young people' or with 'angry adolescents' or 'delinquents', or the 'anti-social' or 'un-clubables', what is it that we are talking about? We could, of course, be talking about different ways of working; ie methods, strategies, approaches, tactics or programmes. We could be advocating the merits and demerits of working in this way rather than that: street work instead of a church group; neighbourhood work instead of an open youth centre; group literacy work as opposed to an evening class; a self-run open hostel instead of a rigid institution, and so on. But essentially we are talking about intervening (to one degree or another) in social settings where someone perceives there to be some kind of problem. Even when we want to claim that our work is 'non-directive' or when our only objective is to enable local people to solve their own problems in relation to adolescents, we are essentially advocating (even practising in our everyday work) some kind of intervention. We may call it interaction or we may think of it simply as 'being friendly towards' people, but we are talking nonetheless about some kind of intervention, since most of us are (in the social, education and 'helping' services) employed so to do. Whatever kind of intervention we wish to practise, it seems to me that the whole arena is problematic.

There are essential and fundamental problems at the heart of what we call 'understanding', or what I will call for the moment (following R. D. Laing) the *politics of intervention into social situations*. These problems can be grouped under the following headings: observation and interpretation (the problem of meaning); interaction (the problem of doing); moral problems (the problem of justice) and problems of reasoning (the problem of being-in-the-world). What I want to do here is to attempt to spell out something of the nature of these problems (and in so doing to indicate something of my own way of 'handling' them), and to draw upon a range of literature that you may like to refer to yourself for further reflection.

Things are often not what they seem to be. *'Social reality turns out to have many layers of meaning*[26]. The discovery of each new layer changes one's perception of the whole. Thus, probably every youth worker's perception or understanding of anti-social behaviour is something different, but more importantly we are often not entirely honest (with ourselves as much as with others) in recognising why we conclude as we do about other people's actions.

We have been 'trained' to accept some kind of need for accurate and as-far-as-possible 'objective' observation. But the observer may be seen as a *cold manipulator — a self-appointed superior man — standing off from the warm vitality of common existence; finding his satisfaction not in living but in coolly appraising the lives of others*[27]. And, though we are not merely observers, we have to recognise that the minute we attempt in a disciplined way to understand what we see around us (ie the minute we try to take a step back and reflect upon what is happening before us, 'rationally') we can — to some extent legitimately — have this criticism levelled at us. Perhaps this is trite since youth workers, teachers and the like might accept the need to attempt to understand more deeply the world we have lived in all our lives — in particular the world of young people.

We need to ask questions not only of ourselves but also as to **how those people involved in the situation see their own actions.** Otherwise we can so easily fall into the trap of judging the actions of others without ever realising that our own values (let alone theirs) are affecting what we see going on. Thus, there is not only a problem involved in our role as observers, but there is a more fundamental problem involved in what we call understanding or in interpreting what we see. We have to ask the question of all behaviour that we see: is this (action/behaviour) comprehensible within its own context? This context transcends the immediate situation (eg the club room where 'trouble' is brewing) and involves the interrelations of a stream of persons significant to the personality of the primary actor(s) (eg the anti-social youngster(s) causing the 'trouble' to brew). Only by seeking out this context can we avoid judging people or even situations before we have any knowledge of them, and only so can we begin to understand why people behave as they do. In doing this we would be equipping ourselves better for our particular activity, our intervention, our work with these youngsters[28].

It is insufficient to be satisfied because we believe ourselves to be growing in understanding; we will need positive evidence of our 'growing' with the job. It is inadequate just to attempt to 'rationally' reflect upon what we see and what we do with young people. It is even inadequate merely to combine this with an attempt to be more aware of our own values and to see how such values relate to our inter-pretations of others' behaviour, in its own context and in relation to our own consciousness of ourselves, since our understanding can only ever be relatively 'objective', 'accurate', 'true' etc. As we seek to know about the relations between self and others (and others' selves and others) that constitute the context that concerns us, our own consciousness is continually transformed (ie we begin to perceive further layers of meaning and reality for the persons who make up those contexts). We are, in this sense, always only approximating towards 'objectivity', 'accuracy' and 'truth', and this because we are inextricably caught up in the same essential processes and problems of 'being' (of existence, of living-in-the-world and expressing who it is that we are) as those with whom we are working. That is to say, since we are all engaged in social life (whether or not we are also working with young people), we are part of the context that we seek to understand. And our seeking to understand that context is itself an element of our part in that context. It cannot be ignored as such (or bracketed or negated) since our mode of being-in-that-context will inevitably affect both what the context is for us, as well as our and others' perceptions of the reality of that context[29].

My second 'problem-area' — though related to the first — concerns the fact that we can never, as it were, wait until we 'understand' sufficiently (though a basic minimum training is, I believe, essential) before we begin to act. But our **actions** and interventions in social situations are themselves problematic[30]. Firstly, what constitutes a **social** situation? (After all, as one stands on the side of Scafell one can be said to be viewing 'a situation', or one reads daily of 'the situation' in Northern Ireland or of the state of the British economy). A **social** situation is one *'in which people orientate their actions towards one another'*[31]. But the term 'action' itself is somewhat ambiguous. It can first of all mean *'the already constituted act considered as a completed unit, a finished product . . . but second it can mean . . . a flow, an on-going sequence of events, a process of bringing something forth. Every action, whether it be my own or that of another person, can appear to me under both these aspects'*[32].

'Action is a series of **experiences** *being formed in the concrete and individual consciousness of the actor'*[33]. We cannot therefore ever assume that we are fully cognisant of the way in which our own actions are going to affect the actions of others in a situation that confronts us. And we have to recognise that, however sensitive or careful we may be when we begin to take part in a situation, our actions do affect others in that situation. Indeed, our very presence can affect others.

All this is not meant to question the validity of action per se (clearly though, we have to think very hard about what action is appropriate or valid in each situation we deem to affect). On the contrary, as youth workers or as educators we have a commitment to 'action', and it is 'action' of a particular kind. Our actions may fall into the 'category' which R. T. Batten calls *'non-directive'*[34]. That is to say, our task primarily (and especially with 'difficult' young people) will be the creation of relationships **of a reciprocal nature** which, **in themselves,** enable 'things' to be generated through which young people (individually and in groups) can develop their social (and other) 'skills', and act in ways which bring **them** enjoyment and satisfaction. Our task, in short, is social education, using activities, facilities, events, even 'the club' itself, as tools to this end. *'Youth workers . . . have always affirmed that they have two basic, underlying purposes in common: the one, to provide young people with opportunities of meeting each other, making friends, and enjoying themselves; and the other to help them develop themselves as persons so that they grow up into happier, more self-reliant, and more socially responsible* *people than they might otherwise be. If these really are the basic purposes of youth workers then every activity or project, or even the actual clubs in which we work, are really no more than* **the means** *through which workers hope to achieve these purposes, and cannot rightly be regarded as purposes in themselves*[35].

But we must notice the somewhat ambiguous and contradictory formulation in Batten's assertions. Firstly, he tells us that the people who work with adolescents are intent upon making certain kinds of provisions (for young people to meet, make friends and have fun together). Leaving aside the fact that this need not be the case — for example, social workers, teachers, youth employment officers, probation officers, community workers etc may see their work in very different terms to these; these terms **may** characterise the objectives of club workers but not of all youth workers — we need to note the paternalistic and somewhat authoritarian overtones of the notion of **providing** for young people. This is contradictory to his second assertion, that we want to help young people to develop themselves. If we engage in provision-making for young people we cannot also hope that this will not limit the extent to which we are able to encourage self-development, in terms of self-reliance, self-direction, responsibility and the like. If these are our objectives, then we would surely be more concerned about young people engaging jointly in decision-making about their own provisions with other sectors of the community.

So having noted our commitment to action, we notice that we cannot imagine for one moment that the quality of that action, or the kind of action that it is, will be anything but supremely important and will, to a very large extent, depend upon the kinds of assumptions we make about ourselves, the work we do, the people we work with, the environment we live in, the locality in which we work, the structure of the locality, job availability, school experience and the like. In short, the quality of that action will depend upon our assumptions about the social world. If action itself cannot be rigorously separated or distinguished from experiences in the process of formation, and if such experience transforms our consciousness of 'what the situation is' (adding all the stories and perceptions that make up our experience of others in the situation), what is it but our experience which underpins not only our observations and interpretations, but also our actions? Even though we may be relatively objective in attempting to appraise the situations that confront us, and even though we may seek to support our interpretations with the rational findings from other situations, the situation that confronts **us** is unique in certain respects, whilst sharing a common structure with those other situations. And whilst an understanding of that common structure is also very important, it will not negate the uniqueness of the experiences being generated in action and interaction in those contexts of which we are a part. The very generation of these experiences, whilst transforming the consciousness of each of the actors to the degree that they are involved in the situation, changes what the situation is.

Having said all this, let me return to my first proposition in relation to our intervention into social situations, and let us take a simple example. We are working with a small group of very 'angry' young people; suddenly the police arrive, there is a 'scene' as two of the boys are arrested; our 'position' is somewhat precarious but we decide that there are things we can do (find out which police station they are being taken to, inform the parents, get hold of information as to 'rights on arrest', get hold of a solicitor if necessary etc). My point is simply this, that there are **immeasurable** ramifications in this simple situation of the consequences of 'intervention' (ie deciding to take action) by both the police and the youth worker. This 'situation' and the 'actions' embodied within it are not final, complete units, they are *'experiences in the course of its formation'*, and to each 'actor' in that situation the experience means something different. Consider: what will this scene have meant to the police officers, the magistrate (when he hears about it), the timid 14 year old girl who gets shoved out of the way as the policemen make their bid to hold onto the lads, the innocent bystander who makes some remark about 'pigs' and gets hauled off as well, the mother of the girl-friend of one of the principal protagonists, the father of the lad who came to the club for the first time that evening etc? What will the fact that arrests were made at the club mean to neighbours, the youth officer, the probation officer, parents, the management committee? What will the fact that the youth worker supports the rights of the arrested mean to the management committee, the police officers, the court etc? We can never assume (i) that our experience of the situation is common to others in or out of that situation, (ii) that 'actions' end within the 'event', (iii) that our 'actions' do not have direct consequences for the lives and well-being of a range of other persons with whom we are 'in relation'.

This leads me to my third essential problem-area, which is again very closely linked to what has gone before. Simply stated it is this: *'By **what** criteria does **who** decide **whose** views are 'right'?*[36] *And from whence do these criteria derive?'*

'No one in the situation may know what the situation is. We can never assume that people in the situation know what the situation is. A corollary to this is: the situation has to be discovered. The stories people tell ('people' here includes all people, parents, children, fellow social workers, psychiatrists, the police, ourselves) do not tell us simply and unambiguously what the situation is. These stories are part of the situation . . . There is no priori reason to 'believe' or 'disbelieve' a story because anyone tells us it. The stories we are told and tell are always significant parts of the situation to be discovered . . . When the situation has 'broken down' (ie when 'difficult' or 'anti-social' behaviour is seen to be a 'problem') not only may some or all of those in the situation not themselves see what the situation is, but also **they may not see that they do not see it.** To realise this may be **very** frightening.

'Social diagnosis is a process: not a single moment. It is **not** an* *element in an ordered set of before-after events in time. Intervention in social situations may have different phases: they overlap, contrapuntally. The phases cannot be chopped up into time slices . . . What one sees as one looks into the situation changes as one hears the story, in a year's time, after one has got to know the people in the situation a little. The story will have gone through a number of transformations (the discovery of the different 'layers of meaning'). Often it will be very different from what one heard, say, a year back. Neither version is necessarily untrue or true. It is a different story'.*[37]

Here, Laing puts very succinctly the major problems confronting us. Our assumptions, attitudes, values and conclusions derive from a social (and political) context, and yet inherent in **all** social situations is the problem he posits ie that *'. . . our definition is an act of intervention that changes the situation, which thus requires redefining; it introduces a new factor. At any moment of time, in the continuous process of looking through, of diagnosis, we see it in a particular way that leads us to a non-definitive definition, subject to revision in the light of the transformations that this definition induces, prospectively and retrospectively'*[38]. It seems to me that any dogmatic assertion about the nature of (in this case) anti-social behaviour, or indeed about the way to 'deal with' or work with these kinds of situation, is **in itself** suspect. All we can do is work continuously to discover and enable others to discover these situations as they develop and interrelate. This is an on-going, dynamic process, and work in this field requires us to be completely honest about our own moral assertions.

We can also be conscious of the ways in which our experiences are being **structured** in our interactions in the social institutions that make up a large part of society — schools, the family, work institutions, the legal and political institutions etc. Often the ways in which our experience of situations will develop (and indeed the situations themselves) will be more or less influenced (even determined) by the structured constraints that work upon us in social affairs. My argument earlier in this paper was very much that aggression can be seen as a relatively rational response to a constricting and oppressive experience of the reality of life in disadvantaged circumstances. But we must also beware of going so far as to say that human beings have no choice about their responses to life. Dennis Wrong has argued cogently that an *'over-socialised'* conception of man has, for too long, dominated our thinking[39]. What I am arguing that we can and must do is to recognise **both** the ways in which our experience is structured and that our responses need not be acquiescent; that our responses can and will, to some extent, make some difference. That this needs to be part of the process of relating with others in social situations perhaps doesn't need restating, but the implications of seeing this to be part and parcel of the work we do will fundamentally alter both the nature and the outcome (as well as the criteria by which we set objectives and assess success) of that work. It will necessarily call into question factors which perhaps heretofore we have said are not part of our concern, and it will orientate our work much more towards precipitating change in the social structure and sub-structure of which our activity is a part.

Finally, I feel bound to attempt to introduce the problems involved in rationality itself. For some years now we have been encouraged to try to be 'objective' in our reasoning about our work with young people, ie we have been encouraged to try 'to put to one side' (not that this is actually possible) our emotional and moral responses to people and situations, in order to think rationally before we make conclusions. We have, that is, been encouraged to reason analytically. Analytical reasoning is linked to the notion of understanding (about which I have already indicated what I consider to be major difficulties). Briefly let me restate the analytically-reasoned model: in order to understand a social phenomenon one needs to know of the 'internal' relations within or identified by that phenomenon (in this case 'anti-social' behaviour) **and** of the relations between that phenomenon and other phenomena (eg between the incidence of anti-social behaviour and, say, working-class background, unemployment, inarticulate speech or poor education etc). To construct ideal types (well-formulated, detailed ideas), statistically probable laws or theoretical concepts, whilst helping to draw attention to the existence of complex phenomena within particular situations, will not of themselves **explain** those phenomena. Casual relations or discursive relations, whilst important, again do not **explain**; they only help to highlight. To explain is to know intuitively from the point of view of the subjects (in this case, the 'angry' young man), ie to be **in** the position of the actors[40]. But since we know we cannot enter **fully** into another's experience, or experience a situation in precisely the same way as another, all our explanations will necessarily be partial. The extent of our recognition of their partiality will evidence our caution in matters of policy. There are always unintended consequences in policy-making and implementation, as Robert Pinker has demonstrated[41]. The point is to minimise such unintended consequences through realising a much wider framework within which both to think and act. Such a framework will necessarily involve the series of problems we have discussed above, but it will also mean a much wider series of involvements between ourselves and others in our work situations. Indeed, it will lead to a re-definition of what constitutes our 'work situation'. Persons perhaps heretofore considered irrelevant will be regarded as having not only different stories to tell about the situation, but also the right to be consulted, involved and responsible for those decisions which affect their lives. What perhaps we previously considered to be our own ('professional') domain, province or speciality is, within such a framework, open both to doubt and to criticism, debate and examination — not only for and by ourselves but also those others with whom we are in relation.

The theoretical approach I am advocating here vis a vis 'understanding' and 'explanation' clearly has an integrated relation with practice. It is not something that can be considered in isolation from practice, since to attempt this is to slip back into making false distinctions between human experience which, as we have already seen, merely lead us into contradictions and anomalies. This approach, more accurately seen as a philosophy, is in the tradition of both Weberian 'Verstehen Sociologie' and Marxist existential dialectics. That is to say, both the emphasis upon empathy evident in Weber's work **and** the emphasis upon the reciprocal impact between the social structure and the species-being in, say, Sartre's work, are not only equally important but are synthesised in this approach to understanding seen as intervention. There have been two strands of social theory which have attempted this synthesis: Schutzian phenomenology and ethnomethodology[42] and the new Frankfurt critical theory[43]. I shall confine myself here to some comments which derive from attempts to reason dialectically in an essentially Sartrian manner.

To begin to approximate towards being in the position of the actor (or, to begin to use the framework I have outlined, in attempting to understand and get close to the 'anti-social' adolescent) is to reason dialectically and not analytically. Dialectical reasoning subsumes analytical reasoning within itself, but it transcends the limits of analytical reasoning. It also, in some measure, reflects what we call a common sense view of the world; that is to say, qualitatively the processes are no different though the level of abstraction may be 'higher'; and, significantly, the taken-for-granted world is not lost sight of, but seen more clearly.

'Dialectical reasoning is the principle of what may be termed dialectical science, which is to be distinguished from natural science. By dialectical science I mean the study of **the reciprocities of persons and groups of persons** in contrast to the study of natural events . . . Persons are always in relation . . . Persons relate through establishing relations with each other[44] and to natural events, while things and organisms appear not to so relate . . . In relating, persons experience the situation in a particular way. They experience it as their situation. They relate; they experience themselves relating; they experience the possibility of knowing the form and style of the relations they make. They experience themselves, the relation **and** that to which they relate . . . this pattern of relating and experiencing may be termed the **form** of personal relating. **It constitutes the relationship as personal and through it the person is constituted**'[45].

In other words, dialectical reasoning is reasoning which is itself the outcome of inter-personal relations; the outcome of the reciprocities inherent in those relations and the experiences generated within those relations. That is to say, dialectical reasoning takes full account of the fact that persons are what they are because of all the relations that have contributed to their being thus and no other, whilst at the same time recognising that those persons are the ones that enable one to create, sustain and contribute to the relations that one enters into. Dialectical reasoning is thus person-bound and notices that persons both create and are created by experience. It is not 'outside' of personal relations as analytical reasoning claims to be[46].

Some of this may seem a long way removed from the everyday business of running a youth club, seeing to a caseload or teaching a classroom full of young people. The problems I have sought to reflect upon are essential and fundamental ones within those everyday kinds of situation we get caught up in during our interventions into social settings, not only where 'difficult' young people are implicated but also in our everyday experience of living in a social world. These concerns, then, constitute not only my anxieties about the so-called anti-social adolescent, but also the central ontological problems of my own being-in-the-world. If, herein, there is something with which you can identify then we can be sure we are moving towards a position where we might be better enabled at least to understand each other. That is no small task in itself.

References

1 **A Dearling**, in 'Hard Cheese Two', October 1973, pp.1-7.
2 **F Milson**, Youth Work in the 1970s, RKP, 1970.
3 **H Prosser** and **P Wedge**, Born to Fail, Arrow Books with the National Children's Bureau, 1973, p.59.
4 **M Young** (Ed.), Poverty Report 1974, Maurice Temple-Smith, 1974; **G Clark**, Whatever happened to the Welfare State?, City Poverty Committee, 1974; Unequal Britain, Child Poverty Action Group, 1974.
5 **B Abel-Smith** and **P Townsend**, The Poor and the Poorest, Bell and Sons, 1965.
6 CPAG conference paper (op cit.) suggests that the number of people currently living below the government's own 'poverty line' is nearer ten million.
7 **R Titmuss**, Income Distribution and Social Change, Allen and Unwin, 1962; **R Blackburn,** 'The Unequal Society' in **J Urry** and **J Wakeford**, Power in Britain, Heinemann, 1973, pp.68-84; **Webb** and **Sieve**, Income Redistribution and the Welfare State, Bell and Sons, 1971; **J Kincaid**, Poverty and Equality in Britain, Pelican, 1973; **D Wedderburn**, Poverty, Inequality and Class Structure, Cambridge UP, 1974.
8 See **P Freire**, Cultural Action for Freedom, Penguin, 1972 and **P Freire**, Pedagogy of the Oppressed, Penguin, 1971.
9 See Social Trends, HMSO, 1973 and **G Clark**, op cit.
10 See **Titmuss**, op cit., and **Webb** and **Sieve**, op cit.
11 Central Advisory Council for Education, Children and their Primary Schools, HMSO, 1967.
12 See **Jackson** and **Marsden**, Education and the Working Class, Pelican, 1966; **J Ford**, Social Class and the Comprehensive School, RKP, 1968; **J Douglas**, All Our Future, Peter Davis, 1968; **Rubenstein** and **Stoneman**, Education for Democracy, Penguin, 1970.

13 **M Duane**, *'Education in Britain Today'* in **Rubenstein** and **Stoneman,** op cit., p.59.

14 Youth Service Development Council, *Youth and Community Work in the 1970s*, HMSO, 1969; Russell Committee, *Adult Education: a Plan for Development*, HMSO, 1973; White Paper, *Employment and Training*, HMSO, 1973; Central Advisory Council for Education, *Higher Education*, HMSO, 1963.

15 **A H Halsey** (Ed.), *Educational Priority*, Vol. 1, HMSO, 1972.

16 **C Jencks**, *Inequality: Family and Schooling in the United States*, Allen Lane, 1973; **B Bernstein**, *'A Critique of the Concept of Compensatory Education'* in **Rubenstein** and **Stoneman**, op cit., pp.110-121.

17 See **Rex** and **Moore**, *Race, Community and Conflict*, Oxford UP, 1967; **P Townsend** (Ed.), *The Concept of Poverty*, Heinemann, 1970; Community Development Projects, *Inter-project Report*, Centre for Environmental Studies, 1974; **D Jackson**, *Poverty*, Macmillan, 1972; **R Holman**, *Socially Deprived Families in Britain*, Bedord Square Press, 1970; **Coates** and **Silburn**, *Poverty: the Forgotten Englishmen*, Penguin, 1973.

18 **B Bernstein**, *Class, Codes and Control*, 2 vols., RKP, 1971 and 1973; **J Klein**, *Samples from English Cultures*, 2 vols., RKP, 1965.

19 **B Bernstein**, in **Rubenstein** and **Stoneman**, op cit., p.113. See also **M F D Young** (Ed.), *Knowledge and Control*, Collier Macmillan, 1971, and **N Keddie,** *Tinker . . . Tailor . . . The Myth of Cultural Deprivation*, Penguin, 1973.

20 See **R D Laing**, *The Politics of Experience*, Penguin, 1969, and **R D Laing**, *Knots*, Penguin, 1971.

21 See **Butterworth** and **Weir** (Eds.), *Social Problems of Modern Britain*, Fontana, 1972, pp.280-286; **C Wright Mills**, *The Sociological Imagination*, Pelican, 1970; **C Wright Mills**, *The Ideology of Social Pathologists*, Bobbs-Merrill, 1949.

22 See **Bernstein**, op cit., **Young**, op cit., **Keddie**, op cit., **A Cicourel**, *Language, Socialisation and Use in Testing and Other Education Settings*, Seminar Press, 1973; **Cicourel** and **Kitsuse**, *The Educational Decision Makers*, Bobbs-Merrill, 1963; **P Giglioli** (Ed.), *Language and Social Context*, Penguin, 1972.

23 See **I Illich**, *'Professions as a Form of Imperialism'* in *New Society*, 13th September 1973; **I Illich**, *The Tools of Conviviality*, Open Forum, 1973; **H Marcuse**, *One Dimensional Man*, RKP, 1964.

24 See Radical Alternatives to Prison, *Children Out of Trouble*, RKP, 1974; **M Kellmer Pringle**, *The Roots of Violence and Vandalism*, National Children's Bureau, 1973; *'Violence and Vandalism'* in *Youth Service Scene*, No. 6, National Youth Bureau, 1974.

25 See **Berger** and **Luckman**, *The Social Construction of Reality*, Penguin, 1972; **M G Winwood**, *'On Understanding Difficult Young People'* in *Youth in Society*, April 1975.

26 **Peter L Berber**, *Invitation to Sociology*, Pelican, 1969, p.34.

27 Ibid., p.26.

28 For a fuller discussion of the notion of social context see **Aaron Esterson**, *The Leaves of Spring*, Pelican, 1972, pt.2; **David Silverman** in **Filmer, Philipson** et al, *New Directions in Sociological Theory*, Collier-

Macmillan, 1972, pp.1-14, 165-202; **Jack Douglas** (Ed.), *Understanding Everyday Life*, RKP, 1971.

29 See **H P Wagner**, *Alfred Schutz on Phenomenology and Social Relations*, Chicago UP, 1972.

30 **R D Laing**, *Intervention into Social Situations* in **Laing**, *The Politics of the Family and other Essays*, Tavistock, 1971, pp.21-42.

31 **Max Weber**, *The Theory of Social and Economic Organisation*, Free Press, 1949, p.118.

32 **Alfred Schutz**, *The Phenomenology of the Social World*, Heinemann, 1972, p.39.

33 Ibid., p.40.

34 **T R Batten**, *The Non-directive Approach to Group and Community Work*, Oxford UP, 1967.

35 **T R Batten**, *The Human Factor in Youth Work*, Oxford UP, 1970, p.166.

36 **R D Laing**, op cit., p.36.

37 Ibid., pp.33-40.

38 Ibid., p.41.

39 **Dennis Wrong**, 'The Over-socialised Conception of Man in Modern Sociology' in *The American Sociological Review*, Vol. 26, No. 2, 1961, reprinted in **Coser** and **Rosenberg**, *Sociological Theory*, Collier-Macmillan, 1969.

40 Theories do emerge, of course, since we do know something of the existence of certain 'regularities of occurrence' in human behaviour, and there are attempts to understand those regularities. The theories are useful as aids to memory or for comparative purposes, but there is the danger that we might think that the theory is 'equal to' reality. This can never be so. What we must remember is that when we recognise the ways in which a situation embodies any 'regularities', we are only seeing part of what the situation is. Such recognitions will form part of our 'working definition' of what the situation is, but we will know it to be partial and will not treat it as though it were the 'truth'. Hence our understanding of the situation assumes a priori that it will be unique, to the degree that the reciprocal relations between the actors have never been enacted in that way, in that time, in that combination, to that degree, before.

Hence our 'theorising' too (which is qualitatively the same process involved in what we have called 'understanding') is situation-specific. So, in our comparisons between situations we will each time have to begin anew or start again to discover what are the essential meanings, stories or definition intrinsic to that situation, as well as recognising the regularities present between different situations. We cannot alone be interested in those regularities, for to be so interested will be to negate the essential unique occurences which largely make a situation what it is for the persons involved in it. Thus, whilst theories may point out ideas or highlight particular elements that we will want to take into account, they will tell us little about the experiential reality of a situation for those actors who make it up. The discovery of something of that experiential reality (the meanings embedded in the relations) will inevitably modify any theories we may be using, in each of its applications to social life. This will give us not only new theories, but a more active, dynamic conception of both the nature and role of theory in our everyday lives, which is itself akin to the processes involved in developing our 'common sense' knowledge of that social world, since it (the process) is inextricably tied to practice.

See **Esterson**, op cit., **Filmer** et al, op cit., **Peter Winch**, *The Idea of a Social|Science*, RKP, 1958.

41 **R A Pinker**, *Social Theory and Social Policy*, Heinemann, 1971, and **R A Pinker**, *'Social Policy and Social Justice'* in *Journal of Social Policy*, Vol. 3, Pt. 1, 1974, pp. 1-19.

42 See **H Garfinkel**, *Studies in Ethnomethodology*, Prentice-Hall, 1967; **Roy Turner** (Ed.), *Ethnomethodology*, Penguin, 1974; **John O'Malley**, *The Sociology of Meaning*, Human Context, 1973; **Berger** and **Luckman**, *The Social Construction of Reality*, Penguin, 1971.

43 See **Laing** and **Cooper**, *Reason and Violence*, Tavistock, 1964; **Tony Manser**, *Sartre*, Macmillan, 1970; **Jean-Paul Sartre**, *Being and Nothingness*, Methuen, 1958; **J Habermas**, *Toward a Rational Society*, Heinemann, 1972; **J Habermas**, *Knowledge and Human Interest*, Heinemann, 1972.

44 See **E Goffman**, *The Presentation of Self in Everyday Life*, Pelican, 1966.

45 **Aaron Esterson**, *The Leaves of Spring*, op cit., pp. 213-214.

46 See titles already cited, and **Robert F Murphy**, *The Dialectics of Social Life*, Allen and Unwin, 1972; **Martin Jay**, *The Dialectical Imagination*, Heinemann, 1973.

Chapter 3

Youth and the Social Environment: Community and Society

AREYH LEISSNER

Areyh Leissner has extensive experience in community youth work, including projects with young prisoners and their families in New York (1955-63), research on street club work in Israel (1963-66) and action research on Family Advice Centres and community-based Intermediate Treatment for the National Children's Bureau in England (1966-75). He is currently Senior Lecturer in Community Work at the University of Keele. He also fulfils several commitments to ongoing projects on behalf of national organisations, including the NAYC project, Youth and Race in the Inner-City, and the Joint University Council Sub-Committee on Community Work Training. Among his published works are 'Family Advice Services' (1967), 'Street Club Work in Tel Aviv and New York' (1969) and (with Herdman and Davies) 'Advice, Guidance and Assistance' (1971).

'A man has only one life and if during it he has no great environment, no community, he has been irreparably robbed of a human right. This loss is damaging, especially in growing up, for it deprives outgoing growth, which begins with weaning from Mother and walking out of the house, of the chance of entering upon a great and honourable scene to develop in'.
Paul Goodman, *'Growing Up Absurd'*, Random House, New York, 1960, p.97.

Youth and the Social Environment

I regard the task of youth work as social education in the broadest, most inclusive sense of the term. Social education, however, does not wait for the youth worker to arrive upon the scene to set it in motion. It is a process which starts at birth. At best it continues throughout life as conscious, creative learning about oneself and others, and as a growing receptiveness and awareness which enriches and extends one's own life and the lives of others. At worst it is a miserably limited attempt to cope with existence in an environment which stunts one's own growth and which distorts one's relations with others. Where it succeeds, social education opens up a wide range of opportunities for self-realisation, for the development and the use of human potential to the benefit of society. Where the process of social education remains inadequate or is suppressed, children grow up to become adults who are apathetic objects of manipulation and exploitation of an increasingly impersonal, self-perpetuating socio-economic and political system of vested interests, of greed, physical coercion and cultural corruption, or they become willing supporters and accomplices of such a system of society. Social education can and should be the process which enables youth to gain awareness of their own role and functions in society, to critically appraise their society, its professed values and its reality, and to exercise the foremost prerogative of youth — to change things that are not what they ought to be.

It is generally accepted that social education starts with the family. But families do not exist in a social vacuum. They live among other families. They belong to social strata or classes of society. They constitute the population of neighbourhoods, of communities. Social education is, therefore, decisively affected by the determinants of social class, and it takes place not only in the family or in the institutions which the social system sets up to act in loco parentis, such as the schools, but also in the community. The conveyors of social education are not only parents, teachers and youth workers, but neighbours and peers, the local shopkeeper, the owner of the nearby cafe or pub, the numerous representatives of society's institutions of care and control who are active in the neighbourhood, the groups and associations which represent certain interests and traditions and, last but by no means least, the mass media which bombard their viewers, listeners and readers with an overwhelming mass of often contradictory facts and fictions, and disseminate often conflicting values, aspirations and expectations.

We are living in an era of crisis and transition and, perhaps, also of opportunities. The children, adolescents and the young adults of the '80s may have to face some of the major changes and adjustments which we still seem to manage to avoid and postpone. There are now, as there were in past generations and as there will be in coming years, young people who feel that it is their responsibility to take a critical look at their world, and to do something about what they see. There are many more who are '. . . *not angry and active, but apathetic and unassertive. . . . Even where few minorities threaten them directly, a deep-seated bigotry often bitterly obtrudes, as they seem to defend the little they do possess. Far from challenging the world around them with an insistent individuality, they seem personally and socially incarcerated; their talents are consistently underrated, their vision constricted, their most personal modes of expression stifled. Each self-image they have created for themselves has been repeatedly deflated, all futures prematurely foreclosed'*[1]. It is to this great number of young people that youth work priorities will have to be assigned, and their number is indeed great: we are told that 'a third of all children in Britain, 4,500,000 million, are growing up in families in the bottom quarter'* of the national incomes stratum[2].

That is not to imply that the children of the poor are the only legitimate concern of the youth worker. There are young people in all strata of society whose social education is being stunted or distorted. It is, however, apparent that it is in the deprived areas of our cities, and in quite a few rural slums[3], that the first priority is the physical environment, the social situation in which children grow up, the neighbourhood and the people who live in it. It is here that the community work focus of youth work is most needed, and potentially most effective.

It is my conviction, based on some years of experience in detached youth and community work, that youth work will only make a far-reaching contribution to the great task of social education if its work with young people encompasses the physical environment and the social situation of the young, and if the participation of the community in the planning, provision and management of services is the primary objective.

45

Community and Society: a Social Environmental Model

'The social environment is more than a source of restraint or deprivation. It is a dynamic complex of forces which participate in the shaping of personality and the determination of behaviour. If we view the individual as being independent of his environment or being set against it, or being what he is despite his environment, we will not be likely to search out and to identify the linkages, the bonds between the individual and the social structure. The social environment is not self-evident and unproblematical; in fact, it is extraordinarily complex and subtle'[4].

'Society is a system of usages and procedures, of authority and mutual aid, of many groupings and divisions, of controls of human behaviour and of liberties. This ever-changing, complex system we call society . . . it is the web of social relationships, and it is always changing[5] . . . Wherever the members of any group, small or large, live together in such a way that they share not this or that particular interest, but the basic conditions of a common life, we call that group a community[6]'.

'Community implies having something in common. In the early use of the word it meant having goods in common. Those who live in a community have overriding; economic interests which are the same or complementary. They work together and also pray and play together. Their common interest in things gives them a common interest in each other. They quarrel with each other but are never indifferent to each other. They form a group of people who meet frequently face-to-face, although this may mean they end up back-to-back. That people in such an area of social life turn their backs on each other is not a matter of chance. In a community even conflict may be a form of co-operation'[7].

For the community youth worker, and for the young people he serves, 'society' is, in practical terms, represented by those of its institutions, agencies and functionaries which are more or less directly encountered in daily life, and whose policies and plans, attitudes and procedures are known to affect the youth worker's ability to carry out his tasks. For all practical purposes the youth worker and the young people he serves encounter society's system of opportunities and limitations, its caring and controlling functions, not only through society's representatives, such as the local councillors, the statutory officers of the local authority departments, but also the voluntary agencies and associations and local dignitaries and professionals. The worker's own employing agency, be that the Youth Service, a settlement house or a church, are part of this system—a social system which the youth worker is himself said to represent.

The impact of the social system is still immediate and visible when it comes from farther afield, for instance from regional and central government departments who encourage or curtail the youth worker's ambitions, provide grants or withhold resources, emphasise and legislate for the care and protection of youth, for prevention and rehabilitation, or insist on conformity and punitive measures. The ways of the social system become more mysterious and intangible when it seems to preach one thing and practise the other, when it upholds the work ethic and creates unemployment, when it asserts equal opportunities for all, but it is obvious that for many the dice are loaded at birth, when it speaks of democracy but excludes those without power and status from effective participation in the democratic process. Especially for the youth worker in the so-called 'deprived' areas, these contradictions may become sources of confusion, frustration, even despair.

The youth worker's 'target area', the area inhabited by the young people he serves, is, of course, part of society. However, some areas seem to be more part of society than others, and the further down the socio-economic scales we go, the more we have to deal with marginal groups, controlled and cared for by society to varying extent, but somehow existing on its fringes. The more marginal the area, the less likely it is to present the picture of a cohesive community, aware of its own identity, conscious of its own responsibility for one another, and with its own traditional networks of mutual aid and its own range of opportunities for self-realisation for its youth.

Jon Rowland wrote: *'A community is based on geographical and social parameters. It may be determined by anything from a main road to a catchment area of a primary school. But although a political decision to do this can be taken very quickly, creating a 'sense of community' is a slow process, taking a period of years*[8].It is my view that a sense of community is a vital ingredient of the process of social education. This sense of community is not just a romantic notion with undertones of nostalgia for the good old days, but, especially for the marginal groups of our society, the basis for participation in the social and political system. This system is basically one of competition for power, status and resources between different interest groups and coalitions of such groups, in which political parties and voluntary organisations, trades unions and employers' associations, cultural movements and social pressure groups all play their dynamic parts and maintain a system of checks-and-balances which is described as the democratic process. Especially for the youth of our poorer areas, their neighbourhood and their community are the first, and sometimes the only context in which they can learn to participate in this democratic process by identifying with, and by asserting the interests and the rights of their community, as well as by sharing concern for the improvement of their social situation with their parents and neighbours. Rights and obligations are an essential part of participation in the democratic process. Young people learn about them by learning about self-assertion and self-realisation, the techniques of active participation, of bargaining and compromise, of confrontation and conflict. The roles and the objectives of the community worker and the youth worker are, therefore, complementary; in the tasks of community youth work they merge.

In the following pages I shall attempt to provide a frame of reference for community work which is relevant to community youth work. A word of caution: models of this type should never be used as neat and convenient receptacles into whose compartments the 'facts' are sorted, whether they fit or not, or whether they are indeed 'facts' at all. The realities of the situation which is being analysed should determine structure and content of the model, and the model should be suitably adapted or scrapped as the reality changes, or as new and different insights are obtained.

Model I: The Community and the Social System

What happens to people in their daily lives, what shapes their present existence and what determines their future, are the result of their personal development as individuals **and** the influence of their environment. The individual and the family are constantly involved with other individuals and families in their neighbourhood. They are, whether they are aware of it or not, part of a **community.** But many vitally important areas of their lives are controlled by the processes and institutions of **society.** These processes and institutions represent, impose and maintain society's social norms, its cultural traditions and its economic and political system.

The community worker helps people to understand, to cope with and, if necessary, to change their situation, in their community, in their county or borough, in the society in which they are citizens with rights and obligations. The community worker helps people to look at and to understand the needs and the priorities of their own living conditions and that of their neighbours. He/she helps people to look at and to evaluate the services to which they are entitled, to communicate their demands to the local and central government institutions **and** to contribute to the improvement of their and other communities' social situation by making their own contribution, by mobilising their own resources and skills in order to **participate** in the improvement of conditions, in the planning and the provision of services.

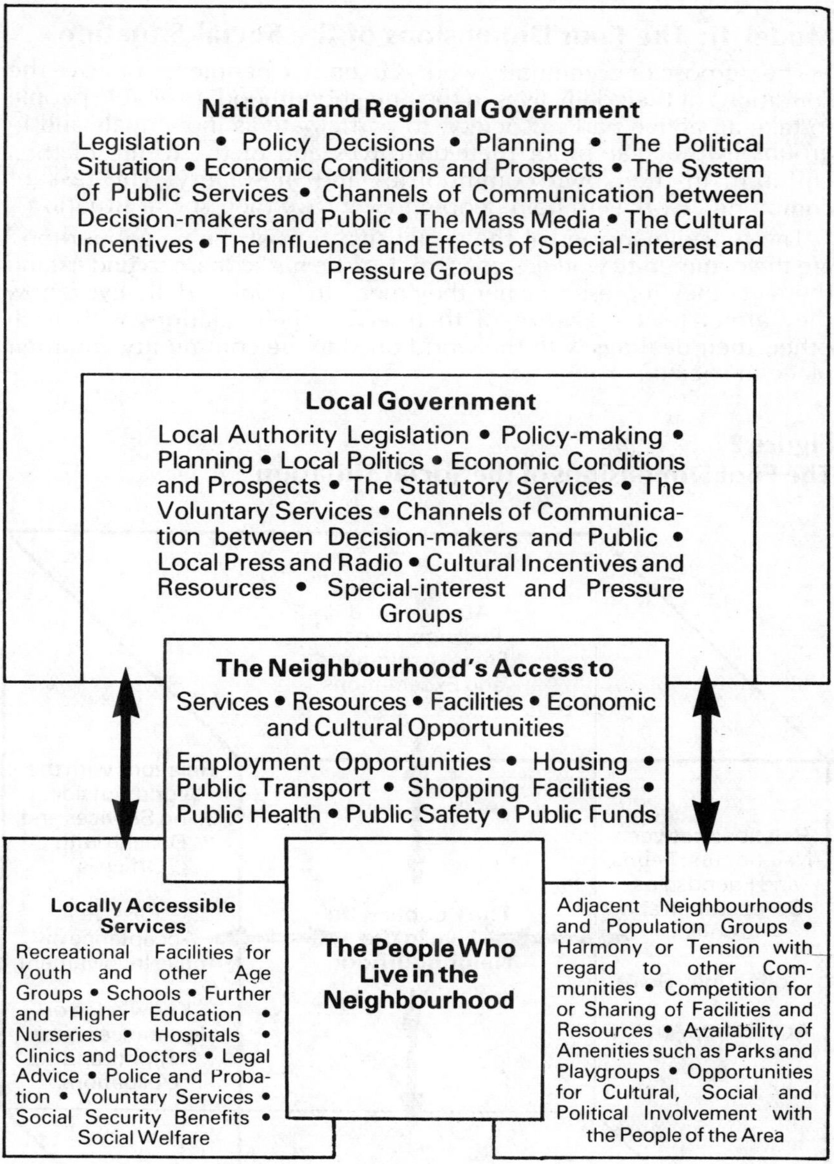

National and Regional Government

Legislation • Policy Decisions • Planning • The Political Situation • Economic Conditions and Prospects • The System of Public Services • Channels of Communication between Decision-makers and Public • The Mass Media • The Cultural Incentives • The Influence and Effects of Special-interest and Pressure Groups

Local Government

Local Authority Legislation • Policy-making • Planning • Local Politics • Economic Conditions and Prospects • The Statutory Services • The Voluntary Services • Channels of Communication between Decision-makers and Public • Local Press and Radio • Cultural Incentives and Resources • Special-interest and Pressure Groups

The Neighbourhood's Access to

Services • Resources • Facilities • Economic and Cultural Opportunities

Employment Opportunities • Housing • Public Transport • Shopping Facilities • Public Health • Public Safety • Public Funds

Locally Accessible Services

Recreational Facilities for Youth and other Age Groups • Schools • Further and Higher Education • Nurseries • Hospitals • Clinics and Doctors • Legal Advice • Police and Probation • Voluntary Services • Social Security Benefits • Social Welfare

The People Who Live in the Neighbourhood

Adjacent Neighbourhoods and Population Groups • Harmony or Tension with regard to other Communities • Competition for or Sharing of Facilities and Resources • Availability of Amenities such as Parks and Playgroups • Opportunities for Cultural, Social and Political Involvement with the People of the Area

Figure 1
The Community and the Social System

49

Model II: The Four Dimensions of the Social Situation

The purpose of community work is to enable people to improve the conditions of their daily lives in their neighbourhood, to enable people to take an active part in society, to participate as individuals and in groups in the shaping of their own lives and of the future of their children, in their own communities and in society. The task of community work is to help people to improve their social situation.

The four dimensions of the social situation of the neighbourhood are the community worker's concern. He/she has to learn to understand the facts they represent, what they mean in people's daily lives, how they affect people's views of themselves, their relations with each other, their dealings with the world outside the community and their place in society.

Figure 2
The Four Dimensions of the Social Situation

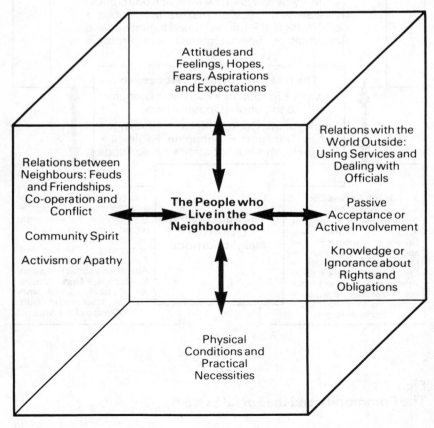

Attitudes and Feelings, Hopes, Fears, Aspirations and Expectations

Relations with the World Outside: Using Services and Dealing with Officials

Relations between Neighbours: Feuds and Friendships, Co-operation and Conflict

Community Spirit

Activism or Apathy

The People who Live in the Neighbourhood

Passive Acceptance or Active Involvement

Knowledge or Ignorance about Rights and Obligations

Physical Conditions and Practical Necessities

Model III: Community Structure

The people of a neighbourhood do not necessarily live as a community, aware of their common interests and problems, willing to share responsibilities and resources, realising that there is strength in unity. Much more often there are divisions and conflicts between different groups, alliances and feuds, concern with one's own problems and indifference to the problems of others. There are 'old-timers' and 'newcomers', 'respectable' people and 'undesirables', people who 'care' and others who can't be bothered. There may be an 'elite' who may feel obliged to help 'the less fortunate', there may be those who are 'stable' and 'self-sufficient' and those who have become overly dependent upon the charity of others. There may be 'leaders' and 'activists', and others who seem 'helpless' and 'apathetic'. There may be 'good copers' who seem well able to look after themselves, and 'problem families' and people with recognised 'special needs', such as the old and infirm, the physically disabled or mentally handicapped, or the children in need of care and protection. There may be people who are regarded as 'assets' to the community and who are liked and respected, others who are disliked and envied, those who are regarded as 'dangerous' or just as a nuisance, such as young vandals or teenage delinquents, and some who are kept at arm's length simply because they seem 'different', because of their 'peculiar ways' or because of the colour of their skin.

The community worker's task is to learn to understand the **structure** of the neighbourhood, to find out what goes on beneath the surface, to identify actual and potential leaders and activists, to point out the psychological and social barriers that keep people apart. His/her task is to enable people to better understand and communicate with each other, to recognise and respect differences between them, to face conflict openly where necessary. His/her task is to enable people to identify and face their needs and problems, and to recognise the contributions **all** can make to help to improve the physical conditions and social situation of the neighbourhood. The community worker's task is to enable people to work together to achieve **common goals**, rather than to be diverted, confused and weakened by useless and needless quarrelling and discrimination among themselves. His/her task is to help people discover that finding scapegoats for inadequacies and injustices brings **no** solutions, identifying those who are really responsible and holding them accountable, **does**. Last but not least, the community worker's task is to enable those who dispense charity to participate constructively in bringing about change and improvement in the community, not to continue the debilitative tradition of doing things **for** people, but to do things **with** them.

A neighbourhood or community is rarely a cohesive, harmonious whole; there are usually groupings and factions, social and cultural differences and economic and political factors which create their own dynamics of co-operation and conflict.

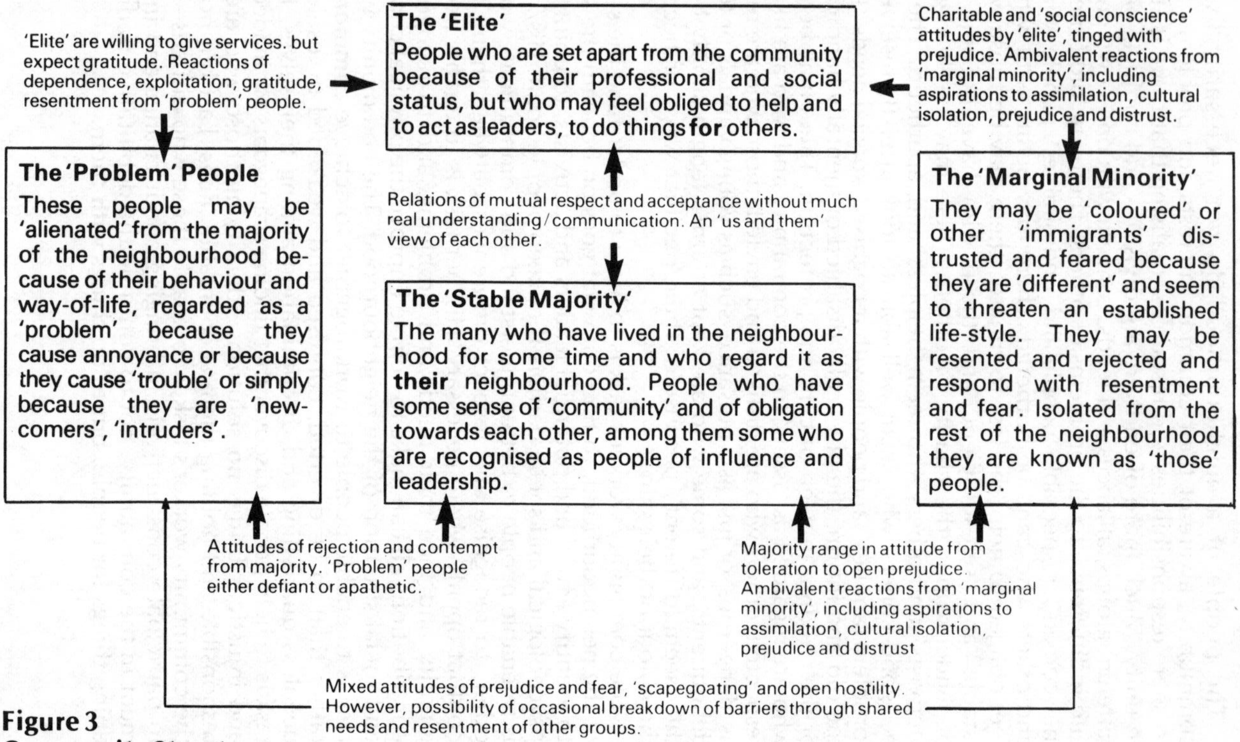

Charitable and 'social conscience' attitudes by 'elite', tinged with prejudice. Ambivalent reactions from 'marginal minority', including aspirations to assimilation, cultural isolation, prejudice and distrust.

The 'Marginal Minority'

They may be 'coloured' or other 'immigrants' distrusted and feared because they are 'different' and seem to threaten an established life-style. They may be resented and rejected and respond with resentment and fear. Isolated from the rest of the neighbourhood they are known as 'those' people.

The 'Elite'

People who are set apart from the community because of their professional and social status, but who may feel obliged to help and to act as leaders, to do things for others.

Relations of mutual respect and acceptance without much real understanding 'communication. An 'us and them' view of each other.

The 'Stable Majority'

The many who have lived in the neighbourhood for some time and who regard it as **their** neighbourhood. People who have some sense of 'community' and of obligation towards each other, among them some who are recognised as people of influence and leadership.

Majority range in attitude from toleration to open prejudice. Ambivalent reactions from 'marginal minority', including aspirations to assimilation, cultural isolation, prejudice and distrust

'Elite' are willing to give services. but expect gratitude. Reactions of dependence, exploitation, gratitude, resentment from 'problem' people.

The 'Problem' People

These people may be 'alienated' from the majority of the neighbourhood because of their behaviour and way-of-life, regarded as a 'problem' because they cause annoyance or because they cause 'trouble' or simply because they are 'new-comers', 'intruders'.

Attitudes of rejection and contempt from majority. 'Problem' people either defiant or apathetic.

Mixed attitudes of prejudice and fear, 'scapegoating' and open hostility. However, possibility of occasional breakdown of barriers through shared needs and resentment of other groups.

Figure 3
Community Structure

52

The three-dimensional model of community work should be regarded as an integrated, indivisible whole, unified by the principle of participation. In this approach the community worker's overall task is to enable people to participate actively and effectively in the social system which controls and determines their daily existence and the future of their children.

Without the unifying and guiding principle of participation, any one of the three parts of the three-dimensional approach may lead to the imposing of the community worker's, or his employer's, will and objectives upon the community or group. This may lead to the manipulation of people to conform to the needs and objectives of one or another agency, organisation or system, rather than enabling people to identify their own needs, rank their own priorities, determine their own objectives and choose their own ways and means of reaching their goals. Moreover, without the guiding principle of participation, even the most competent and effective services provided by the community worker can only be of temporary benefit. Depending mainly upon the expertise of the community worker and the resources and support he can mobilise, matters are most likely to revert towards their previous state when the worker leaves.

Any selective division of one or another part of the three-dimensional approach must, of necessity, be artificial, because the three-dimensional approach reflects the reality of the inter-relatedness of the social situation as a whole. People's needs and problems do not exist in compartmentalised sections of 'self-help', 'service delivery' and 'service co-ordination', but in a social reality in which these factors are interdependent.

Over-emphasis on self-help objectives carries with it the temptation (and in some cases the intention) of restricting people to their own mutual-aid networks and resources and the charity of voluntary outside help, thereby depriving them, in practice, of the will and ability to identify and to assert their rights to, and make the best use of the statutory services.

Over-emphasis on service-delivery improvements without simultaneous development of the self-confidence, the internal resources, the organisational and negotiating skills of the community, and/or the special-needs group, may lead to pseudo-participation in policy-making and administrative structures, aimed at streamlining and economising to the detriment of minority needs, adjustment to local conditions and accountability to the consumers.

Over-emphasis on co-ordination without sufficient strengthening of the organised influence of the community, and/or special-needs group, also entails the danger of token participation and may lead to the manipulative misuse of community workers and community leaders to ensure conformity with the preconceived objectives and deadlines of planners and administrators.

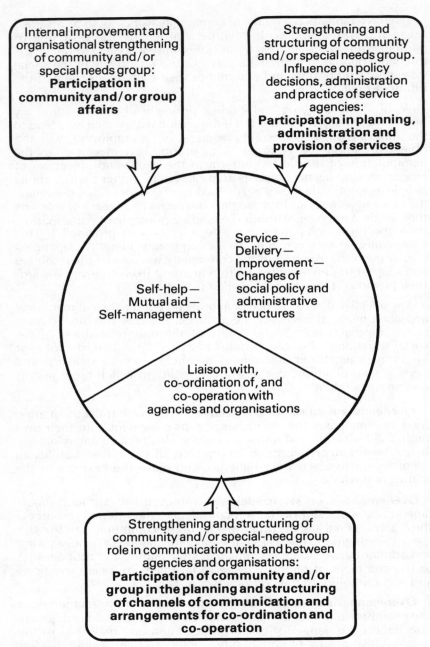

Internal improvement and organisational strengthening of community and/or special needs group: **Participation in community and/or group affairs**

Strengthening and structuring of community and/or special needs group. Influence on policy decisions, administration and practice of service agencies: **Participation in planning, administration and provision of services**

Self-help —
Mutual aid —
Self-management

Service —
Delivery —
Improvement —
Changes of
social policy and
administrative
structures

Liaison with,
co-ordination of, and
co-operation with
agencies and organisations

Strengthening and structuring of community and/or special-need group role in communication with and between agencies and organisations: **Participation of community and/or group in the planning and structuring of channels of communication and arrangements for co-ordination and co-operation**

Figure 4
The Three Dimensions of Community

Social Change: the Strategic Goal and the Realities of Limits

No community or group exists in a vacuum, but is subject to the determining influences of, and the limits imposed by society as a whole. Any far-reaching and lasting improvements of the physical conditions and the social situation of the community or the special-needs group must, therefore, seek to change conditions in the wider sense; this may mean the need for change in the socio-cultural, economic and political conditions which determine the present situation and the future perspectives of individuals, families and groups.

There is a range of possibilities for change provided for within the limits imposed by our system of society. Within this range the limits are rarely clearly-defined. Limits are often arbitrarily or accidentally imposed, and obstacles to change in some areas may be imposed by one interest group, while a group or organisation with conflicting interests may be ready to assert its power to remove such obstacles. Our system of society is based to some considerable extent upon a balance-of-power equilibrium, constantly challenged by conflicts of interest, and always seeking to re-establish its equilibrium by negotiation, accommodation, compromise or change. This leaves some considerable room for manoeuvre and for introducing new factors, such as an organised and purposeful community or a special-needs pressure group, into the local, regional or national arena.

Community Action and Social Action: Testing the Limits

Perhaps the most important function of community work is that of applying its knowledge and skills to the continuous process of enabling communities and groups to effectively test the limits which seem to be imposed upon any need or demand for social, economic and political change.

This testing-the-limits in itself consists of an action, or a series of activities, which may lead to the emergence of a new power factor. For instance, the progression from diffuse anxiety and anger over inadequate housing conditions to organised protest may lead to planned community action by several hundred, or even thousands of council tenants, and this would no doubt constitute a significant new factor in the local political spectrum, which could attract allies and worry opponents in the local power structure. The political clout of pressure groups in testing the limits imposed upon the demands for improvements and fundamental changes for people with special needs (the handicapped, for example), or of national interest groups such as trades unions, employers' associations or farmers' lobbyists, is well-known.

While **community** action tests the limits on a local level, **social** action on a wider scale may do so regionally or nationally. The objective is always to establish what the limits to any proposed change are,

55

who or what imposes and defends these limits (obstacles to be removed, opponents to be confronted), or possible partners (for bargaining), and who is indifferent to, or opposed to these limits (potential converts and allies).

Success, or partial success, may come when it becomes clear that the limits to change which were generally believed to exist and/or to be insurmountable, either turn out to be just a figment of someone's lack of imagination, or can be overcome with some degree of concerted and sustained effort; or when it is found that such obstacles to change can be side-stepped and made irrelevant, rather than met head-on; or when the limits are pushed back through negotiation and persuasion, or removed through direct confrontation. This kind of success can be, and has been, achieved with regard to issues as different as obtaining permission to use a piece of local authority-owned waste land for football practice, or widening eligibility for the government's mobility allowance for the parents of disabled children.

In many cases the achievements of community and social action may be regarded as 'trivial' by those who see the only solution to all social problems in terms of fundamental changes in the socio-economic and political system. Pending such far-reaching revolutionary change, successful testing of the limits on a smaller scale is often of very considerable value to individuals and families, groups and communities, and perhaps to the standards of humane behaviour and social justice in our society. It is, however, of the utmost importance for the community worker to realise and accept the fact that there **are** limits which **cannot** be removed with the methods and resources of community work. Such limits may be imposed by economic and political factors which seem to be beyond anyone's control, as in the case of unemployment and inflation. Others may be limits which serve to preserve the socio-political system itself. No society will permit political and social action which is aimed at its own destruction. Whatever the ideological commitments and personal political affiliation, in his or her professional role the community worker must face and accept these realities. By refusing to do so he or she will, at best, confuse and mislead, and at worst endanger and help to defeat the people who seek his or her advice and guidance. The community worker's realism and sense of professional responsibility become most decisively important when called upon to help the community or the group to understand whether they are facing obstacles to change put in their way by interest groups, which can be confronted or bargained with, or whether they are facing the limits imposed by factors or powers which they can neither hope to control nor defeat.

References

1 **B Davies,** 'Non-swinging Youth' in New Society, 3rd July 1969.
2 Royal Commission on the Distribution of Income and Wealth, Report No. 6, Lower Incomes, No. 7175, HMSO, and **R Layard, D Piachaud** and **M Stewart,** Background Paper No. 5, The Causes of Poverty, HMSO, as reported in The Times, 25th May 1978.
3 See, for instance, **G Weightman,** 'The Making of Modern Slum Estates' in New Society, 29th June 1978, and **A Larkin,** 'Ghettos of Rural Poverty' in New Society, 18th May 1978.
4 **Stein** and **Cloward** (Eds.), Social Perspectives in Behaviour, Free Press, 1958, p.15.
5 **MacIver** and **Page,** Society, Macmillan, 1962, p.5.
6 Ibid., p.15.
7 **Ronald Frankenberg,** Communities in Britain, Penguin, 1973, p.238.
8 **J Rowland,** Community Decay, Penguin, 1973.

Recommended Reading

R Plant, Community and Ideology, RKP, 1974.
Naish and **Filkin,** 'What does a Community Worker need to know? What does a Community Worker need to be able to do?', Occasional Papers in Community and Youth Work No. 2, University of London Goldsmith's College, 1974.
G W Goetschius, Working with Community Groups, RKP, 1971.
A Barr, 'The Practice of Neighbourhood Community Work', Papers in Community Studies No. 12, Department of Social Administration and Social Work, University of York, 1977.
D H Thomas, Organising for Social Change: a Study in the Theory and Practice of Community Work, George Allen and Unwin, 1976.
Chetham and Hill, 'Community Work: Social Realities and Ethical Dilemmas' in British Journal of Social Work, Vol. 3. No. 3, Autumn 1973.
Glen, Pearce and **Booth,** 'Resources for Social Change', Papers in Community Studies No. 14, Department of Social Administration and Social Work, University of York, 1977.
A Leissner, 'Participation: Issues of Strategy and Tactics' in **P A Evens** (Ed.), Readings in Social Change Vol. 1: Community Work Theory and Practice, Alistair Shornach, 1974.
A Leissner, 'Social Action and Social Realities' in Social Work Today, Vol. 9, No. 4, 20th September 1977.
A Leissner, 'Community Work and the Volunteer' in Social Work Today, Vol. 3, No. 22, 8th February 1973.
A Leissner, 'Models for Community Workers and Community Youth Workers' in Social Work Today, Vol. 5, No. 22, 6th February 1975.
D M Cox, A Community Approach to Youth Work in East London, YWCA, 1970.
A Leissner, 'Community Youth Work: a Team Work Approach' in Community Health, Vol. 5, No. 5, March/April 1974.

A Leissner, 'Participation and Pseudo-participation' in *International Child Welfare Review*, December 1971.

A Leissner, 'How Youth Work can Involve the Community' in *Youth Review*, No. 25, Winter 1972.

T Powley, 'Detached Youth Work and the Community' in *Youth in Society*, No. 8, November 1974.

D Evans, 'Community-based Provisions for Young People' in *Health and Social Service Journal*, 10th April 1976.

Leissner, **Powley** and **Evans**, *Intermediate Treatment: a Community-based Action-research Study*, National Children's Bureau, 1977.

Wedge and **Prosser**, *Born to Fail?*, Arrow Books, 1973.

A Leissner, 'Parents and Children in High-need Areas' in *The Parental Role*, Papers given to Annual Conference, National Children's Bureau, 1972.

E V Davies, *Neighbourhood Families*, London Council of Social Service, 1977.

Recreation and Deprivation in Inner Urban Areas, HMSO, 1978.

Humphry and **John**, *Because they're Black*, Penguin, 1971.

S Taylor, 'Racism and Youth' in *New Society*, 3rd August 1978.

V Goldman, 'If the Kids are United' in *Sounds*, 22nd July 1978.

Chapter 4

Schooling and Pastoral Care: Resistance to Schooling and the Welfare Reaction

TONY HILL

Tony Hill entered teaching after periods of clerical, manual and commercial labour. After some time in secondary art and craft, he began to specialise in work with 'maladjusted' pupils. He worked in a residential school in Essex, and ran a withdrawal unit in South London. He is now in charge of a sanctuary unit and has active interests in a number of organisations involved in this type of work. He is currently Editor of *Socialism and Education*.

4

Introduction

Although 'there is in English schools a strong tradition of pastoral care'[1], that tradition has led to major transformations in pastoral organisation over the past 20 years, which absorb an increasing proportion of the education budget and deploy a rapidly growing number of people who function in schools in a complex and problematic relationship with traditional 'academic' work. An increasing amount of time is being taken up **within** the academic curriculum, and within the routine working day of the class teacher, to effect some form of 'pastoral' concern for pupils. A lot of media space is given over to the complex discussion surrounding pastoral care in schools, in particular its focus on 'disruption' and general work with 'difficult' pupils. The media tend to simplify and polarise this discussion, as do the professional teaching unions. As with other contentious social concerns, one finds far more heat than light in the debate.

One developing feature of pastoral care, the 'Counselling Service', derives from the rapid growth business in America which is itself linked to 'correctional reforms', such as the famous Massachusetts model. This is largely responsible for what the 'Schools Council Working Paper No 15' refers to as 'a quickening of interest and activity'[2] in what has become a career structure on its own. A pastoral career structure is available to those who are perhaps disinclined to subject teaching, who may prefer the close contact with pupils and the less formal mode of work. In this they are similar to colleagues in youth and community work and other peripheral education areas. The CEO of ILEA has recently stated that experience in work with 'disruptive' pupils will make the path to senior positions more easy to travel — one measure of the importance of such work with education authorities.

Although there is a growing number of trained and qualified 'counsellors', the main thrust of the pastoral effort is still through the ordinary school staff and, as 'Teachers' Action No 3' points out, substantively through women teachers[3].

There tends to be a professional division between pastoral and academic work in schools, one which calls into question the distribution of higher-scale posts and the sharing of the educational work-load of schools. Although subject teachers understand the support given by pastoral care, they see pastoral care as more of a 'welfare' concern, and one which ought perhaps to belong more properly to the social services and other related agencies, leaving the schools free to 'teach'. On the other hand, although the pastoral area is well staffed, often over-staffed in the schools themselves, there is little specialised administrative or advisory oversight of pastoral practices. Those with academic priorities often have some pastoral responsibility tagged onto their commitments, wherever the need might be felt.

The Schools Psychological Service has helped to fill the resulting gap as it did with remedial education, and this had contributed to a psychologically over-weighted ideology of pastoral care, and a weak body of knowledge about 'disruptive' activity in schools. In recent years teachers in special withdrawal units, both on-site and off-site, have made attempts to organise themselves, and the ILEA's new policy on sanctuary units is bringing divisional inspectors, advisers and administrators alongside head teachers in an attempt to control and account for the somewhat random provision and practices in units for 'disruptive' pupils. This specialised field of pastoral work is the one attracting most interest at present, because it deals most directly with the contemporary 'problem' of classroom disruption. So far the focus of this burgeoning interest has been on secondary schools, though it is moving quite quickly into the primary sector, and largely in working class areas, particularly urban and inner-city regions.

There is a need to 'know' just what is happening within this complex and contradictory movement in schooling; a need to open up the ideology underpinning it and to analyse the activities in the classroom. This paper is intended as a small, introductory contribution to what will become a major debate in the future of education.

The Practice of Pastoral Care

James Ferman, writing in the ILEA Magazine 'Contact', referred to pastoral care as 'that ill-defined if noble ideal (that) is too often a euphemism for the buck that society passes to its teachers'[4]. If the 'ideal' is ill-defined, the practice is certainly ill-assorted, and it would not be possible to make a definitive statement on the pastoral practices in schooling today. Pastoral systems vary, though they tend to cluster around either a 'house' or 'year' system with a hierarchy that flows down from the head teacher, through a pastoral deputy head, senior master or senior tutor, and on through heads of school, heads of house or year to a front line of year or form tutors. Generally the pastoral function decreases in 'purity' as we descend the hierarchy, and the pastoral role of tutors usually becomes inextricably tied to their role as general teachers.

The pastoral function can be seen at work when special 'relevant' lessons and projects are prepared, in so far as these might be aimed at keeping certain pupils 'busy'[5] on a programme of learning so that they do not create problems for teachers who wish to teach 'proper' subjects to those who are more amenable. This is perhaps what Marland means when he refers to pastoral care as having a 'central educative purpose in itself'[6].

It is certainly not practically possible to separate academic and pastoral work in the urban secondary school, as many teachers would prefer — and as the career division suggests — though the creation of trained 'counsellors', who typically spend 80% of their time in face-to-face interviews, is tending to force a division, one which is actually threatening the existing pastoral structure. In practice the pastoral care system can be justified as 'enabling' the school to carry on its traditional 'grading, skilling and disciplining' functions, by removing or modifying those elements which pose a threat to those functions. This is not to deny the more general 'welfare' role of pastoral care, but to point to a specific tendency within it. A tendency which focuses the pastoral skills on 'disruption' in the classroom.

'Teachers' Action No 3[7] mentions the 'trivialised' routine practices of the pastoral teacher who must deal with school-rule enforcement, sending pupils home if they're not wearing a tie, and so on. The class teachers are seen as using form and year or house teachers as a disciplinary back-up system; sending pupils along to them who are making teaching difficult, and thereby setting in motion a system of sanctions, lines, detention, issuing of report forms, waiting outside of doors and so on. There may be a dash of counselling thrown in, often finger-wagging paternalism, but the process usually facilitates a move from 'normal' class work to a surveillance and control area which marks or confirms the pupil as a 'troublemaker', 'deviant', or whatever label may be utilised. In a sense, the pastoral staff are often operating as the whips and timekeepers; the 'production control' elements of the school workplace. Many of the pastoral functions overlap with the careers service in schools, and there are several contingent services linked to pastoral care, the Education Welfare Service, Schools Psychological Service, Social Services and, more tenuously, the Juvenile Bureaux of the police force. It usually follows that the more intransigent the 'problem', the more support is sought from other services; just as within the school itself the 'problem' engages the attention of more people according to its perceived 'seriousness'.

Apart from attendance checks, the issuing of passes and the making up of reports, the pastoral staff attend case studies and care conferences, education welfare meetings and so on, as well as routine staff meetings and home visits. The senior pastoral staff frequently have an air of harassment about them which is generated from the multitude of demands made on their time and skills. Lee Rainwater has referred to such teachers as society's 'dirty workers'[8], and it must be said that many feel pushed around, asked to do too many things etc. If the pastoral role is being played in a special school, withdrawal unit, tutorial unit or any such agencies from the range of educational and social safety nets that are strung around the periphery of schooling (they may be seen as micro-'educational priority areas'), then it is usually more simple to carry through, because it is more focused, and less cluttered with institutional demands.

In such units curriculum work tends to have a strong remedial bias, and the underlying approach seems directed at social control, modification, social education and therapy. The *'Times Educational Supplement'* recently gave four pages over to a study of some of these units[9], and it is clear from this that such units tend generally to deal with the 'middle range' of problems, leaving the 'heavies' — the 'clinically maladjusted', the 'bloody-minded' and the utterly bored — to find some other exit from a system that aggravates and often antagonises them. This might be by way of truancy, suspension or expulsion, a residential unit, community home or whatever. Or, perhaps more typically, by bargaining for 'easy street' outside of the classroom, playing dominoes, drifting between teachers who can 'handle' them, waiting interminably outside of offices or being tossed into whatever provision can be found for them. In this way many pupils learn as much about the demands and responses of the world of work as their friends who knuckle down to routine class work.

The middle range of pupils are seen as being in need of something resembling a 'short, sharp shock', or perhaps personal and group therapy, or 'behavioural modification'. Units tend to set themselves up under one methodological banner or other. Pupils pass through them for a sort of 'turn round' behavioural servicing, so that they can return to the school and tick over more smoothly. This 'servicing' entails a log of routine paper-work, but at least the teachers don't have the school hierarchy bearing down, or the manifold routine demands of a large comprehensive school clawing at them, such as marking, lesson preparation, supervision, meetings and so on. There are, of course, other demands arising from the generally closer involvement with the community, though it is easier to pace the response to these demands. Most units do need to secure some sort of working arrangement with the pastoral staff in referring schools, and this usually means that the school disciplinary system locks itself in to the unit, with some flexibility which can be negotiated by the unit teacher using the argument for 'therapy'.

Unit teachers are quite often found supporting the free school creed in one degree or another, in particular the ideas of A. S. Neill and his followers. This brings them into conflict with the demand to return the pupil to school and to seek some resolution of this demand, in the vague notion that the mainstream school system can be changed by utilising the pedagogical practices of the unit. This is most usually found amongst teachers who work in the off-site units set up under voluntary bodies and supported by LEAs. Teachers working in the on-site units and those more closely controlled by the LEA often respond to the demands made upon them simply by accepting the task as defined by the school, by acting as an extension of the school.

I have tried to argue that by working closely with schools, but claiming some autonomy, the unit teacher can help to transform some of the key social control practices in the school, and can alert teachers to alternative practices. This works best with individual cases where the unit teacher is able to furnish a more complete and supportive context within which to discuss a pupil or a problem. It is possible then to make such discussions routine in the school. Obviously there are many accommodations to make, and many unit teachers find this impossible for political reasons.

Pastoral work enlarges the 'surveillance' of dissident youth in schools, and one might suggest historical reasons for this. Young people are being dealt with in their communities where 'direct' total care is not possible, but where a whole network of caring 'welfare' agencies can ensure that restive youth is 'gentled', the 'negative' influences of family and social environment are filtered out or remedied in the effort to get pupils to conform to the school's varied social behavioural requirements.

If the social deprivation thesis is taken seriously, then this approach to 'problem' pupils is unproblematic, but seen as Ingleby regards it, the total surveillance of working class youth and families is a reactionary tendency[10]. The intervention in 'extra-school factors' of working class pupils is repressive, and when the school system is linked to the factory system of work[11], or is seen as one of the key agencies for the 'reproduction of hierarchies', then the vital work of pastoral care as a facilitator of social control is revealed more clearly. In the final analysis, it all depends on whether one accepts that there is a social class struggle still going on in our society, or whether one believes that class is a dead or irrelevant concept.

The extent to which the territory of social control is spreading may be seen in the Central Lancashire Family and Community Project, started in 1965[12]. Following the Seebohm Report of 1969, many authorities used the 'Lancashire' idea of social work in school, many now having their own social worker as well as an education welfare worker. The Lancashire project sums it up as *any kind of work which operates through personal relationships to help children and their families to solve and adjust to personal problems*. Which shows that the 'child saving' ideology is still with us[13]. One may lightly sketch a picture of crumbling institutions with masses of working people trapped, the managers having fled, and the welfare and pastoral workers busy patching up broken heads and crushed spirits, but seeing the injuries and harrowed looks as warts, infections and hernias, brought about by too much lying underneath rubble, with insufficient intellectual or spiritual protection to endure prolonged suffering. Here the need to carefully administrate the procedures displaces the need to change or rebuild the structures.

It must be said that many workers in the 'welfare' areas recognise the contradictions they live and work with, and many struggle to effect changes in their workplaces; but the 'radical' position is very difficult to locate in practical terms, it is far easier to theorise about[14]. Most workers are left to muddle towards radical practices whilst luxuriating in radical theory and action **outside** of their workplaces. I see this as a crucial weakness in the struggle towards a socialist society, one shared at every level of education. It is perhaps less excusable amongst intellectual workers, who may urge the practical worker to take a more radical approach whilst avoiding the reactionary constraints on their own intellectual 'practices'.

In the present social-economic climate we are witnessing a strong bureaucratic response to 'radical' ideas and practices in education. 'Accountability' is everywhere manifest, linking the 'progressive' educational scene to some mythical picture of a time when education was the simple, easily measurable and widely successful experience of youth. What is being dealt with in this reaction is not the success of 'education' as an intellectual or technical activity, but the loss of social control in an educational system which is being openly challenged by pupils, teachers and parents, albeit in different ways. Even the claims that our technological society requires an ever more skilled work force are an inversion of the truth[15]. Pupils seem to 'know' more about the truth in this respect:

'What a capitalist society requires at this stage, is a more disciplined and tractable workforce which will trade its technical and creative potentiality for a mess of 'leisure' provisions, and for 'waiting around' in a reserve army of labour.' 'Disruption' in any productive context challenges that requirement'[16].

It is teachers who must find a response at the 'chalk-face' to policy changes and the difficulties faced in doing that are, as yet, barely understood. The LEAs seem prepared to pour resources into work with 'disruptive' pupils but are, as already mentioned, seeking more direct control over the disbursement and utilisation of those resources. There was never so much concern over resources for curriculum development, resources which are now being cut. LEAs and teachers' unions are still talking about the 'few' pupils whose disruptive behaviour makes things bad for the others. This is a patent falsehood in the experience of most inner-city teachers. These bodies still clearly believe that by rooting out a few 'rotten apples' from the body of pupils and a few 'rotten apples' from the teaching force, then all manner of things will be well, especially with community 'welfare' machinery ticking over (just) and a rigid 'policing' of communities and social institutions[17]. This all depends, of course, on a particular interpretation of 'disruption and violence' in schools.

Disruption and Violence in Schools

Strangely, it is difficult to assess the extent and character of 'disruption' in schools. A couple of years ago an ILEA educational television programme discussed the 'disruptive one per cent', though one of the participants gave the lie to the figure by mentioning an impressive range of resources available to deal with the *'five or six in any one school'* who are being 'disruptive'. On the other hand there has been a vast amount of coverage of urban school 'problems' in the local and national mass media, indicating that, at the very least, there is a moral 'panic' on about disruption[18].

As a sobering start to an analysis of the problem, it might be usetul to look briefly at the historical context of disruptive behaviour in schooling. Struggle against schooling is as old as schooling itself. In 1669 a 70-page 'Children's Petition' was presented to Parliament by 'a lively boy' in which, amongst other things, there was reference to the stern authoritarian teachers of the day, who had *the liberty to use such a kind of discipline over us, that the spring time of human life, which in all other creatures is left at the greatest freedom to be sweet and jocund, is defloured and consumed with bitterness and terror, to the drying up of the sap which should nourish our bodies, and those more lively spirits which should animate our minds in our future life unto brave actions*[19]. An adolescent upsurge in a privileged class perhaps . . . but thrust into a political context with political intentions. There were revolts at Eton. One of these was a stirring incident in which the whole school, led by the prefects, walked out and refused to return for two days; other incidences included 'rebellions' at Rugby and 'mutinies' at Winchester — all in the eighteenth century. In 1818, one such 'rising' was put down by two companies of soldiers with fixed bayonets. In 1876, not long after the first successful moves towards compulsory state education had been made, a group of Greenwich teachers put their voice to that of the pupils in a petition to the school board, protesting about corporal punishment. Unfortunately the burden of teaching huge classes of recalcitrant pupils proved too much by 1880, and the 'in loco parentis' position on corporal punishment was established in the state teaching profession. A most interesting struggle took place in 1889 when *militant schoolboys from Kennington and Lambeth met on the Albert Embankment. They resolved not to return to school unless they were granted four demands; free education, one free meal a day, no home lessons and no caning*[20].

One can see in these sorts of demands the notion of schooling as a service, as part of the 'social wage'; a notion which is very much part of social democratic thinking on education, and which remains dominant in educational debate today. If 'alternative' possibilities had been readily available, one can assume that the demands would have changed accordingly. In recent years the struggle has taken a more overtly political line — the rash of pupil strikes in 1911 perhaps opening a new era. These strikes were largely in sympathy with striking parents, though they were all too easily and contradictorily put down by many of the parents themselves[21]. The strikes and 'sit-ins' of the 'Lycéens and Technics' of Paris schools in 1968 were a stirring recent example of organisation around a belief that schooling is socially divisive and against the true interests of the working class[22]. It is of some interest to note that the Paris schools have stirred once again more recently, though not in the more open form of struggle which characterises the Italian experience of schooling.

There are also recent examples in England. In 1968 three pupil power groups emerged, each claiming a membership of some 500 or more. Only the NUSS remains as a group with a voice — a voice sometimes amplified by the strains of traditional NUS activity. The NUT still refuses to recognise the NUSS, even though its own membership's actions all too frequently disrupt the pupil's educational work. In America, even as I write, organised action by teachers is disrupting the work of half a million pupils. For socialists this is a particularly unfortunate contradiction.

Pupils at Emanuel School in London recently staged a 'sit-in' to protest against comprehensive reorganisation, a reactionary struggle which helped to reveal the class base of what might appear to be a common struggle. Forty students at Nottingham staged a 'sit-in' because they felt that their teachers regarded them as 'lost causes'[23]. At about the same time 200 pupils went on strike at a school in Burnham, Essex, 100 of them marching into the town centre to protest against the wearing of school ties and the banning of trousers for girls[24]. The school received a lot of publicity in this action and the head subsequently banned 'journalism' from a careers convention held at the school[25]. Police were called in to handle this strike. In another action involving the use of police, pupils from Kidbrooke School, South London went on strike and marched to disrupt several other schools in the area, seeking solidarity[26]. In Tower Hamlets in 1978, the social services and other community agencies joined with pupils in calling for a pupils' strike in solidarity with harassed Asians in the area. Very few teachers seemed to understand or appreciate the political implications of the strike, and there were the usual charges of 'irresponsible' and 'unruly' behaviour flying around affected schools. The much debated action at William Tyndale Junior School in North London perhaps offers the most interesting possibilities for political analysis in recent years, though the action was complex and contradictory, and the lessons have not yet been properly drawn from the experience.

The actions cited above are the more visible 'politically' disruptive actions, but what of the countless thousands of smaller actions going on continually in schools? Some of these are organised, such as the attempt to remove 'boring teachers' by petitioning the headmaster (parents giving active support in one South London school); classes refusing to work or leaving the school premises; organised efforts to bait and divert teachers; protest about curricula, conditions of work, school food and so on. Then there is a vast amount of ill- or non-organised protest going on, some of it collective, some of it individual, all of it 'disruptive'. Often the 'changes' being sought through protest are changes towards anything other than what is currently being experienced, but there are more articulate demands to be found in the disruptive behaviour of pupils, and if the current vogue for political education is to have any real meaning then we must recognise the political education that is taking place as pupils live out their lives in school[27] and on the streets.

Just as I am suggesting that the voice of the pupil should be heard, so do I suggest that the teaching unions listen more carefully to the 'chalk face' teacher. At present the unions are dominated by head teachers who are caught in the trap of 'hierarchy'. Teachers, by and large, do not seem to understand what is going on, and in consequence are letting themselves be deafened by the orchestrated blare of the Black Paper writers and reactionary trades union leadership, or be lulled by those social-democrats who claim that the school system is an exploitable market place for 'shop'-happy parents, or is part of the social wage that the working class must earn by behaving themselves.

There is a struggle going on within the institution of schooling, and if the right wing reaction is in the ascendant, it is because the left is divided and confused; and the broad mass of teachers, who falsely claim that education is 'non-political', are simply weary of a struggle that makes no kind of sense to them. Their inaction only nurtures reaction. Dissembling the ideology of schooling is of the utmost importance in the struggle.

The Ideology of Pastoral Care

'Caring for the flock' is surely as old as the earliest social formations, and will just as surely extend beyond current revolutionary social movements. As long as people gather together (something which the capitalist system does not provide for except through social class divisions), such forms of response to need will always be utilised. We do not necessarily have to criticise the ideology of 'care' at that level, only to examine its nature and extension over time and its utilisation in specific sections of society, at specific historical moments and in specific social institutions.

If the society is fairly stable (and in particular if it is in the mode of 'mechanical solidarity' located by Durkheim in 'The Division of Labour'), then the caring functions will be enshrined in 'rituals', and the functionaries will thereby be able to maintain social order with relative ease. If the society is unstable, breaking down and reforming itself (something not covered adequately in Durkheim's notion of 'organic solidarity'), then the 'natural' functions of care will assert themselves in the direction of protecting the vulnerable areas of society and, at one and the same time, protecting the established and valued institutions. In this way it is possible to control the 'resistance' and the 'reforming' process of a society under stress. 'Care' is then appropriated by one section of society to defend its interests from the threat of change, regardless of how noble the welfare ideals used in developing it in particular ways. Such a defence is very costly, and at times of economic crisis a whole mass of contradictions is thrown up, much of it serving to counteract any effort to unite people in the face of that crisis. It is my contention that behind the 'caring for people' is a 'caring for capitalism', and they are almost inseparable at this historical moment in England, at least in **practice.**

The biological root of pastoral care must not be forgotten. Darwin and Spencer gave us the notion of 'adaptation', or 'adjustment of the organism to its environment'. If the social environment is God-given, universal and immutable, then we can legitimately concern ourselves for the social adjustment of those who have 'strayed'. If the environment can be seen as man-made, culture-specific and transitory, then it seems quite proper to ask questions about a society which is generating high levels of 'maladjustment', in particular where those levels are related to the social class divisions of that society or to generational differences (which, incidentally, replicate themselves).

In particular schools, as in other workplaces, we can legitimately ask questions about the negative effects of the environment, not in terms of its level of material deprivation, but in terms of its defective normative structures which are disruptive of its own organisms[28]. The notion of 'total welfare' of children, sympathetically advanced by Michael Marland in his book *Pastoral Care*, is seen as a coping in the face of the *'massive influence of extra-school factors'*, the most significant of course being 'primary socialisation' into family life. The family institution reproduces resistance to being socialised at a particular level, and that always has to be countered. Hence the importance to capitalism, or any other society, of the 'secondary socialisation' in schooling.

A root can be found in residential care, where children are removed from their families, their communities — in a word, from their 'environment'. With community-based action one would expect to see the pastoral care system moving into the communities, and this is what is happening as the system of separation and punishment or 'modification' fails to come up with the goods.

The practices in the variety of peripheral educational resources dealing with disruption are, as I've already suggested, very jumbled; a tangle of roots can be found which reach into Freudian psychoanalysis, the behavioural work of Thorndike and Skinner, and the encouraging, more recent fashions for 'touch therapy' (a bizarre privatised way of overcoming 'alienation') and Kleinian psychotherapy. What these practices might gain individually will be lost collectively, because they are not addressed to the 'problem' of disruption as a political problem rooted in a specific social-economic formation, but instead focus on the individual presenter of the 'problem' as deviant.

The historical thrust of pastoral care has been, like other aspects of welfare in the service of capitalism, largely concerned with repairing, servicing, modifying and tuning the workforce in a system which functions by way of an exploitative social division of labour. It could not logically be otherwise, but as we move inexorably towards a socialist society we must properly understand and utilise the welfare provisions in the service of that emergent society, and a pre-requisite of that is to recognise the political nature and class characteristics of 'care' in general, to demystify it. To claim that welfare is somehow non-political, theoretically underpinned by objectified scientific knowledge, is to support the social-economic system **against** the wider, collective interests of the individuals, families and communities to whom that welfare is directed.

The present 'phoney' phase of development we refer to as 'social-democracy' is a phase of great upheaval, in which welfare, and controls on welfare, are extending across the entire socialising, working and leisure life of the working class in particular ways, as successive administrations wrestle with the problem of crumbling social institutions —family, work, schooling and so on.

Such welfare is massively a task of surveillance, and it utilises a vast bureaucratic system which will be all too easy to computerise in the near future. Anthony Platt underlines the role of pastoral care in a society which fears its youth and, having no effective punitive response to their struggle against authority, offers a bureaucratic welfare reaction. *'Rather than increasing opportunities for the experience of legitimate power by adolescents, public agencies have opted for closer supervision as* **a means of decreasing opportunities for the exercise of illegitimate power'**[29]. (My emphasis.)

One of the key commentators on pastoral care in England today, Michael Marland, reveals the fragile nature of the process as he seeks a way around the possibility of schooling crumbling into irrelevance. Making use of Erik Erikson's anthropological approach to social research, he has this to say: *'School learning, however intrinsically interesting we may endeavour to make it, is an inevitable but perhaps regrettable layer we have had to insert between the child and his adult life'*. It is a layer necessarily **preliminary** and **obscure**, as Erikson stresses; it therefore develops its own goals and limitations, its achievements and disappointments. To help re-focus the experience and relate it to later life (which has come to be thought of as 'real life') is a pastoral need for twentieth century youth, and one which cannot be accomplished by pure teaching[6].

Clearly Marland has no interest in demystifying the process he advises on, and comes very close to offering an apologia for capitalism by default. For him, pastoral care becomes a 'compensatory', even placatory offering to pupils who cannot or will not accept that education, **as given**, is of value to them. Many pupils see through pastoral care and use it as a 'soft option' in schooling, which suggests to me that neither punitive nor caring measures will ultimately prove effective in dealing with disruption, not while the response to 'disruption' is based on a false or inadequate analysis of it, and certainly not whilst 'disruption' in society at large is politically active.

Paul Willis, in research which shows pupils preparing themselves for the inevitable struggles at work by developing an effective 'oppositional cultural form' at school, draws on a different view of disruptive activity. *'To the outsider, it* (conflict over uniform) *may seem a fatuous argument about differences in taste. Concerned staff and involved kids, however, know that it is a continuing tussle about authority, a fight between cultures, and ultimately a question about the legitimacy of school as an institution'*[30].

What of the pupils themselves, how do they see disruption? One might court individual views and secure a wide variety of responses from the irresponsible to the plain daft, but one section of pupils has thought its ideas through and is organising with the aim of intervening politically in the educational system. This is the National Union of School Students, and in a letter to me, a past Vice President commented on disruption in this way: *'School students* (not 'kids' it will be noted) *are organising with us to set up union branches in schools, linked on an area level, in the struggle for improving our education. By doing this we hope to build up enough strength to be able to demand that school students are brought into the process of organising and running schools. As far as we are concerned, until this happens, whilst every school student feels alienated from the system which imposes control on them seven hours a day, five days a week, there will inevitably be disruption in the classroom. School students are already registering their discontent with the system, playing truant, vandalising school and generally being disruptive. What we in the NUSS hope to achieve is to channel this discontent into positive action which will build rather than destroy'.*

This is the voice which frightens the teaching unions with its threat to the traditional 'paternal' role of educationists and to the 'professionalism' so dearly sought in a vocation which thrives on the separation between intellectual and manual labour in a capitalist society. As a socialist I find this voice more clear and more hopeful than the hysterical outbursts and confused carpings of the teaching unions and of others.

In this paper I have tried, in a faltering way, to show that 'disruption' in schools is a complex and contradictory phenomenon, and that the response in pastoral care is similarly complex and contradictory. The search for 'certainties' I leave to those reactionaries who seek refuge in the certainties of the past in fear of the dawn of socialism in England. I have also tried to show that there are alternative ways of practising pastoral care in schools, limited and difficult though they may be. As a worker in the area of pastoral care I cannot claim academic or 'scientific' distance from the phenomenon, though I value the thoughts of those who might wish to make such a claim. Instead, I have tried to root out some of the contradictions which beset my routine practice, by tracking back and forth between theory and practice, by utilising an historical context, by studying accounts of disruption from a variety of sources and, above all, by struggling to set the subject in a social-economic context.

As a socialist I can conceive of no other way of working towards an understanding of this most enervating and wasteful feature of contemporary school life in England.

References

1 'Counselling and Guidance', ILEA Pamphlet, 1976.
2 'Schools Council Working Paper No. 15', Schools Council, 1967.
3 See 'Pastoral Care: Concern or Control?' in Teachers' Action No. 3, Winter 1974.
4 James Ferman in 'ILEA Contact', ILEA, January 1976.
5 For a discussion of 'busyness' as an aspect of social control, see R Sharp and A Green, Education and Social Control, RKP, 1975.
6 M Marland, Pastoral Care, Heinemann, 1974.
7 Teachers' Action No. 3, op cit.
8 L Rainwater, 'Revolt of the Dirty Workers' in Transaction, November 1967.
9 Ibid.
10 D Ingleby, 'The Job Psychologists Do' in N Armistead (Ed.), Reconstructing Social Psychology, Penguin, 1974.
11 P Willis, Learning to Labour, Saxon House, 1977.
12 See British Journal of Guidance and Counselling, Vol. 3(1), 1975.
13 A Platt, The Child Savers, University of Chicago Press, 1969.
14 S Cohen, 'It's Alright for You to Talk' in R Bailey and R Brake, Radical Social Work, Arnold, 1975.
15 H Braverman, Labour and Monopoly Capital, Monthly Review Press, 1974.
16 P Willis, op cit.
17 S Hall et al, Policing the Crisis, Macmillan, 1978.
18 S Cohen, Folk Devils and Moral Panics, Paladin, 1973.
19 P Newell, A Last Resort, Penguin, 1972.
20 Ibid.
21 D Manson, 'Children Strikes of 1911' in Ruskin History Workshop Pamphlet No. 9, 1973.
22 C Rosenberg, Education and Society, Rank and File Publications, 1973.
23 See The Morning Star, 6th March 1976.
24 See The Guardian, 4th March 1976.
25 See The Times Educational Supplement, 19th March 1976.
26 See Teachers' Action No. 3, op cit.
27 G Whitty and R Johnson, 'Political Education' in Socialism and Education, Vol. 5, No. 5, 1977.
28 M J Power, 'Delinquent Schools' in New Society, 19th October 1967.
29 A Platt, op cit.
30 P Willis, 'How Working Class Kids get Working Class Jobs' in Schooling and Culture, No. 3, ILEA Cockpit Arts Workshop, 1978.

Chapter 5

De-schooling Youth Service
FRANK BOOTON

Frank Booton began voluntary youth work whilst in the RAF during the 1960s, and after leaving university became a full-time youth and community worker in Sussex. He conducted research on youth work as an aspect of education development for a PhD at the University of Sussex, after which he returned to the field as a youth officer in London. He is currently a tutor on the Youth and Community Work course at Sunderland Polytechnic.

Youth Service as it has historically evolved, and to the limited extent to which it has been officially determined, is a public service within the education system. Its purpose is to undertake and supervise the social development of the adolescent by means of offering facilities for leisure and recreational pursuits, in a social context, and in a manner which encourages the growth to maturity of the individual. This is otherwise called 'social education'. Within the general structure of the public services in this country, youth service is unique. Its peculiarity derives principally from three organisational characteristics of crucial importance: (a) the concept of voluntary and statutory co-operation (the 'partnership'), which is intrinsic to the evolution of the service; (b) the institutionalisation of the youth unit in respect of the validation of the 'youth club' as a recognised requirement in every community; and (c) the non-vocational, non-academic and non-compulsory commitment on the part of the young person using the service.

The partnership concept involved the recognition by the State of the early efforts made by the voluntary organisations which, prior to the Physical Training and Recreation Act of 1937, were responsible for virtually all work with youth in Britain. Historical association has given the idea of the partnership a deeply rooted relevance within the evolution of youth service. Today, the contribution of the 'voluntaries' is considerable, embracing as it does the many hundreds of very different types of organisations, ranging from the internationally-linked uniformed movements such as scouting, which counts its membership in the hundreds of thousands, through the national club-based organisations such as NABC, to the humble local group in which two or three parents run a one-night-per-week club for neighbourhood kids in the tenant's hut or church hall. Recently, this framework of Youth Service 'voluntarism' has been extended by the incorporation of a further element, that of youth projects established under the various programmes of urban renewal. They are usually in the form of 'alternative' provision, such as detached work, coffee-bar projects, information units or specialist (ie. unemployed) services. Many of them are not identified with the LEA service in their locality, though, strictly speaking, they are not voluntary organisations either, since the source of their funding is statutory. Their objectives are often short-term, their resources temporary, and their target groups almost exclusively working class. Consequently, in ethos they are closer to the voluntary sector than any other. Given the uncertain future of the urban programmes, those that survive beyond their original phase may do so only because they become 'voluntary organisations' in the conventional sense.

The administrative title 'Youth Service ' encompasses all these forms which, together with statutory provision, usually manage to co-exist in partnership without either compromising their own individuality or becoming victims of conflicting interest. Most 'work with youth' undertaken in our society is effected through voluntary agencies. The extent of this commitment is not known precisely, though one source, in a recent costing of estimated voluntary labour at the lowest part-time paid rate, arrived at a national figure of £27,165,300 per annum[1]. There is no doubt that the overwhelming majority of attachment to the service, on the part of youth itself, is through the voluntary sector. In some areas of the country this may be as high as 75%, whilst in none is it likely to be less than 50%. Moreover, the statutory element of youth service still relies upon voluntary part-time staff for a significant proportion of its total labour force, and the Service as a whole is dependent upon voluntary initiatives for project exper-mentation and the innovation of techniques. The partnership thus has a complicated but practical validity, and though doubts concerning its effectiveness are periodically raised — including, in 1975, doubts by the DES itself which conceded its *inadequate realisation*[2] — it survives; a continued testament to the democratic notion of mutually co-operative goodwill. In other senses, too, the concept has a unique relevance. Youth service is the last remaining area in the education services of this country where local government and private initiatives realistically combine. Though the sectarian nature of some voluntary youth and community work, or individual motives behind it, may be questioned, the important fact to consider is the essentially **democratic** character of the partnership, and, in particular, the potential for further demo-cratisation through the possibility, only yet partially realised, of public access and involvement. In other sections of the public services — particularly in the field of social welfare — the ethic of voluntarism has generally suffered as a result of statutory expansion, though, in the growth during the past ten years of local councils of voluntary service, there are indications of a rediscovery. However, in their support of voluntary youth and community work, many local authorities maintain a level of grant-aid which, though invariably made from the smallest proportion of the education budget, frequently exceeds that made in total by other departments, such as Social Services.

The second, most important factor which describes the organisational peculiarity of youth service is the contemporary acceptance of the youth unit as an essential element of community provision. In one form or another, what we recognise as the youth club developed historically from the same institutional origins as the school, the earliest examples pre-dating the Forster Act of 1870. However, though victorian in its origin, it is only comparatively recently that the State has sponsored the development of youth units — has formalised, as it were, its responsibility for the social development of its youth. Consequently, we must conclude that it is the effect that the youth club has had in social terms, or the function of youth work itself, that is responsible for this gradual legitimation of its relevance within modern public planning, as well as the increasing desire on the part of society at large to supervise the behaviour of its youth. It would seem that irrespective of whatever form it may take, industrial society can no more do without its systems of youth provision than many other institutions of a similar size, the primary school for instance, or the welfare clinic.

The nature of the involvement of the young person with youth provision in this country is traditionally non-academic, non-vocational and completely non-compulsory. Youth service in Britain has always existed as an extremely differentiated range of opportunities for the individual adolescent. They may choose to do one of a great number of things by joining different groups or clubs or, most importantly, **they may choose to have no involvement at all.** This constitutes an unusual type of relation, on the part of the young person, to the Service, and it ensures that at any time a typically successful youth club will be fairly cosmopolitan in both its interests and, hopefully, its membership. Despite the vagaries of young fashions and tastes, the majority of youth clubs retain the flexibility to adapt in order to meet rapidly-changing needs. The actual proportion of the adolescent population using youth provision is not known with any certainty, but the research done by the Social Survey Division in the early 1970s suggested that overall attachment had not changed markedly since the 1940s[3]. Today, fluctuations in attachment are more likely to be located in age than in social characteristics. A majority (65%) of all young people were thought to use some form of provision regularly according to the Bone Report[4], and almost all (93%) have contact during the age-period 14-20, though the proportion using youth service agencies frequently was considered to be probably no higher than one in three. Considering the general impoverishment of resources at the disposal of the average youth worker, the fact that much 'youth work' is merely a recreational provision, and the enormous manipulative demands for the time and attention of young people made by commercial provision and the media, an attachment ratio of one in three is good. It is perhaps surprising that teenagers in our society look to attend youth clubs at all.

One of the more significant developments in English youth work during the last 15 years has been the emergence and growth of what has become known as 'school-based youth work'. Described briefly and in necessarily general terms, the concept of school-based youth work entails the establishment of statutory youth provision on the campus of a school. The youth unit itself is usually purpose-built, and the school almost invariably secondary. The unit, normally called a youth wing or youth centre (and, perhaps interestingly, not so often a 'youth club') is operated according to similar procedures as those usually found in the local authority centre. Full-time and part-time staff are customary, though it is likely that a majority of part-time leaders are themselves teachers. In most cases the full-time worker is one of the permanent staff of the school, and thus subordinate to the head. Occasionally the staff member responsible for youth work has head of department status, usually depending upon the size of school roll, and most have additional teaching or curricular responsibilities. There are virtually no unqualified school-based workers, however the number that have actually received specialist youth work training, equivalent to that of the qualified worker in the non-schooled sector, is probably less than 20% of the occupational group. Analysis of appointments advertising shows that the variety of titles offered in school-based posts reflects a tendency to amalgamate the roles of teacher/youth worker, or to incorporate the youth and community specialism into a school hierarchy, though perhaps not altogether successfully: tutor-warden; teacher-leader; youth tutor; community education worker, etc. Though few local education authorities seem able to offer a defined career structure for the school-based worker without reverting to a full-time teaching role, he or she is often very advantageously placed economically in comparison to youth work colleagues elsewhere in the Service. This, however, is at the cost of several well known occupational inadequacies, of which role-confusion is probably the most serious[5].

In England the historical development of school-based youth work stems primarily from the ideas of Henry Morris, the originator of community education theory. Other debatable influences are certain European experiments (in particular the Folk High School[6]) and the multi-usage or 'campus' concept of secondary education planning from the USA, with its embodiment of pastoral care. Economic expediency has also been an important factor. The 1944 Act implicitly obliged local authorities to maintain provision for youth, but neglected to offer either a definite policy for, or a philosophy of, social education. During postwar educational reconstruction the local authorities themselves faced the extremely difficult task of providing for a doubling of the secondary school population, as well as a considerable increase in adult and further education demand, plus the establishment of sub-services such as separate youth and youth employment services, all within less than one generation. Pervasive uncertainties as to comprehensivisation, the failed promise of the county colleges and coercion by successive ministers through the regulation of the building programme, meant that educational planning was all too often encouraged to short-circuit developmental problems by adopting such practices as multi-purpose usage and, in particular, the building of much larger schools. Inevitably, during the 1950s the physical size of the secondary school grew. This period also saw an increasing pressure for more public access to the enormous investment of 'dead' educational facilities. Together these bestowed upon community education theory a convenient popularity. It is significant that prior to 1969 official reports concerned with Youth Service (ie McNair, 1944[7]; Albemarle, 1959[8]) did not especially recommend an expansion of school-based youth work, whereas reports concerned with mainstream education did (ie

77

Crowther, 1959[9]; Newsom, 1963[10]). A case is frequently made that the YSDC report, 'Youth and Community Work In The 70s'[11], was above all the document that advanced the concept of school-based Youth Service. However, the report itself remained officially unadopted, but, more importantly, by the time it was produced the pattern of development of school-based work, which was to confirm its expansion throughout the 1970s, was already firmly established. The report merely recognised and confirmed an existing situation.

By the early 1960s it seemed logical to many local authorities to deploy Youth Service resources in a manner more closely allied to developments in secondary education. It is generally thought that the immediate post-Albemarle period of Youth Service expansion provided something like £50 millions worth of function-designed plant. For a while during that decade every local authority in the country was erecting 'purpose-builts', and the whole ethos of English youth work became building-conscious. In effect, much of this development ended up within the school-based sector of provision. By the late 1960s other areas of youth work were claiming attention, in particular detached provision. Since 1970 the building of statutory non-schooled youth units has all but ceased, though the building programme for school-based units has continued because of its relation to secondary expansion. Thus, it is correct to assert that, generally, development of the school-based youth units has often been at the expense of other forms of statutory provision.

In any event, school-based youth work has expanded to the point where a majority of all local education authorities now operate such a policy, though not always exclusively. However, its actual extent nationally is still not precisely known and is difficult to assess. The DES Youth Service Register records the number of full-time youth work posts, but does not appear to distinguish between schooled and non-schooled provision. The professional associations, NAYCEO and CYSA, undertake periodic surveys of the total national displacement of staff, but sample returns are seldom high enough to do other than merely indicate. For example, an 'Education' digest published in 1973, but using the previous year's figures, gave the number of school-based posts as '700 and growing'. The NAYSO (later NAYCEO) 'Staffing Report' for 1974/75, which had a reliable 95% return, reported 625 school-based posts. Other sources show that in 1974 the 'Times Educational Supplement' carried 968 advertisements for full-time youth work (non-officer) posts, of which 369 were school-based, from 69 authorities. The following year — the first year of zero-growth in Youth Service — 62 authorities advertised 338 school-based posts from a total of 893. A reasonable estimate would seem to be that at the present time perhaps 30 to 40% of all statutory youth provision in England is school-based, and that proportion must still be increasing, albeit less rapidly than at the beginning of the decade. Increasing then, but with what implications, and at what cost?

The early advocates of schooled youth provision were quick to emphasise the points of similarity between the schooled unit and the non-schooled statutory or voluntary centre. Essentially, the argument ran, the kids are the same kids, they have the same needs and aspirations, and the same methods will be used to meet them. Other considerations thought to favour the schooled approach are based on concepts of 'total' education, such as the now-prevalent community education theories. In addition, there exists the simple 'expediency' case which claims that the centralisation of composite educational facilities of a campus type are either more practical, cheaper, or both. These and other arguments have all been proposed in support of the singular contention that is most frequently made on behalf of school-based youth work, that in essence the concept is not fundamentally **different** from either (a) the remainder of centre-based statutory provision, or (b) the overall ethos of work with young people that other sectors of youth service objectify. The literature supportive to the concept is large and readily available, there is no need here to repeat those arguments. Reasoned critiques of the concept, however, have seldom been attempted. This seems odd, especially considering that the rate of development throughout the 1970s indicates, quite clearly, that if it were to continue a majority of all statutory youth service provision will be firmly tied to secondary education by the mid 1980s.

Schooled provision clearly cuts across the traditional precepts of English youth work. The Service must continually adapt its resources and techniques to meet new challenges, yet the burden of pioneering experimental approaches falls heavily on the voluntary organisations; in part for reasons of their willingness as much as their own flexibility, more often perhaps because, during the period since 1970, statutory youth budgets have included virtually no funds for innovation. Certainly during the 1960s local authorities were enthusiastic in their support for voluntary expansion as 'developmental'. Detached youth work, youth counselling, community industry and homeless projects are examples of such developments that, together with the techniques deriving from them, arose from specific voluntary initiatives. There are now grave doubts as to the future practicality of the partnership concept, and it must be recognised that school-based provision has contributed to its recent erosion. The voluntary agencies have little physical access to schooled facilities, less to the support expertise that skilled youth tutors might provide, and virtually none to the material back-up, such as equipment and transport, that could — and should — be available as public utilities. Moreover, the school units themselves appear to shun innovation. Within the statutory sector as a whole, experiment is limited, but within school-based work it seems all but non-existent. The expectations upon the voluntary organisations to innovate is thus now unreasonably high. In this respect the immediate future seems particularly depressing. For example, the school-based sector appears to be doing little or no work with unemployed youth. Similarly, though a few school-based IT schemes have been attempted, generally there exists no identifiable attempt to work with the increasing number of young offenders in the secondary age group. Perhaps more surprisingly, in view of the recent developments of multi-worker community education programmes in city areas, there seem to be no school-based youth work examples of detached projects. It can only be construed as a serious misplacement of priorities, in that the 30-40% of statutory youth service that claims the newest buildings, some of the most lavish resources, and the highest salaried section of the workforce does not have to meet the same expectations as the remainder of the Service.

Since the concept of school-based youth work owes so much to the theories of community education, it is worthwhile examining it from that point of view. Morris conceived the ideas from which the philosophy of an education process *coterminous with life itself* largely derives. However, the scattered collection of jottings which constitute his writings — including the well known *'Village College Memo'* of 1924 — are quite devoid of specific planning for youth. Perhaps this can be explained partly by the fact that during that period work with youth did not enjoy the validation within social policy — and certainly not within education planning — that it has since acquired. Perhaps, more to the point though, Morris himself saw the social needs for recreational and leisure provision being met by the utility-purpose community centre. He considered that such a building would satisfactorily meet all the requirements of local youth, as well as servicing the wide variety of adult needs which arise in the healthy community. It is from this element of Morris's thinking that community education in its non-academic sense has evolved, though the specific youth unit is a latter day amendment, Morris himself did not speak of separate provision for young people. His scheme, of course, was primarily designed to function in the small decaying communities within the depressed areas of the rural county. Beyond this, however, Morris's scheme displayed a sort of socialist application, implicitly expressed but not fully worked out. It has been applied nationally in recent years through adaptation in an attempt to meet the problems of modern suburbia — a very different range of social implications. On the other hand, Morris was undoubtedly correct in predicting that modern societies would have an increasing need for educationally-based community services. It is well known that Youth Service itself has, since the 1960s, become heavily involved in community work practice, albeit at a comparatively low level of competency. It is now generally reckoned that most, if not all, youth work should be conducted within a community context, and this, of course, is the primary rationale of school-based youth work itself. However, the schooled sector of the Service has engaged itself in very little authentic community work, despite its strong ideological links with the modern educative notions associated with 'community', and its superior resources. More often, regrettably, when the school youth wing is not being used specifically for youth activities it becomes a teaching annexe or, worse, in the name of pupil participation, a 'common room' for privileged sixth formers. Despite the large investment in community education the school is still a closed institution to the vast majority of our population, and very often the school youth wing is no less so to the kids. The term 'community' does not denote an educational reality in our society, and the schooled youth unit is actually retarding the educational process, since its primary function is to reinforce the identity of the 'school' rather than 'society'.

The strongest area of doubt concerning the effectiveness of the school youth unit centres upon its institutional character, and thereby the nature of social relations enacted within it. The school itself, of course, is an institution of immense social influence, and as the literature of educational sociology shows, its relationships are highly complex and not easily reducible to generality. Several points though can be made to demonstrate a simple hypothetical comparison between 'typical' examples of the statutory youth centre and the school-based unit. It should be recognised immediately that certain fundamental characteristics emphasise a basic difference. The secondary school has become the recipient — also, perhaps, the victim — of an almost incredible level of material input, and now its actual size is instrumental in determining its efficiency. Administratively and organisationally it cannot possibly function as a **social** centre, indeed to do so would frequently give rise to an incompatibility with its own academic objectives. Within the modern secondary school the level of human exchange is of necessity structured, disciplined, and inevitably sustained by compulsion, and it is doubtful if a 'good' school can ever really fulfil parental expectations of academic achievement without it being so. The school-based youth worker's skills may help to modify that relationship, but most often it probably does so on behalf of the school as an institution, and not on behalf of the adolescent. School-based youth work must either reflect the nature of this basic relation conflict in its work with young people or, by denying it, engender irreconcilable tensions among the academic goals of the parent institution itself. In practice, it is likely that any conflict will be displaced merely by **accepting** a basic divergence of aims and coercing the worker in the situation to absorb the results as a role-stress. It is doubtful if this basic ambiguity of role between teacher and leader can ever be satisfactorily resolved. Special staff designations within school contexts, and the inevitable assumption of special tasks, responsibilities and techniques, cut across the best initiatives towards the development of the **whole** school as a facility for the **whole** community. It may be argued that **all** teachers, not merely teacher/youth workers, should have training that enables them to relate to their clients as **persons,** and not merely pupils. Generally, institutional specialisation more often consolidates trends towards isolation than not, and the process of integration of the school with its community is not therefore likely to be advanced by the deployment of specialist youth staff.

Institutionally, the school youth unit cannot be separated from the school, indeed the whole argument for such provision is based on its essentially integrated identity. In contrast, the typical statutory youth club or centre possesses a very different institutional character. It is physically very much smaller, and seldom experiences the basic conflict of objectives which seems to be intrinsic to the school youth wing, even allowing for the usage inefficiency which is widespread through-out the Service — and the obvious inadequacies of the 'containment' function behind some of its programming. Moreover, the statutory club is much more intensely cost-effective; three leader posts are still rare, and even dual worker posts are by no means yet the norm. Its size, its relative simplicity of operation and the democratic accessibility of its resources are all factors which outweigh its obvious material inferiority. Moreover, one could suggest that its institutional scale is analogous, in terms of human relations, to the concept of an 'inter-mediate technology'. The best youth clubs are still primarily **social** places, and whilst the principle of voluntary attendance is adhered to they should remain so. The traditional Youth Service concept of the open youth club — a voluntarily-attending, freely-associating social grouping of young people — is the context for social education which most closely approximates to the natural peer groupings that the adolescent encounters in society. The concept is fundamental to centre-based youth work, and where it succeeds it does so because kids relate **by choice** to the institutional nature of the club, and inside it to each other, within their own culture but without having been coerced, and, more importantly, without having to compromise their own social identities. It cannot be doubted that most kids function within one culture inside school and a different one outside it. Youth Service does not experience this institutional culture conflict because its work has always depended upon meeting the kids on their terms. It is precisely this inherently difficult aspect of social education that constitutes the evolving central objective of youth work in a democratic society. The worker has the responsibility of ensuring that his centre facilities encourage social interaction, with special support or guidance for the individual or group if required. We must accept that very many young people now experience great difficulty in relating to the institutional demands of the school. We should also realise the obvious reluctance of the professional education bureaucracy — despite DES urgings — to **open** the school to society at large, and not merely selected portions of it. We must then ask if it is likely, in view of these facts, that schooled youth provision can possibly educate the adolescent socially as successfully as other modes of provision in Youth Service have so far managed to.

At the present time the answer, in general terms, must be 'no'. Given what we know about the modern secondary school, given the basic role confusion of the worker, his or her restricted professional autonomy and the hierarchical accountability of a formally 'educational' nature, given the fundamentally different relationships between the worker and the kids, and both to their respective institutions, it is not merely reasonable, but **logical,** to assume that the school-based sector is not making a contribution to the social education of young people commensurate with that found elsewhere in the Youth and Community Service. Perhaps it can be stated even further. It may well be that, eventually, research into numerical usage, types of programme and social categorisation of membership will show that school-based youth units, when compared with non-schooled statutory provision, are less well attended, generally incline towards activity-based rather than social-based programmes, occupy the interests of a narrower cross-section of the youth population, and are not at all effective with kids who, for whatever reason, do not or cannot enjoy a 'good' school experience. The summary is simple: the development of the schooled unit has, to some extent, actually jeopardised the concept of the 'open' youth club, and with it the Youth Service philosophy of social education.

References

1 *Working Party Report on Resources to the Youth Service,* Youth Service Forum, 1979.
2 *Review of the Youth Service: Summary of Views Expressed in the Discussion,* Department of Education and Science, 1975.
3 *The Youth Service and Similar Provision for Young People,* HMSO, 1972.
4 Ibid., p.1.
5 **P M Hayman,** *'The Youth Tutor'* in *Youth Service,* Vol. 10, No. 5, May 1970. See also **Bernard Davies**, *'School-based Youth work'* and **Harold Haywood OBE**, *'School-based Youth Service'* in *Debate: a Collection of Professional Papers,* Youth Service Information Centre, 1969.
6 **P Manniche**, *Denmark: a Social Laboratory,* Pergamon Press, 1969.
7 *Teachers and Youth Leaders,* HMSO, 1944.
8 *The Youth Service in England and Wales,* HMSO, 1959.
9 *'15 to 18': Report of the Central Advisory Council for Education,* HMSO, 1959.
10 *'Half our Future': Report of the Central Advisory Council for Education,* HMSO, 1963.
11 *Youth and Community Work in the 70s,* HMSO, 1969.

Chapter 6

Building Worlds — Creating Fictions

TED BOWDEN

Ted Bowden studied at Gold-smith's College and the London Institute of Education, after which he taught for several years in the East End. He has also done part-time youth work in Bromley, and more recently,

became Editor of *'Hard Cheese: a Journal of Education'*. He is presently attempting a PhD at the Department of Sociology, Goldsmith's College, on the practical accomplishments of educational psychology.

6

Introduction

What follows is my construction of a participatory experience in a secondary school during the present school year, and is an attempt to raise questions about definitions arising in the context of the teachers' day-to-day work[1]. More specifically, I am looking at that school's attempt to come to terms with its first-year intake.

From the beginning of the present academic year the school, in common with many others, had been faced with difficulties of staff recruitment. The shortage of staff resulted in many time-table alterations and eventually the implementation of part-time schooling as an attempt, albeit limited, to provide some sense of permanency to the timetable. Further, it had been indicated by the head that a certain number of staff, who in normal circumstances would not have been employed by the school, had been appointed. The number of probationary teachers in the school was also deemed to be high. The impression gained was that these teachers were seen as inadequate in some way or another. An added complication was the previous biography of the school which, according to one member of staff, was the main reason for the school failing to attract its fair share of 'good calibre' first-choice applicants from the locality. According to calculations, well over 50% of the school's first-years were in the low-ability banding range.

These factors were acknowledged by the head, the head of first-year and certain other senior members of staff as not being conducive to what they saw as the 'well-being' and 'good social order' of the first-years. They were, it seemed, also a potential threat to the 'well-being' and 'discipline of the whole school'. Having been defined as a 'problem year' the first-years were therefore to be the subject of a staff inquiry.

Two meetings were held with all the teachers involved with this year. The original intention was to discuss a list of 54 children (all defined as 'problems' in one sense or another) drawn up by the head of first-year. However the first meeting (meeting one) remained at a fairly general level, whilst the second (meeting two) was devoted entirely to discussing name by name the 54 'problems'.

Meeting One — February

The general assumption at this meeting was that the first-years did not seem to be working as efficiently and smoothly as they should have been by that stage of the year:

'The problem is to find the best way of training/civilising the vast majority of the first-years'.

One should not, it was suggested, have children shouting at teachers across the room, children should not be wandering aimlessly around the room, should not drop litter, make the furniture look untidy or be chewing. These practices were not, it was argued, associated with that frame of mind which exhibits a sense of involvement and interest in school and, by implication, school-work. It was recognised though that a fundamental contradiction had to be solved: 'Children should be interested and involved but there are differences between children, thus the problem of managing them as a unit'. However, this was not achieved because of a preoccupation with tackling the year as a whole: 'From my observations it is the general standard that worries me, not just one class or individuals'.

The children, it was argued '. . . should know what is expected of them in very mundane things — entering and leaving a room. Many of the problems of indiscipline are a result of a lack of preparation and planning from a teaching-technique point of view. Consistent following-up and repetition is needed. Relationships and respect with classes has to be built up over trifling things like giving out books. Should one have to be told to tell the children to take off their coats? It is these basic rules that one needs to look at, that is, be pernickety about these things'. These notions were further stressed: 'We should know what acceptable/unacceptable behaviour is. Act on it — take the initiative. Come down to the mundane points with the first-years at the start of the morning. Ten minutes with establishing rituals that are necessary for first-years — pens, chewing etc. . .

A preoccupation with order as a panacea for discipline[2] was very evident, and it was suggested: 'In class see that the children are down to work at the beginning of the lesson to keep order, then involve them later'. Also: 'You need order in the room to take a register and set the atmosphere for the day — training them in communication'.

One suggestion was that the first ten minutes of the day could be used as a form library period in order to induce a worklike atmosphere. However, it was replied: 'Is this useful for them when we have such a high proportion of non-readers?'

During the course of the meeting a feeling of senior/junior staff differences seemed to be emerging; one senior member of staff suggesting: 'Experienced teachers are lacking in sympathy to newcomers'. Another senior member of staff suggested: 'Young staff don't realise how powerful they can be — they need to exert themselves. If the attitude is that you're going to have trouble, you're going to get it'.

One of the so-called junior members of staff replied that he'd found double standards: 'Will I or will I not get support from another member of staff? For instance in the general running of the school, for example, seeing kids in the hall — some teachers say 'yes' and some say 'no'. This also applies to lining up outside the classroom'.

The problem of differences in staff interpretations was then touched upon. It seemed to be decided that although it might be useful, one could not have written guidelines as to what practices were rules and what were not. When one junior member of staff suggested that for her it might have been useful to have had some guidelines, one of the senior members retorted: *'It would help if young teachers approached a problem instead of abiding by a set of rules. Does it matter how order is kept? Therefore we must hesitate in laying down hard and fast rules'.* However, the same member of staff went on to suggest: *'There is a system of discipline in the school that has got to work, that is through head of year, head of department, deputy head and head. Do not ignore discipline'.*

One possible solution was offered by another so-called junior member of the staff: *'It would be a good idea to promote a sanctuary unit for problem kids — short or long periods of time'.*

The problem as to who should be placed in the unit, if started, was then touched upon. The consensus indicated those children unable to function normally for background reasons or because of themselves — in other words not the discipline problems per se. *'If we do have a sanctuary unit it will not be a dumping ground. In terms of low- or very low-ability children, the back-up service to the school is very limited. We've got to look after that child'.*

An example of the overloaded back-up service was given by the head of first-year, who said that at the end of the previous term four children had been referred to the educational psychologist; however, only one had been seen so far. If, though, any junior members of staff had trouble with the first-years it was once again stressed that they should use the school referral system — report first to the form teacher, then head of year or the head.

At this point it was suggested that the meeting close and that the second meeting ought to deal exclusively with the 54 'problems'.

Meeting Two — March

For this meeting the staff were presented with a class-by-class list of the 54 'problem' children. Before proceeding to discuss the individual children a few general remarks were made by the head of first-year. He said that he had worked out a simple key for the 'problems' — the problem categories not actually being marked on the list for security reasons, loss etc. The key was:

    R   — remedial, the really lowest kids
    EP — emotional problems
    NE — non-English speaking
    B   — behaviour problems
    BOG — kids with parents on school's board of governors

This, it was stressed, was being mentioned as a point of information. He continued: *'Some children have double problems. Most classes have an IQ range of approximately 40 or more — sub-70 to 120. It is therefore very difficult to plan lessons. We need to look at our own lessons and to see how we can improve them for the bright, intelligent and sharper kids. We have a wide spread in every class. The kids we tend to fail badly are the brighter ones, who in the third or fourth year become behaviour problems. We need to cope with this spread of ability — we must not neglect the brighter kids'.*

The individual 'problems' were then introduced/discussed by the head of first-year, with additional comments being made by other members of the staff. Fourteen examples are given below:

Pupil One
Head of year — *'A little madam. Friday non-attender and lesson truant'.*

Pupil Two
Head of year — *'Behaviour problem, any information welcome. This pupil is a bully — tends to thump people'.*

Pupil Three
Head of year — *'A nuisance who gets very uptight when told off. Don't allow him to give lip'.*
Teacher A — *'Should not be allowed to get away with anything, especially with women staff'.*
Teacher B — *'One is faced with the problem of West Indians wanting stiff discipline'.*
Teacher C — *'Given suitable work he will do it, as will most of the first-years'.*

Pupil Four
Head of year — *'Disturbed, sly and vicious, so says his mother. Behaviour problem if let ride. Okay if clamped on. Emotional problems'.*

Pupil Five
Head of year — *'Visited me ten times in his first week in school. Has the record ever since — four times in one day'.*
Teacher B — *'Works well in my subject because a high standard is not demanded. All his form work well in finding their own standard/ level'.*
Teacher D — *'He worked and tried hard in the remedial group'.*
Head of year — *'I suspect he's bright. Reported last June as non-English speaking so he must have learnt English through the summer holidays'.*
Teacher A — *'Extremely disobedient. Not frightened of authority. He is going to be very difficult'.*
Head of year — *'Was moved from another form at the beginning of term. Our policy was to put kids from the same primary school in the same class. This didn't work with that particular form. Next year we should know in advance of the problems and who should be split etc'.*

Pupil Six
Head of year — *'Poor home background. Remedial, can read vaguely. Can't write and form sentences'.*

Pupil Seven

Head of year — 'A nuisance. He is sly with it — not noticed first off. Slightly remedial. Works at weekends'.

Teacher E — 'His behaviour has improved recently'.

Teacher F — 'He's influenced by (pupil eight)'.

Pupil Eight

Head of year — 'Emotional to put it mildly. Bright but can be a bully. Likes his own way. Vicious temper and needs to be sat upon. He is a case for immediate referral to the hierarchy if he blows his cool. He has a record of nasty tricks — threw darts at other kids in the playground. He is sailing close to a lengthy suspension'.

Teacher G — 'Vital that he be kept working all the time as he is a clever boy'.

Teacher F — 'Take this pupil out of this form and it would be a wonderful class. This pupil has no redeeming feature'.

Teacher B — 'He is over-mature and foul, especially as regards the pornography that he gets from his elder brother'.

Head of year — 'He is on daily report. Happily in September we will have a sanctuary unit — we should have the physical space for a first-year unit. This will help though not necessarily with pupil eight. It will help with some of the more extreme cases'.

Teacher A — 'I have a reasonably good relationship with the mother. He is more intelligent than his brother. In times of stress do not give him a case against the teacher, especially in the case of physical chastisement. Don't touch him, hit, push or shove him in any way. This causes more harm than good. It is the last thing to do to him. The one redeeming thing is his mother'.

Pupil Nine

Head of year — 'One of a group that can cause trouble. Needs to be sat on especially with Smith (not on list). Was briefly moved to another form but now back'.

Pupil Ten

Head of year — 'Emotional. Poor home background. We've been asked by the educational psychologist to contain him in school until it becomes impossible. He has a wicked temper — boils over. Avoid confrontation in class as he plays to the audience. Lots of kids don't want to lose face. He is potentially violent with women teachers'.

Teacher D — 'But he will work hard in class. He's just very emotional'.

Teacher F — 'He's dynamite. Dangerous because one can't foresee the problems'.

Head of year — 'Minor incidents are to be expected'.

Teacher H — 'He tends to bully other kids'.

Teacher F — 'Be consistent with him — never vary'.

Teacher D — 'Split him away from others'.

Teacher A — 'But he can get at people after. If we can't control him we're not having him. Demand standards. If he threatens safety report it, especially the well being of others'.

Teacher B — 'When gestures occur get him out of the room'.
Head of year — 'We could use the lever of his keenness on sport to improve his behaviour. It might work but his temper is still there. In a sense there has been a considerable improvement overall. He is the most explosive kid in the year, in terms of damaging himself and others with his temper. Walloping is a waste of time. It reinforces the bullying as he gets so much at home. I'd like to hear everything about him that is worthy of note. Father wallops him if he is late home from school. Needs to have prior warning, as do all the first-years'.

Pupil 11
Head of year — 'Prize nuisance. Excellent at lying his way out of situations, so do not take his word on anything. Wretched nuisance. To be watched as he gets into major trouble'.

Pupil 12
Head of year — 'Remedial and emotional. Uptight about the fact that he can't read and write properly. To be watched'.

Pupil 13
Head of year — 'Emotional and behaviour (problems). Poor attender. If she decides she won't do something, she won't. For example, she stayed away for six weeks at one point. Difficult family. Home not the best. Take her gently as far as possible'.

Pupil 14
Head of year — 'Remedial and daft sometimes. Caught stealing from local shops'.
Teacher I — 'Depends on the phase of his mood. Has gone off recently. He started badly, then improved, but now slipping back. He is frightened of punishment. The scheme of the 'good fairy' with (Teacher F) helped out. I came in at the last minute and saved him from being caned by (Teacher F). He is a physical coward and will refuse to accept punishment. Needs to have his ego boosted. Responds to encouragement quite well'.
Head of year — (Teacher I's) scheme of the 'good fairy' often works a treat, particularly with the first-years'.

In conclusion, it was suggested that unless the school did something it would be 'lumbering itself' for the future. One possibility was for a withdrawal system to be set up. On being asked why it was that the school had such a high number of non-readers, the head of year indicated that one local primary school head who had a poor opinion of the school sent only non-readers. Teachers F and I argued that the children were not in fact being taught anything in primary school, thus the pace with the school's intake had, of necessity, to be slower and more patient. Parental choice, it was argued, certainly militated against the school. The final remark was made by teacher A: 'Having seen some of the parents, I have to sympathise with the kids'.

Rather than include everything that was said at the two meetings, an attempt has been made to include what I feel were the important strands of the discussions concerning the first-years — the 'problem' year. In order to raise questions about definitions arising in the context of the teachers' day-to-day work, I have had to consciously choose certain extracts of the discussions; however this does not detract from the substance of the two meetings. One further methodological note: the meetings were not taped (recorded), but full notes were made during them and transcribed as soon as possible afterwards, whilst the memory of what was said remained fresh in my mind.

Theoretical and Practical Implications
Socialisation and Social Order

It can be argued that these two meetings presented an explication of a normative perspective on socialisation. Thus, according to Mackay: *'Children are incomplete — immature, irrational, incompetent, asocial, acultural, depending on whether you are a teacher, sociologist, anthropologist or psychologist. Adults, on the other hand, are complete — mature, rational, competent, social and autonomous, unless they are 'acting like children'*[3]. In other words, this is a theoretical formulation reflecting an adult conception of children as incomplete beings (inadequate adults), which then has practical implications for the way in which teachers 'deal with' children in schools. The grounds, in this instance, for the normative perspective seem to be based on a belief that the efficiency (social order) of school is dependent on a given taken-for-granted pattern of operation; rules, regulations and behaviour are the means by which the acquisition of roles by the 'to-be-socialised' child can be further enhanced by the teacher.

These rules and regulations were, in this instance however, subject to a little confusion amongst the staff. When it was suggested by one member of staff that, for her, it would have been useful to have had written guidelines as to which practices constituted rules, a senior member of staff, who had previously stressed the need for establishing ritualisation of certain practices, then suggested that it didn't really matter how order was kept — implying 'as long as it was kept'. Thus order is only defined in terms of orderly conduct, yet there is no notion as to what dis-order may be.

Having accepted that the chief problem was seen, in this case, as a need to train and civilise the majority of the first-years, a tacit acceptance was given to the notion that social order is a result of good discipline and that this is grounded in mundane practices such as lining-up outside classrooms. Thus, it appears that the process of socialisation (training and civilising) is achieved by the inculcation of 'good practices' and 'work habits'. If this is the case then teachers are, as socialising agents, very powerful indeed.

However, the staff's analysis is probably far too simplistic, based, as it is on definitions accepted from the tradition and grounded in the notion of viewing schools purely as 'schooling' agencies which operate on a 'banking' concept of education — teachers as 'depositors' and children as 'depositories'[4]. Before 'banking' knowledge, though, it would seem that teachers are to 'bank' good practices and work habits — it having been suggested by one teacher that in class: *'One ought to see that the children are down to work at the beginning of the lesson to keep order, then involve them later'.*

This overt preoccupation by the staff with social order is perhaps a failure on their part to 'do philosophy' — to question what they are doing, what others are doing, to question what teaching and learning involve, for all concerned. In other words, to question the everyday reality and practical accomplishment of teaching in any meaningful way (for both learner and teacher). Not one teacher, for instance, questioned what the notion of socialisation could actually involve, yet all at least glossed over the subject in one way or another.

The normative paradigm of socialisation misses one important factor because of its adult conception bias, that is, it dismisses notions of any capacities that a child may have when he comes to school. Adults, rather than prescribing a way for children to view the world (school) — as ordered, regulated and rule-governed (a prerequisite for learning) — should, perhaps, first accept that children already have a view of the world and its knowledge based on the same interpretative abilities as held by adults. This view also encompasses a notion of 'differing cultures' (different worlds or forms of life) of children and adults, not based on attributes such as social class, but instead resting on a notion of 'differing interpretations' by social beings[5]. Similarly, motivation to learn can then be seen as developing from a conception of what the child sees he is doing.

In this sense, the staff at the two meetings were, perhaps, operating on the wrong level in so far as the views are taken as 'given' and not susceptible to change. It is all very well trying to achieve a social order, but not as an end in itself, and not if there are basic discrepancies as to what this should entail by the very people who are trying to institute it, that is, the members of the organised collectivity of the school.

A general 'cultural view' of these particular children also seemed prevalent amongst many of the staff — particularly those senior members with a considerable length of work experience in this one school. This view was related specifically to notions of discipline, and could be seen and found, in written form, in the school handbook[6].

'Many of our more serious disciplinary incidents arise from a failure on the part of the teacher — a failure to appreciate the East End children. Under the surface, they're exactly the same as any other kids, but there are some important special characteristics on the surface'.

'Children are, on the whole, gang animals, but the gang is more real and immediate and essential here than in most other places (and the connotations of 'gang' are far from being all that bad)'.

'The East End gang child, when in the presence of other members of the gang — the normal classroom situation — is as touchy about a point of honour as a golden age spanish grandee, and as humiliated

by a loss of face as an oriental. What, in many areas, children accept as a tolerable attitude or remark on the part of the teacher, is here regarded by the pupil as a challenge which must be taken up: in the extreme case (which is not all that rare!) it may be met by obscene abuse of a young woman teacher or a threat of violence (or actual violence) against a man teacher. The point to appreciate is that, very often, the child honestly feels aggrieved and justified'.

'Avoidance of such situations is a matter of experience and tolerance, and there can be no easy short cut to this ideal. A good rule to bear in mind is to remove the showdowns, when they have to occur, from the public place. Sometimes it is necessary to cut an offender down to size before his mates, but it has to be done by the right person on the right occasion'.

Whilst on the one hand one seems to be expected to allow for a differing culture approach (though its interpretation is somewhat dubious, to say the least), one is reminded of the ethnocentric stance that one must take towards the children — the stated culture is to be devalued in favour of that (nebulous) culture to be presented in the school: a culture synonomous with discipline (imposed and not self), social order and good work habits as a basis of civilised pursuits (seen as the basic problem in meeting one), rather than a 'negotiated' culture based on that of the children.

What one seems to have is a two-part conception of the children in the school grounded in:
(a) an adult conception of children — a normative construct of socialisation.
(b) a general cultural view of the children from the locality — somewhat romanticised.
These two conceptions appear as the general rationale for the inculcation of the civilising ways of the school, as exemplified by notions of social order already described. Once more it seems that the staff are exhibiting a tendency to 'not-do-philosophy'; rather they are working on a taken-for-granted tradition of 'schooling' (in contra-distinction to 'education').

Expectations and Typifications

Though implicit in both meetings, meeting two provides us with specific typificatory examples and their generation within an educational setting. Five categories were presented by the head of first year: remedial children; children with emotional problems; non-English speaking children; children with behaviour problems; and children whose parents are on the school's board of governors(!).

The rationale, as stated by the head of first-year, for this meeting was to inform staff of the 'problem' children. Certain children, it was claimed, were causing concern, thus needing to be brought to the attention of those members of staff who were involved in the teaching of first-years. The problematical feature of this kind of procedure though, remained unexamined — that is, the potential for this information to become a self-fulfilling prophecy and a reinforcement of already-present expectations held by members of staff.

If, for example, a teacher is faced with a child in a classroom who, according to his information, is *'sly and vicious'*, a *'behaviour problem'* with *'emotional hang-ups'*, then what are the teacher's expectations of that child when he, for instance, perpetrates a 'confrontation' with the teacher as an 'authority figure'? This very 'confrontation' could, in fact, be the direct result of some action taken by the teacher or other pupils in the classroom in a particular lesson. But, if the teacher is not careful, he could easily define the child's action as resulting from that child's 'emotional hang-ups' (which, if 'clamped on' in class, can be easily contained). The grounds for that child's 'confrontation' remain unexamined because of the nature of the initial information on the child made available to the teacher by, in this case, the head of the first-year.

In other words, the teacher is provided with an easy way of explaining, in some cases, the deviant' actions of particular children, because of 'labelling reference points' that he has access to. Similarly, so-called 'deviant' action becomes expected of certain children. This can be seen in instances where, for example, a teacher, when demanding the attention of a group, usually refers only to one or two children as the main culprits: *'Well it must be John or Pete making all the noise (because they have emotional and behaviour hang-ups and are therefore always causing a nuisance!)'*[7].

The information (labels) given on children provides a means of explanation for classroom interaction at a very superficial level only — a coping level for teachers. Labelling enhances a sense of power and security (control) for teachers in the classroom. The actions of children become easily definable through reference to these dubious labels, which are often pathological in nature and can often form the basis of defining children as 'maladjusted'[8]. At this point one perhaps needs to examine more closely the actual definitions used in the labelling of first-year children. What exactly are 'remedial', 'emotional' and 'behaviour' problems?

The teachers at both meetings appeared to be grounding their definitions in taken-for-granted assumptions as to what, for instance, counted as a 'remedial' child. A 'remedial' child was, in this instance, seen generally as one who was not at the level of other children in academic work (and 'behaviour' it also seemed!). There appeared to be an overt preoccupation here with the inability of many of the children to read or write properly, but even this notion remains to be explained clearly by those who define the inability. What standard are we to work from, and who sets this standard? We can also, it would appear, speak of 'under-achievement' without ever really questioning what the child is 'under-achieving' from.

'Behaviour' problems, on the other hand, were more clearly definable

— those children it seemed with whom, at a classroom-interaction level, certain teachers couldn't cope. However, in this instance, this remained at a relativistic level; those who could cope glibly offered panaceas for 'social control' in classroom activities to those who couldn't. Another way, it seems, for a child to become a 'behaviour' problem was through his or her being referred to the head of year for creating some disturbance. Thus those with the 'arch-behaviour' problems were the pupils who had been seen the most times by the head of year — four times in one day being the current record! Could this then involve some conscious deliberation on behalf of the pupil?

Because the definition of 'behaviour' is rationalised by reference to 'discipline', we only have a simplistic gloss on the notion. Apart from the suggestion, by the head of first year, that perhaps a key factor lay in the planning and preparation of interesting lessons, no other indication of interest could be found as to why so-called 'discipline' problems arose in the classroom. Could not, for example, the basis of these so-called problems be grounded in the actions of specific teachers in the classroom?

'Behaviour' and 'remedial' problems were, however, rarely treated as separate entities; rather, along with 'emotional' problems, they were applied generally as a two-fold analysis to quite a number of children. Thus, for example, pupil 12 is described as having 'emotional' and 'remedial' problems, pupil 13 has 'emotional' and 'behaviour' problems and pupil seven, 'remedial' and 'behaviour' problems.

The notion of 'emotional' problems remained the least explicated, and seemed to be applied to children willy-nilly — chiefly as a home-background trait. 'Emotional' is apparently a concept that all teachers 'know' and 'understand', and which can be applied as an explanation of, for example, disruptive behaviour in school. The question needs to be asked as to why easily-roused strong feelings become problematic for teachers in class, and why 'emotion' then assumes a derogatory connotation. As with 'behaviour', the reasons for a child expressing strong feelings were never examined or questioned, but were accepted as 'given' dangerous traits in terms of teachers commanding a social order over children in classrooms and schools.

The problem of non-English speaking children is, in a sense, more readily acceptable, in so far as the lingua franca of the school is English. However, the 'BOG' category is, to say the least, a peculiar point of information to be made public for the staff. Are we to assume that these children are to be given preferential treatment in terms of, for example, school reports sent to parents or teacher attitudes towards them in the classroom?

Sanctuary Units

In the course of meeting one it had been suggested that it would be a good idea to promote such a unit for 'problem' first-year children.

Similarly, meeting two provided a further suggestion, by the head of first-year, for some kind of withdrawal unit for 'problem' children.

Though one member of staff stressed that such a unit should not be a 'dumping-ground', a certain amount of confusion was evident amongst the staff as to exactly what such a unit could/would be. Whilst, on the one hand, one of the staff argued that such a unit would be for those children who *could not function normally for background reasons or because of themselves',* other staff seemed to be operating on 'remedial'- and 'discipline'-level criteria. Certainly, when the question of categorisation of pupils for such a unit was raised, the issue was quickly glossed over by the staff. Presumably, having a taken-for-granted basis of labelling categories, these would be used, although modified to a certain extent, to decide which children would become 'sanctus' pupils[9].

In view of the previously-outlined problematic nature of the head of first-year's 'problem' categories, it would seem that any unit formed on such a basis will also be problematic (as will a reliance on referrals to the educational psychologist) in its conception. The notions of 'sanctuary unit' and 'sanctus pupils' must not become unquestioned realities, in so far that they become 'coping' strategies for the staffs of schools faced with so-called 'problem children'. Those teachers interested in the formation of sanctuary units must 'do philosophy' when planning them — at least for the sake of those children whom they plan to place in them. We must not encourage covert streaming by use of dubious labelling procedures such as have been described. There is, of course, the further problem as to who should be the arbiters of those children who are to become 'sanctus' pupils.

Conclusions

In seeking to raise questions about definitions arising in the context of the teachers' day-to-day work, I have attempted to show the problematic nature of such definitions as they arose in this school's attempt to come to terms with so-called 'problem' children. I have been concerned with an analysis of the everyday reality of generating and building a world of 'problem' children. These 'problems' then, I have suggested, become 'fictions' on which to act and prescribe remedies. However, this process of construction and reification is grounded in taken-for-granted assumptions about children and schooling which, because of a perceived need by the head of first-year (in particular) and staff to be able to and be seen to cope, remained largely unexplicated and unexamined. It can be argued that the discussion served merely as a 'labelling' exercise, thus reinforcing pre-conceived expectations of the children from the locality.

Finally, then, this paper is an attempt, albeit limited, to raise questions rather than provide answers/solutions. The solutions must emanate from teachers 'doing' philosophy that is reflexive and questioning — a philosophy that challenges traditional assumptions and realities. The questions embodied in such solutions (however makeshift) provide for the possibility of the moral future of the business of education in our schools.

References

1 **M Greene**, *Teacher as Stranger*, Wadsworth, 1973.
2 **C Jenks**, *A Question of Control: a Study of Classroom Interaction in a Junior School*, University of London MSc thesis, 1971.
3 **W Robert Mackay**, *Conceptions of Children and Models of Socialisation* in **R Turner** (Ed.), *Ethnomethodology*, Penguin, 1974, p.181.
4 **Paulo Freire**, *The Pedagogy of the Oppressed*, Penguin, 1973.
5 **Mackay**, op cit.
6 At the time of this participatory experience, the school handbook was defunct and had been for over a year. However, it would be fair to say that it had once assumed great significance amongst many of the teachers present at the two meetings.
7 **Kim Johndon**, 'Expectations in Classroom Interaction' in *Hard Cheese One: a Journal of Education,* 1973.
8 An example of this in practice can also be found in the same school. A list was drawn up of pupils from another year group who were, it was claimed, *'causing considerable concern'* and *'exhibiting numerous symptoms of maladjustment'*. They were classified as follows:
   1 Drop in standard of work
     a. caused by truancy
     b. underachieving
   2 Restless — unable to concentrate
   3 Aggressive, often in the absence of provocation
   4 Irritability and sulkiness
   5 Delinquent acts — stealing articles of little value, often repeats this behaviour in spite of correction
   6 Clowning to attract attention
   7 Emergence of speech defect
   8 Day-dreaming
   9 Rapidly changing moods, depression and excessive anxiety
  10 Clumsiness — lack of co-ordination
  11 Failure to build a relationship, to make and keep friends
  12 Over-sensitivity when criticised or corrected. Further, it was added:
     'In the light of information gathered over the past months, and having listened to colleagues, I have compiled the above list; I would welcome your comments on its validity and judgements made in it. Please remove or add other pupil's names who you consider **should be brought to the attention of the educational psychologist** *(my stress). It will be on the collected judgements of colleagues that action will or will not be taken'*
9 The school has previously operated a sanctuary unit which, when

originally started, was for all the school age range. Since then, (presumably) because of administrative difficulties, it has become chiefly limited to second- and third-year children. Upon commencement of this unit, in conversation with the teacher responsible for its inception, I discovered that three types of child were to be catered for; the three categories were:

a Behaviour problems.
b Remedial problems.
c Non-English speaking children.

When asked how this could operate, the teacher replied that pupils would be referred by form and year teachers in consultation with himself and the headmaster. In practical terms he did not see any problems arising with the use of these three categories. Many teachers, however, remained dubious about this project and tended only to refer discipline (so-called) problems and newly-arrived immigrant children with a poor standard of English (spoken and written).

In effect then, there already existed a model on which the head of year could work (and seemed to be working on) without fully considering the implications of starting such a unit. (Fortunately this is not as bizarre as a sanctuary unit that I discovered to be operating in another local school; the unit was a numerical one, in so far as it was designed to cater for ten children only—from a school population of over 1,000. It was explained to me that the two '**worst**' children from years one to five in the school were to be **sent to the unit!**)

I'd like to thank Chris Jenks (Goldsmith's College) for his many useful comments on an earlier draft of this paper.

Chapter 7

Community Development through Social Education

MARTIN STRUBE

Martin Strube is a Canadian
anthropologist currently
working with the Watford
Social Education Project.

The best preparation for 'responsibility' has always, and will always be the allocation of responsibility. The unquantifiable burden under which western democracies are straining is the immeasurable weight of the ignorance and disenchantment of their constituent members. This ignorance and disenchantment doesn't arise by chance — it is not a natural human reaction to a complex situation. It arises out of very early experiences with hierarchical decision-making structures, in the form of (a) the family and (b) the school which very rarely, if ever, allow for direct experience in shared decision-making.

Social education has been defined variously as *an explicit educative process* and *'learning about oneself, the social structures, and skills required to deal with these structures'*, but its methods must be considered in more than one light. There tend to be two basic approaches to the field of social education (SE). One is the community development (CD) approach which, along the lines of good community work, is preoccupied with the instillation into pragmatically-defined groups of the ability to recognise common problems, to organise and determine common solutions, and ultimately to set about seeing that these solutions are implemented in one way or another — the entire process having the long-term objective of ensuring that members of the group will continue to recognise the potential (in themselves, in the group, and in other groups they may be part of) for self-organised and co-operative decision-making and action. The other is the 'therapeutic' approach, which is preoccupied with the analysis, in groups, of individuals' feelings and motives in relation to outside institutions (notably the school and the future work place), with a view to coming to grips with what is actually called for in the **individual** struggle for self-betterment and progression through stages of life.

These approaches are not necessarily clearly defined and/or separated by the various social education practitioners, and unconscious and arbitrary combinations of the two seem to be common. Both approaches tend to break down similarly (see Figure 5), but with slight differences in emphasis; the CD approach tending to emphasise **process** and the therapeutic tending to emphasise **product.** Additionally, the CD approach tries to emphasise the value of culling the support of the group as a whole, and adjusting individual requirements to facilitate working towards a commonly-held objective, whereas the therapeutic approach might well emphasise the need for one-to-one contact and the importance of adapting the individual to outside institutions.

This paper will be limited to a consideration of the CD approach and its implications for the educational system and, ultimately, the state of participant democracy in our society.

Essentially, the CD approach at the Watford Social Education Project has developed in two ways — the long-term (a year, plus) and the short-term (six to eight weeks, plus). The long-term work involves an introduction to group self-organisation and decision-making through simulations such as the Moonshot Shuffle* and variations of Railway Pioneer* and Risk*. Working closely with the teacher, situations are created whereby negotiation, representation, delegation, formal discussion and voting are used to actually determine the next stages of the simulation. Certain bodies are empowered to consider fundamental situational issues, such as orders of priority, rule changes and termination of the simulation. This goes on for several weeks, until such time as members of the group start to question its relevance and begin to voice an interest in moving on to something more practical. As this programme takes place in a 'Humanities' or 'Community Studies' slot in the school timetable, this usually means getting on with the planning of some sort of study or action involving direct access (through project transport and contacts) to the community at large. This planning then begins to take place through the structures which the group has been experimenting with in the simulation work. Elections are held and a chairman and secretary are elected to run the meetings, at which plans are discussed and voted on. The teacher and the worker become voting members of the group and also act as resource people when called upon by the group.

The short-term work involves an introductory session, run along fairly formal lines, whereby two project workers present a way of running a school class to a group of students already embarked upon some form of study (eg consumer affairs, local government etc). The workers offer project resources (van, video tape recorder, typing and duplicating) to the group on condition that they can resolve the distribution of these resources themselves in a democratic fashion, as demonstrated by the workers in their mode of presentation. As its first exercise in decision-making the group is asked to decide for or against this involvement, in the absence of both teacher and workers. If they decide for, the class elects a chairman and secretary, resumes as a meeting and tries to sort out a plan of action. The meetings can be called and adjourned at any time during the session for formal discussion or decisions.

Needless to say, these can be very confusing and frustrating processes, and introductory methods are in need of much experimentation and improvement. However, it is interesting to note that attempts with secondary school students are no more nor less confusing and frustrating than attempts with, for example, the staff of the local Youth Service, where democratic practice is not extensive and is considered somewhat suspect.

---

*See descriptions below

103

What these two approaches will mean to the schools and individuals participating remains to be systematically noted. At the moment, all that can be done is to theorise some prospective long-terms effects.

An effort along the above lines to combat the 'unquantifiable burden', ie the ignorance, inarticulacy and disenchantment of the voting populace, undertaken in the schools should lead to a general enlightenment with regard to current democratic procedure. The current fashion for condemning 'committee meetings' stems from frustration, which in turn arises from a complete lack of understanding of what committees actually try to do, ie to develop common policy, and of what kinds of unavoidable human communication problems they are inevitably faced with in such attempts. People totally devoid of any kind of shared decision-making experience are not only struck by the apparent complexity of the performance they see taking place, but can also be destructive to that performance when they actually do try to take part. One can often see this occurring when an enraged individual takes his complaint for the first time to a local meeting, and goes away further frustrated and more cynical at the process involved, determined never again to participate in such foolishness. Initial experiences with such foolishness should be taking place very early on in the school setting, where efforts can be made to explain to individuals the kinds of complications which are involved and the kinds of rationale which led to their being involved.

School experience of this nature, operating in a responsibility vacuum, will simply lead to disillusionment. Responsibility **must** be allocated, and the fruits of group decisions, good or bad, must be clearly visible. Exposure to **real** responsibility, as has been proven again and again, is a maturing process and the most effective counter to disenchantment and apathy (groups must also experience the deferral of people normally in authority (teachers, heads, etc.) to the authority of whatever group they might be attending; students must see that others, too, have a belief in democratic process and accept its constraints).

Attempts have been made in some schools to provide a practical democratic experience in the form of powerless student councils. This form of introduction is usually of interest only to more or less academically-inclined students and is, in fact, usually restricted to students who qualify in academic terms. This precludes, even at the rudimentary and vacuous levels, the very people who aren't getting what they need from their education, and who will continue to be powerless with respect to their needs being met later in life.

Whether or not this sort of system proves effective in educational terms, any evaluation or criticism of it must attempt to be objective. Firstly, it is not being suggested here that the outcome will be better examination results for more people. But it is being suggested that the outcome itself, and the means by which it should be assessed, must arise out of the same system; not be held over from the previous one. Secondly, the system is meant to be an educative reflection of the way society is run. If the system appears to produce no success, even in its own terms, then it is not simply the system which must be criticised, but the society it is attempting to educatively reflect.

Assuming that the correct types of conditions prevail, the long-term optimistic outcome of social education in the schools will be

Figure 5
The Two Approaches to Social Education

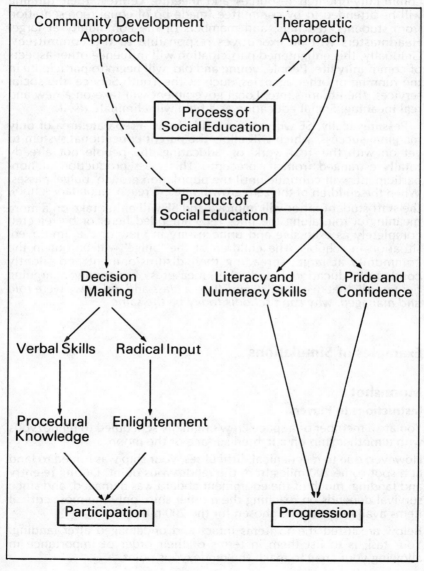

chain-reactive. SE will gradually evolve as a method rather than as a type of community studies subject area. Students will have more say in the running of their classes; teachers will take on a more clearly-defined role as group members and resource persons; schools as institutions will relax generally. There will be more flow between school and community, more and more members of the community at large participating as teacher/learners. Schools will again become community-oriented resources and meeting centres; their running will be attended to by committees made up of equal representation from students, teachers, and members of the community at large. Headmasters will be executives responsible to the committees. Gradually, this enlightened participation will influence other aspects of community life. People, young and old, will begin to participate in the running of other agencies, such as the Youth Service, the social services, the libraries, etc. Local government will take on a new and real meaning. Social education as a field will eliminate itself.

Pessimistically, SE will remain a sideshow; a separate area of only marginal success, which will allow the parent educational system to get on with the 'real work' of 'educating' the people not already totally estranged from its precepts. This mass production of non-participants will continue until the population growth 'bulge' passes. When the children of the zero-growth rate era reach secondary school, the staff-student ratios will improve and SE will either take on a more meaningful role along the lines recommended here, or be rejected completely as excessive and unnecessary in view of the 'improved' situation in schools. The children of the 'bulge' will be out in the community at large, spreading their disillusionment and silently condoning educational (and other) measures of economy — arguing righteously that 'we were 30 and 40 to a class and did as we were told and managed, why can't schools today be the same . . .'

Examples of Simulations

Moonshot
Instructions to Players

You are a member of a space crew originally scheduled to rendezvous with a mother ship on a lighted surface of the moon.

However, due to mechanical difficulties, your ship was forced to land at a spot some 200 miles from the rendezvous point. During re-entry and landing, much of the equipment aboard was damaged, and since survival depends on reaching the mother ship, only the most critical items available must be chosen for the 200 mile trip.

Below are listed the 15 items intact and undamaged after landing. Your task is to list them in terms of their order of importance in allowing your crew to reach the rendezvous point.

Place the number **1** by the most important item, the number **2** by the second most important item, and so on through to number **15** for the least important item.

Order of importance

. . . . .   Box of matches
. . . . .   Food concentrate
. . . . .   50 feet of nylon rope
. . . . .   Parachute silk
. . . . .   Portable heating unit
. . . . .   Two .45 calibre pistols
. . . . .   One case of dehydrated milk
. . . . .   Two 100lb tanks of oxygen
. . . . .   Stellar map (of the Moon's constellations)
. . . . .   Life raft
. . . . .   Magnetic compass
. . . . .   5 gallons of water
. . . . .   Signal flares
. . . . .   First aid kit (containing injection needles)
. . . .   Solar powered FM receiver/transmitter

The Moonshot Shuffle

1   The lists are handed out to each individual member of the group. They complete and hand in.

2   The group is divided arbitrarily into sub-groups of five or six. Each sub-group completes a list, agreed jointly. (Observers can be assigned to each group, which gives rise to 2a.). They hand in.

2a The observers are asked to report who in each of the sub-groups made most of the decisions. The groups are then re-organised so as to put all the 'dominants' (the ones who had made the decisions in the previous groupings) together and all the 'non-dominants' together (to give the quieter ones a chance to influence the proceedings). They hand in.

3   The group elects a chairman and secretary and attempts to work out one list of priorities in accordance with democratic procedure. The chairman calls for nominations for first priority, sees that these are fully discussed, and calls a vote. The secretary notes down the nominations and voting. The chairman moves onto the next one, etc. The list is handed in.

4   Between sessions, preferably, the results are collated and organised graphically by the worker and teacher, and the lessons are drawn from discussions at the following session.

Adaptation of Risk

1 Sub-groups are formed within the main group. The teacher and worker play together as a single sub-group.
2 The game is played normally except for discussion between groups which takes place through negotiators, as in Railway Pioneers.
3 Play is discussed. Egalitarian role of teacher-worker sub group is noted. Possibility of all-round balance of power is studied.

This adaptation is still being worked on. The co-operative element is not yet satisfactorily emphasised, and much work needs to be done.

Adaptation of Railway Pioneers

1 The group forms sub-groups which become railway 'companies' and 'the bank'.
2 Each company has an income and 'lays track' on the map in accordance with how many 'units' they have to spend.
3 Where 'tracks' from one company interfere with the plans of another, each company must appoint a negotiator to represent their views and interests to the other.
4 On issues in dispute and non-negotiable, or on matters involving rule changes, a council made up of one representative from each company and one from the bank meet and discuss and come to agreement. The other group members are allowed to watch and listen but cannot participate other than to ask that the meeting be adjourned so that they can consult further with their representatives.
5 The whole simulation is discussed and lessons drawn.

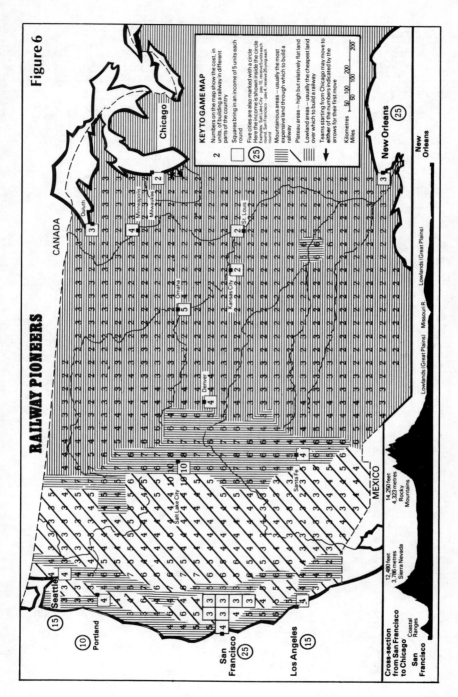

RAILWAY PIONEERS

Figure 6

KEY TO GAME MAP

2 Numbers on the map show the cost, in units, of building a railway in different parts of the country

☐ Squares bring in an income of 5 units each round

㉕ Five cities are also marked with a circle Here the income is shown inside the circle. Examples: Salt Lake City — pay 10, receive 5 units each round. San Francisco — pay 4, receive 25 units each round.

▨ Mountainous areas — usually the most expensive land through which to build a railway

╱ Plateau areas — high but relatively flat land

▦ Lowland areas — usually the cheapest land over which to build a railway

→ Teams starting from Chicago may move to either of the numbers indicated by the arrows for their first move

Kilometres 50 100 200
Miles 50 100 200

CANADA

Chicago

Duluth

Minneapolis
Milwaukee

St. Louis

Omaha

Kansas City

Denver

Salt Lake City

Santa Fe

MEXICO

Seattle   ㉕
Portland ⑩

San Francisco ㉕

Los Angeles ⑮

New Orleans ㉕

New Orleans

Cross-section from San Francisco to Chicago

San Francisco — Coastal Ranges

12,490 feet 3,786 metres Sierra Nevada

14,250 feet 4,323 metres Rocky Mountains

Lowlands (Great Plains) — Missouri R.

Lowlands (Great Plains)

Lowlands (Great Plains)

Chapter 8

Inexperienced Adults: Youth Work in the Community

LESLIE SILVERLOCK

Leslie Silverlock is 34 and has been a playleader, youth leader, teacher, school-based youth worker and residential neighbourhood community worker in London, Ipswich and Manchester — all jobs he shared with his wife, Marion. He is at present a Community education officer in Somerset. A past chairman of the Community Work Committee, he is now vice-president of the Community and Youth Service Association and a representative on the Parliamentary Youth Affairs lobby.

8

Young people are isolated. Untrue? Isolated at a time when they most need to be integrated — during adolescence. Fatuous? Adolescence is a time for imitative behaviour, a time when you aspire to be an adult and to have adult status. What you most want to do during adolescence is go to work, earn money, drive vehicles, socialize, drink alcohol, have sexual relationships, take holidays and make your own decisions. To do these things you need experience — practice. During adolescence the only previous experience you have to lean on is that of childhood. For adults, drawing on experience is considered mature behaviour, but in adolescence it is called regressive, reverting to childhood.

To become a practising adult and to understand how adults do things, you need to share experience with them. It is impossible to achieve competence in any activity without practice. Such practice is available, for example, in the unofficial learning process for drinking alcohol; most adults learn to drink alcohol before they are eligible to do so in law. As a child you drink at home on special occasions. As a teenager you drink at parties and occasionally in pubs. Drinking under-age is a kind of privilege, and that is restraint in itself on your over-doing it. Through this process many adults learn to drink when still too young. This is an example of a 'folk' practice overriding the law.

Few activities, however, allow young people this sort of graded learning process. Our society isolates them from most such experience and practice. It isolates them in a period of dis-ease, known as adolescence; a trap between childhood and adulthood during which they are encouraged to retreat into peer groups. Society has rules, but if you are not educated or experienced in using them then how, when young, can you know if you are breaking them? However, if you do trangress you will be punished. Reward and punishment, rather than experience, become the yard-sticks by which young people learn.

The development of the concept of adolescence as a special growth period, and the subsequent planning of services to meet a range of needs supposedly peculiar to adolescence, has been in part a dis-service to young people. It delays their integration as part of the community. It isolates them and their needs from those of other people in the community, both younger and older. Many of the needs of adolescence are mirrored in adults, and some in children. Yet our system of social organisation tries to meet adolescent needs within peer groups. Separating young people from the rest of society cannot improve their understanding of it. To attempt to meet needs from a basis of shared ignorance seems a weak starting point. The Youth Service, for its part, puts a small ratio of adults into contact with young people. This is a process of professional or semi-professional social intervention. The attempt to be detached in this work, called 'professionalism', depersonalises the Service still further and diminishes the possibilities of the emotional needs of those young people being met.

The importance placed on peer-group relationships during adolescence exacerbates the isolationist policies of adult society towards young people. Sticking together during adolescence may be as much a by-product of the structure as it is an expression of adolescent need.

Meeting the needs of young people, from the basis of community activity, in cross-generational groups, would be working from shared experience rather than shared ignorance. At present, our society actively blocks young people and the community from such contact. It isolates young people politically, educationally, socially and in employment.

The Political Isolation of Young People

Young people have a lot of protections, mistakenly called 'rights', which are administered for them by adults. They can see their community operating around them — buildings erected, services provided, traffic administered, play spaces eroded — but cannot affect that process. At 18 they may vote in public elections, but any experience of voting before that age (ie understanding and using the criteria and information for selection) will have been mostly haphazard 'hands up' in class debates or youth organisations.

Voting in elections is the tip of the political-participation iceberg. What room do young people have to participate in the affairs of their own community, and within their families, peer groups, school and work? How much influence can they exert upon the issues that interest and concern them; as members of a committee at a youth club, on a youth council, a school council, an area youth committee, school governors? If you know one young person who comes into contact with such participation, then that young person is extremely rare. If they truly participate, then it is a miracle. Participation for young people in the decisions which affect their lives is exceptional. Such involvement seems threatening to adult society — vis-a-vis the furore that action by the National Union of School Students usually creates. Even the National Union of Students scares most adults, who think that students are privileged, should be grateful and should get on with their work. Being seen and not heard is still an accepted, if not wholly endorsed, maxim. But if you don't practise participation how can you demonstrate anything but apathy or alienation in later life? In a society in which the state is assuming responsibility for the individual's choice in media control, transport movement, recreation and leisure, housing, employment and education, we need to produce more adults who understand how the system works and how they can participate in it. If most young people aren't given the opportunity to practise in local politics, our exceedingly complicated bureaucracy can only hope to be understood by a very small minority in the future.

If the young people of the '80s are not to be the unconcerned or the anarchists of the '90s then we need to ensure their involvement and participation in the structure of our society. It will be the responsibility of adults who, at present, make the decisions to transfer some of that power to young people. Involvement leads to responsibility, and responsibility is what young people need if they are to fulfil themselves and find their roles as adults. They should become involved initially at a simple level — in their local communities, on committees of all kinds.

No decision on the development of leisure and recreation provision should be taken in a parish without consulting the young people in that parish. A system which provided the gradual assumption of voting rights might be introduced, starting with parish councils. The presence of 14 year olds in parish politics during the '70s might have made a significant difference to the provision of skateboarding facilities and the erosion of play spaces. If some roads were closed as effectively as many skateboarding areas have been, then driving would die out as quickly as skateboarding has in certain places. Would the motoring voter allow that?

At 14 the law recognizes that young people are old enough to know their own minds (for example, where they want to live), therefore they should begin to have significant powers of voting at that age with which to practise. Parish councils are powerful. Although few people realise this yet, they are the community's forum, the group responsible for maintaining the healthy state of local life. Space could be made for young people to be involved at this level initially. At 18 they could be eligible as candidates (at present 21).

Adults who are sympathetic towards young people's involvement will need to form lobbies, at a district level, on behalf of young people to campaign for their involvement in local affairs. GUST, in the West Country, is a body of adults formed to create political awareness of the need for young people to participate. GUST means, 'Give Us a Say in Things'. Adults are taking the lead, on behalf of young people who are disenfranchised. Somebody must form their lobby for them initially. Bringing together people interested in forming local lobbies is a role the Youth Service could play.

The inexperience of young people in political affairs, and the mistakes they will inevitably make, should not be an excluding factor in their rights, as people, to participate in political decision-making. Young people should be involved in the affairs of parish councils, district councils, youth councils, schools councils, labour unions, apprenticeship unions, the National Union of School Students. It will be up to sympathetic adults to campaign for a policy of positive discrimination, on behalf of young people, if any changes are to be forthcoming.

Political education is most likely to become the new panacea in the '80s for youth participation. It will satisfy many adults that the young are being involved in the processes by which their society is governed. However, recent trends towards the inclusion of political education in the school curriculum suggest that it will be just another subject, carefully watched lest any political party should seek to gain an advantage. A party-broadcast to pupils, sixth form governors, and a trip to the district council chambers may be an improvement, but that is hardly experiential political education. Most likely it will be largely meaningless, and probably boring. All young people need the opportunity to 'play' with political concepts and responsibilities. Taking decisions about the running of their school, their class, their youth club, their adventure playground and the services for them in their local community will educate them far more than a subject-based political education (read party politics), which will be nudging religious education and other peripheral subjects in an overcrowded examination-based school curriculum.

The Educational Isolation of Young People

Up to the age of 16, young people are incarcerated within a compulsory, statutory system of mostly classroom learning. The criteria for ultimate success within that system are set by a remote educational agency, with which very few young people will come into contact — the university. Unable to meet those criteria, most young people will choose to compromise and pick up what skills, qualifications and benefits they can, or those which are forced upon them. The experience of this compromise, or, in many cases, failure, will leave them feeling that education is something which takes place up to the age of 16, has now finished and has never to be endured again — thereby alienating many from further planned, even participatory, learning.

Within that system, young people will be isolated from the rest of the community. 'Ordinary' adults, apparently out of organisational necessity, are kept out of this formal education structure. Young people will meet only a narrow range of adults known as teachers. They will be isolated from cross-generational contact by being placed in classes based on age. This isolation may be further aggravated by streaming according to intelligence, ability and motivation. While at school they will be unable largely to work on the issues which interest and concern them on any particular day, or to influence the subject-matter which they are studying. Not listening or not going is as much participation as some young people will ever experience in education. After their experiences in school, most people would have to do a mental somersault to see the educational process as the life-long experience that community education is trying to promote.

The community should be invited into the school during the day; to study, use the facilities, share lunch and work in groups with young people. By introducing into schools adults with the freedom to choose, and practice in making up their own minds, young people will be gaining experience in subject-areas little taught in schools, but in much demand in adult life — working the system, finding answers, standards and morals. School-based youth work and community education could take a lead in bringing the community into the schools during the day thereby providing a community atmosphere there. The idea that life is about working on your own with books and pens needs to be dispelled. Very few young people will follow those pursuits in adult life; most people spend a lot of time working with groups of people of all ages, engaged in physical transactions — buying, selling, swapping, talking and watching.

Those on the fringes of educational services, whether they call themselves youth service, community education service, youth and community service, careers service or school counsellors, must develop conscious strategies for the involvement of young people in their educational lives. The recent fashion of 'knocking' formal education, and expecting the teachers and schools to take the brunt, is myopic and should stop. Teachers and schools are isolated too, and they need help in involving the community. A travelling educational circus could be introduced; taking films, lectures, discussion groups and examples of good practice in community involvement to the teachers and the schools. Teachers' centres and the fringe educational services could contribute in this development.

The further isolation of young people in many areas, who are 'bussed' from their communities to school, should be reversed, not for economic reasons, but for the social health of the community. Young people, taken out of their communities, cannot play a part in them or contribute fully to local activity, improvement and development. There are no merits in bussing. Bigger schools do no necessarily provide greater educational opportunity, either in the curriculum or in extra-curricula activities. Small schools, like small communities, are the life blood of our society, and must be kept open — they do not cost more.

The lead taken by pre-school and primary education in the development of play as a learning medium should become significant in adolescent education. The need to role play, fantasise, dramatise and tumble about is just as great during adolescence (and probably in adulthood too) as it is in childhood. If the world of primary education has succeeded in using motivation to meet people's own needs, then secondary education, relieved of some of the pressures of a university-manipulated curriculum, could do likewise. The need for play exists in all of us — adolescence is not the time to 'condition it out'.

Involvement and participation in educational life up to the age of 15 could produce a great thirst for self-education in those years of learning, gathering and understanding information between late-adolescence and the early 30s. We must develop an education system which enables everybody to take advantage of opportunities during that period, not for just the handful of people who play by the rules and succeed by an almost blind obedience during adolescence.

The Social Isolation of Young People

During this period of inexperienced adulthood, adolescents need to be with adults more often to observe, imitate and experiment. Most of the services offered to young people seek to isolate them from adults. The Youth Service has played its part in this social isolation of young people, though to its credit it has provided a broad range of adults for young people to relate to.

Youth clubs were created as a response to the deprivation of young people (who had nowhere to go), and perhaps also in response to an adult need to keep young people out of the way. While praiseworthy that someone is concerned for young people (in this case the Youth Service), it might be better to campaign for integration within the community. By the '70s, the Youth Service had not achieved the overwhelming support of young people, and suffered from under-expenditure and restricted growth.

Young people are excluded, largely, from the major arena of adult social life — the pub — leaving them the choice of the youth club (if it is open), street corner or market square. Occasionally, commercial provision exists in the form of a dance hall, cafe, cinema or sporting event. Most community groups or organisations centre on the needs of adults, usually exclusively. Then, of course, there is home! However important the peer group, parents are still the most significant factor in a young person's life. S/he needs to 'grow away' from them without guilt and pain — abandon them without separation. S/he needs other adults, other 'parents' to help in this process and to make comparisons.

Young people are also isolated sexually within our society. At a time when sexuality is dawning, they will find little information or guidance on sexual behaviour or manners. While the media will make sex glossy and romantic, and heighten expectations, their first experiences will probably be hounded by guilt (lest the community discovers). They will meet little honest talk of sexual activity and much humbug on moral values. Sex is the hardest adult secret society for young people to penetrate, and when they eventually do, if ever, it may be with a mistakenly hurried marriage or an unplanned child to their credit. Greater contact with more adults earlier on might have helped.

Any organisation concerned with the development of young people, which provides **for** them, is doing young people a disservice. Participation in the social structure, in order to watch how adults relate to one another, is an essential feature of the adolescent's social education. Young people are well motivated towards such learning during adolescence — they want adult status. We should provide them with as many opportunities as possible for experiential learning — opportunities to 'play' with the social network.

Two areas of our society have something to teach us in this matter. Churches and village life provide good examples of cross-generational

117

contact with young people. This integration of all age groups arises from a significant reduction or shortage of people in both settings. Churches, with dwindling congregations, involve young people at most levels of their operation. A young person belonging to the church is likely to be able to sing, play an instrument, serve, organise events, join discussions and participate in the congregation alongside adults. The opportunities for social learning for young people are varied.

In village life, the small population results in many young people having the opportunity of a place in the social network which their urban and suburban counterparts do not enjoy. When dances and festivities are held young people are found everywhere, both as organisers and participants. It is often an economic necessity (enough money to make the event pay), and a social one too (enough people to make it a success). There is not the tradition of leaving young people at home in village life. These multi-generational groups (as well as peer groups) are found in village life, sharing their different levels of understanding and experience — watching, learning and developing together.

Age barriers, which prevent what happens in churches and villages from occurring elsewhere, need to be broken down. The social climate eventually produces changes in the law (vis-a-vis abortion, homosexuality, sexism, racism); changes which further speed the development of social awareness. We therefore need a number of changes in the law to combat that ageism which the law maintains. The law has taken responsibility away from the community for decision-making for itself and its members. It has, in this process, diminished the responsibility of society for its young people. Young people are ready to drive, take alcohol, have sexual relationships, marry, own property, travel, pothole, climb, ride horses, join trades unions and leave home, all at different stages of their development. Yet the law says quite arbitrarily the age at which they shall do some of these things and ignores the existence of others. A young person will not get on a horse or go down a dark hole in the ground unless s/he feels ready to, or unless there are heavy social pressures to do so. If something goes wrong or s/he doesn't like it s/he will avoid that activity in the future. The same is true of those activities where there are laws — for example, drinking, having sexual relationships, driving — except that the existence of laws creates additional social pressure, they mark desirable symbols of adult status for young people.

Although laws have the status of being objective, they are usually based as much on emotion, political manipulation and discrimination as any other response. They demonstrate their own imperfection and inflexibility by relying on case law when the main law can no longer apply. Laws are given the status, particularly where young people are concerned, of protecting people often from themselves and their own 'wickedness'. Yet most of the ageist laws relating to young people have the effect, while possibly protecting them, of isolating them from responsible decision-making for themselves within their families and their communities. Laws diminish responsibility.

Let us in future have adults who, because they have practised during adolescence, know more of what they want and like, and who can participate in the structure of society. Politicians constantly bemoan the existence of apathy towards participation, which they themselves endorse by maintaining responsibility for other people's decision-making. Let young people, in the future, exercise some of the freedom in driving, drinking, sex and trade unionism that we allow them in travelling, potholing, climbing and riding horses. Horses are more difficult to control on the road than motorised bicycles. Let them drive the latter when **they** choose. Don't ban them from mobility for political expediency, but rather teach them how to do it well and safely. Let them mix with adults in pubs whenever they wish or whenever the adults will have them — leave the decisions to the locals. Let them experiment in sexual activity when they are ready to, whether that is 13 or 22, and let them become involved in trades unions, parish politics, schools councils and other political arenas which concern them.

Young people's services will need to be the vanguard of political change on their behalf. Those services, in the process, will have to challenge the double standards of political activity, particularly at a local level, ie politics are respectable for politicians but subversive when others become involved.

In the meantime, community groups should be encouraged to take young people into their ranks. The Youth Service has a role to play, asking community groups what they can do for young people, developing opportunities for young people to share and learn special skills alongside adults, whether in the arts, horticulture, politics, sport, mechanics or whatever.

Those services which are designed to help young people should examine their own paternalism towards the young. There is no merit in organising social activities — discotheques, football matches, outings, film shows — **for** young people. On the one hand it diminishes their responsibility for themselves by spoonfeeding, and on the other wastes the opportunity for experience and participation which they would gain, with varying degrees of support, from organising such activities for themselves. There should be no role for the Youth Service in aping commercial enterprises. If young people have to be wooed to the Youth Service by commercial-style provision, then the Youth Service in its present form is not what they want or need.

Youth workers, community workers and playleaders might be better employed promoting ideas like community houses. These are not purpose-built, cold, isolationist centres, but normal buildings within the community within which peer groups and multi-generational groups can operate side by side. As needs change, rooms change and houses change. The community house is neither an expensive nor unreasonable expectation. The alcoholic public house is an example of similar provision which facilitates free association for people in small self-selecting groups. Such buildings exist on every corner, often the number of them appearing to out-weigh the needs of the nearby community. Unfortunately, these houses are ageist. Nor do they provide, as community houses might, for that vital adolescent need, at present largely unmet, for short residential periods away from home.

To develop provision that includes young people, community workers will need to infiltrate structure plans. Planners are looking to improve the health of communities — they want ideas. It is the responsibility of those in work who care about people to promote new, flexible initiatives for the future which include young people.

A Role for the Youth Service

What part can the Youth Service play in relieving the isolation of young people? Physically and operationally it is small; its effect, however, is pervasive. Every community expects to have either a small part-time youth club or a large full-time centre. Society hopes that these will socialize young people. The practitioners hope they will meet the social-educational needs of the adolescent. Young people themselves, however, have not used this provision much. In consequence there has not been a strong response from adults for the financial support of the Youth Service, either locally or nationally. The result has produced a club-based service which has remained under-provided with resources and staff.

In making this provision the Youth Service has partly 'done as it was told' by society. It has occasionally answered back for the limitations of youth club work with experimental initiatives in detached work, counselling, project-based work, play provision and mobile projects. A recent initiative to move towards the rest of society is epitomised in the rise of the phrase 'Youth and Community work'. This, however, is a misleading term. Youth work is a part of community work and a much needed specialism within it.

There is no great mystique about the practice of youth work. Most adults have something to offer to one another. Similarly, they have something to offer to young people. To enable those members of the community to make their contribution, the Youth Service must de-professionalise. This is not to say there will not be full-time, dedicated, highly-trained experts, but that the Youth Service will not look exclusively to them or their part-time equivalents. There is an abundance of goodwill towards adolescents among adults in the community. This goodwill may often be confused, inarticulate or may lean on apparently out-moded values. However, these are not reasons for rejecting this interest. The Youth Service should harness community spirit to the advantage of, and for the growth of young people. To do so, the Youth Service full-time expertise will have to be allocated less time in youth clubs and more time in the community, mobilising resources — encouraging football clubs to run youth clubs, encouraging pubs to have youth rooms, encouraging senior citizens and people with time to 'take on' young people, to offer counsel, advice, support and group work, running training courses for the community (not just committed part-time leaders) about the needs of adolescence. A campaign on the lines of 'sport for all', 'year of the child', 'look after yourself' could be mounted which invited adult community groups of every type to 'make space for young people' — physically, emotionally, intellectually and socially — including greater sports provision outside schools and the Youth Service — in the community — development of community houses in towns and mobile resources in rural areas, and encouragement for greater participation and involvement in decision-making for young people in the family, in employment and in the community.

To achieve this the Youth Service will have to employ more people as community workers, who would be used to stimulate community involvement in realising the needs of young people, and community involvement **for** young people. They would support community groups and encourage indigenous leadership, by people in the community who understand the communication patterns and network of relationships within the locality.

Using manpower successfully and cheaply is a skill in which the Youth Service has excelled. Though organised by full-time staff, the Youth Service has been maintained by volunteers. Whether you call it leisure time or unemployment, blame microchips or robots, there will be a lot more members of the community about in the future with time to spare — perhaps for young people. If a family of two children needs two parents and the ideal school class numbers 12, then young people during adolescence also need a high ratio of adult support. The Youth Service can contribute to breaking down the generation gap and enabling interaction to take place.

A feature of adult society is the need for organisation and discipline. A feature of adolescence is the need to question organisation and discipline (how else do you learn if you don't ask questions?). Many young people, through schools and organisations, will have had a bad experience of organisation and discipline, and may even have suffered at the hands of it. The Youth Service could teach people about this problem. It could encourage adults to realise that young people still want relationships with them. It could articulate the needs of adolescents to the community and help different generations to overcome the blocks to communication that exist between them.

Without stimulating community involvement we can expect the further alienation of young people within our society in the future. With more time to spare, more young people are going to become frustrated by the lack of status and involvement they have in community life. During the 1980s the Youth Service has a responsibility to change its direction, from a sticking plaster service to one which integrates and involves young people in community life. Let the Youth Service of the '80s say that it organised nothing **for** young people, but that it helped young people and the community to organise themselves. Let it set up courses, conferences, discussions groups and issue guide notes on the involvement of young people in community life. Let it use some of its resources to pay people in the community, part-time, to take an interest in youth affairs. Pay people to 'wander' the community in the same way as it pays people to 'wander' clubs. Let it say it opened channels of communication across the generations. Let it politicise in adult arenas on behalf of young people, within those areas of the law, education, social life and politics which discriminate against young people. To achieve this, an alternative policy of positive discrimination in favour of young people is required.

Why should the Youth Service bother? Why should society bother? Because, as a matter of social organisation, it cannot afford an inexperienced or confused generation in the future; because it is in the economic and social interest of adults to see that the next generation of young adults are committed and participant, not silent or violent.

A Future for the Professions

'Effective youth work in the 1970s presupposes that there will be no barriers between those who teach, work with, influence or in various ways support young people in our society'.

The isolation of young people is mirrored by the isolation of the services designed to meet their needs. In a community-based Youth Service some established traditions will need to be martyred. It is ludicrous that such a small-scale service as the Youth Service has such a heavy bureaucracy. The hierarchy of personnel needs to be re-deployed. To employ so many officers and administrators in a service so short of field staff is poor use of resources. Team work approaches should be developed, wherein work and skills are shared. Specialisms designed to meet particular needs need not be eroded. The lobby that wants youth work maintained as a specialism is right to want so; practising youth work in the community will not lessen its speciality, though it will broaden its base. Fiercely maintaining youth clubs, as the main provision of youth service, is not the only way of maintaining youth work as a specialism.

The Youth Service and other services with which it has much in common are all small — providing play, community development, adult education, community arts, community information. These services have a common ground — their clients use them from choice and often participate in structuring the style of service. As services, they are all 'fringe', initiatives developing often from the limitations of other major services, voluntary and statutory. 'Community work' is the general term which covers these services; they are all driven by the desire to assist the community either generally, or through particular age groups or with particular problems. All these services, with varying degrees of commitment, put responsibility, resources and decision-making into the hands of the community. Each of them is driven at some level of its operation by the belief that people should have more control over decisions and resources which affect their lives.

Because most resources and decisions are controlled centrally, the time has come for the component parts of community work to unite and seek the decentralisation of resources and decision-making. In order to achieve this, fringe services in community work need to come together locally, regionally and nationally. The distribution of resources and the responsibility for decision-making are mostly based, at present, in centralised agencies (for example, government departments and local authorities). A unified voice from the community work field is vital if any decentralisation is to be achieved. The return of responsibility and control to community groups, mistakenly taken from them by bureaucracy and democracy in recent decades, is the goal.

To achieve this unity, those organisations, associations and unions concerned in community work need to establish a base from which the ideology of community work can begin to have more influence — a confederation of their specialist interests. The necessity for this is clear. Without such organisation and commitment, the fringe services always suffer, politically and economically. If you believe that community work has something to offer in the development of involvement and participation — that people working together, deciding for themselves what is relevant to their needs, making their own decisions, is important — then a stronger lobby for the growth of community work is necessary. What community work must learn from the growth of education, social services, health services, and the law is that the resources must be controlled by the users. Community work could achieve this. It could relieve the isolation, alienation and apathy of many people, put ageism in prison with sexism and racism, and gain participation and involvement for many more people, including young people, in employment, social life, education and politics.

Chapter 9

The Social Control of Young People

COLM NOLAN

Colm Nolan took his first
degree in the social sciences at
Middlesex Polytechnic, after
which he worked in North
London on a mobile/detached
youth work project. He is
currently at Sunderland
Polytechnic, engaged in
research into the participation
of young people in social
institutions.

Introduction: The Youth Problem

Most sociological theories of youth have tended to categorise youth as problematic for contemporary society as well as for the individual experiencing adolescence; to focus on defining the nature of the problem and on offering suggestions for the more successful integration of young people into the wider society. As such, the problem is often defined as delinquency, or failure to conform to adult norms; explanations involve the traumas of adolescence and societal pressures; solutions are intended to counteract adverse influences and help make the progress to responsible adulthood a smooth and enjoyable experience.

Thus, particularly in the late'50s and early'60s, with the advent of a distinct youth culture, theories were submitted bearing reference to the new conditions of youth in the 'affluent society', where young people were understood to be suffering from the worst effects of marketing pressures and in their increased leisure time were succumbing to the superficial pleasures offered by, for example, the record and fashion industries. In order to provide an alternative, it was suggested that more attention should be given to the needs and problems of young people through the agencies of schools, youth clubs and community welfare organisations, wherein it was hoped they could be offered direction and guidance by responsible but sympathetic adults.

This approach has informed numerous government reports, projects and committees. For instance, T. R. Fyvel, whose particular concern in 1961 was with the effects of the affluent society and 'Rebellious Youth in the Welfare State', points out that both the Crowther and the Albemarle Reports[1] were influenced by this theory.

Yet in a society of mass production, whose processes demand a rapid turnover of goods and the exploitation of all avenues of marketing, the youth market, which both feeds on and helps promote a distinct teenage culture, is an important and powerful source of profit. As such, it is an integral part of the economy with which no government would interfere. 'State intervention' in the socialisation of young people, which does not interfere in what the state perceives as the basis of the problem, ie the youth market, and which is interested, in fact, in maintaining that market, is suffering from a contradiction which implies impotence.

A major factor said to affect the vulnerability of young people and the creation of a youth subculture was suggested by Talcott Parsons, who maintains that delinquency is a symptom of youth's economic and political powerlessness. Young people, says Parsons, tend to suffer from *'the fact that the major agents for initiating processes of change lie in other sectors of society, above all, in large scale organisation, in the development of science and technology, in the higher political processes and in the higher ranges of culture. . . . This would suggest that . . . the adult agencies upon which the youth most depends tend to some extent to be 'out of tune' with what he senses to be the most advanced development of the time. He senses that he is put in an unfair dilemma by having to be so subject to their control*[2].

Once again, a government which seeks to maintain the status quo is in no position to offer power to youth to help solve its problems. In a society where power depends primarily on property relations, all those divorced from ownership of the means of production are denied real power. Yet the particular position of young people denies them any power even in their everyday relations. For instance, status and power within the family or local community may depend upon level and type of employment as well as income. Although physically mature at about the age of 14, young people must accept compulsory schooling until the age of 16. The present high incidence of unemployment among school leavers only serves to make this problem more acute. Government policy, which of necessity reflects the requirements of the economic system, maintains a situation which enhances the powerlessness of youth.

Using the above liberal-type theories, the government is thus forced into a position where it must consistently be seen to be dealing with the problem of youth, while at the same time its remedies can only be superficial at best. Thus we read in *'The Times'*, 21st September 1976, under the heading *'Whitehall suggests a new style body to study juvenile crime'*, that:

'Leading magistrates, educationists, social workers and policemen may be invited to serve alongside a team of ministers who, it is suggested, will pool their departmental responsibilities in **reviewing public concern** *over present trends in the behaviour, treatment and punishment of young persons'* (Emphasis added).

The liberal theories of youth, prevalent in the period of the affluent society, have shown themselves inadequate in dealing with the phenomenon of adolescent rebellion, although these theories continue to inform a great deal of public policy concerning youth. Since the period of 'affluence', the student revolts of the late '60s, rising juvenile crime and mass unemployment among school leavers have given rise to a number of Marxist-type analyses. Debate in this area has focused upon whether or not youth constitutes a class in itself and the relationship of young people to the traditional classes in Marxian theory.

In their paper entitled *'The Political Economy of Youth in our Generation'*[3], the Rowntrees have argued from a late 1960s' American perspective that the class nature of the youth movement has been obscured by the liberal notion of generational conflict and that, due to its unique relationship with the education system (an expanding industry) and the armed forces (another expanding industry), youth is suffering a particular form of exploitation — a surplus labour force absorbed by education and the army, both underpaid — which has given rise to a 'youth class'. Unfortunately for this theory, what was true of America in 1969 cannot be shown to be true of Britain today. In Britain in 1976, both Education and Defence are major targets for cuts in public expenditure and can no longer be classed as expanding industries. Moreover, there are theoretical flaws in this analysis which stem from the desire to make Marxist theory fit a perceived empirical situation. Indeed, the authors provide their own criticism by contradicting their own thesis:

'Classes, more or less rapidly, create and destroy themselves in political struggle, and a youth class, by its natural process of ageing, is inherently a very unstable class formation. It is clear that **the youth class is only a part of the total working class** *in the United States. At the present the overlapping of class exploitation with traditional youth roles provides a focal point for extraordinarily rapid class formation. That is to say,* **the youth of the youth class is a secondary rather than a primary characteristic. The contemporary movement is a movement of students and soldiers;** *their class definition results from their roles in the production of technology and violence'*[4] (Emphasis added).

While it is possible to accept that youth as a social group is being exploited in particular sectors of the economy, it does not necessarily follow from this that such an exploitation has given rise to a 'class' of youth. Even if one accepts the thesis that the educational system and the army are particularly exploitative (it is possible to argue against this) and that, therefore, young people involved in these areas are potentially revolutionary, then this only leads to identification of a potential revolutionary vanguard within the working class. Take the definition of class offered by Bowles and Gintis:

'A class is a group of individuals who relate to the production process in similar ways. A class structure emerges naturally from the institutions of U.S. capitalism. Property relations are an essential aspect of class; no less important are the relations of control. Considering the class structure in the broadest outline, capitalists own and control the means of production. Workers, conversely, do not own the products of their labour, nor do they own or control the tools, buildings and facilities of the productive process'[5].

It is possible to suggest that if young people are concentrated in particular areas of production, their class nature depends on the property and power relations prevalent in those areas, not on their youth. Following the Rowntrees' thesis, youth can constitute a part of the working class with particular characteristics — it does not form a class in itself. It does not follow from this that young people are inconsequential in movements for social change.

This paper argues that the liberal analysis of youth is both superficial and inadequate on a number of levels. It has a tendency to ignore historical development and neither understands the contradictions in the productive process which create changes, nor the dynamic of the development of institutional and ideological controls which operate to subvert or contain social movements for radical change. The contention here is that youth is problematic today because of both the general imposition of certain socio-economic conditions upon it, and the situation of particular groups of young people in relation to other struggles.

The theory will be presented largely through the context of the social institutions of youth — particularly the formal and non-formal education systems. It will proceed with an analysis of the relationship of young people to the productive process and the divisions within youth itself. The role of formal education and the current problems it faces will be shown to be related to ideological contradictions with respect to youth, to the subsequent conflicts between youth and the state and to the development of a non-formal structure of education as a means of counteracting the conflict. The analysis will ultimately show that this attempt to contain the dissatisfactions of young people is itself contradictory and bound to perpetuate the growing consciousness of youth of its exploitation.

Part One — Reproduction of Social Relations

A society which reproduced in replica the social relations of production in each succeeding generation would demonstrate an ideal model of cultural transmission. The activities, ideologies, personalities and interests of the older generation would be learned completely by the younger generation and deviation would be impossible, or at least, exceedingly rare.

To a certain degree, such a process can be observed in some primitive societies where the younger generation are early integrated in production and accorded a high social status, while seniority, which speaks of wisdom and experience, plays an important part in the regulation of behaviour. In such societies the divisions between young and old, which are prevalent in the western world, are scarcely noticeable. Aries has attempted to show that such a situation was once true in the West[6]. Prior to the industrial revolution, young people were seen simply as miniature adults. This has led to Musgrove's widely quoted statement that *'the adolescent was invented at the same time as the steam-engine'*[7].

Speaking of the Tikopia tribe in the 1920s, R. Firth relates how the young were early integrated and involved in the central concerns of the island's economy:

'The child soon comes to take part in the work of the community, and so useful is it that a household without one is at a distinct loss. At first it goes out with a relative to the cultivations and intersperses its play with fetching and carrying things. Gradually, most of the economic minutiae are allotted to it by its elders, including others than parents, and its performances, small in themselves, act as the emollient which

allows the household machinery to run smoothly[8].

Firth found no evidence of revolt or deviation among the young and, returning in 1952, he found the Tikopia little changed, in spite of widening contacts with the outside world.

Musgrove has deduced from such anthropological evidence that in those societies in which the status of adolescents is high, change will tend to be slow and the *'blandishments of an alien civilisation resisted'*, while in societies where the young are denied social status there is likely to be a predisposition to change — the young may respond readily to the opportunities offered by an alien culture to follow alternative and quicker routes to power and influence. This has led Musgrove to the conclusion that *'it may be one of the ironies of the human condition that any society must choose between social conservatism and rigidity* **or** *the oppression of its young'*[9].

However, while Musgrove's evidence may be useful in describing factors which influence social change in primitive societies in contact with the West, he pays insufficient attention to the productive processes existing in these societies and the social relations these processes demand. In an economy which requires little technical knowledge other than that gained in participation, where simple processes allow all age groups to be involved, the volume of work requires that as many members of the community as possible be involved, the early economic integration of young people is demanded, no separate education is necessary and little pressure is exerted for social change. The effect of contact with the West must depend upon both the prevailing state of production at the moment of contact and upon the relative merits of the influences of the West for the primitive society.

Contrary to Musgrove, Karl Mannheim has emphasised the important role that youth must be allowed if progress and change are to be achieved. In 1943 he suggested that *'static societies which develop only gradually, and in which the rate of change is relatively slow, will rely mainly on the experience of the old'*[10]. A dynamic society, on the other hand, would accord youth a high status. This is a fairly commonly expressed view, which reflects the situation of modern society wherein new ideas appear to affect the young rather than the old, where it appears that the young lack the depth of commitment to the established social order that characterises most adults and are more willing to overturn traditional values to replace them with a new dynamic moral order.

This type of debate, revolving around whether youth is fundamentally conservative or dynamic, and what social circumstances cause it to be so, can be summed up by the statement that *'change can be measured by the degree to which the culture of the young and the culture of the older generation is not continuous, integrated and coherent'*[11].

Such statements not only ignore the processes which create change and the means by which social relations are reproduced, but they also fail to perceive that 'change' can either be superficial in terms of the basic structure of society or it can be fundamental in radically altering the productive relations. Similarly; the word 'youth' is used as a blanket category covering different social classes, races and sexes, involving all people somewhere between the ages of 12 and 25. In order to present an adequate analysis of youth and social change it is necessary to clarify the terms used and to place young people within the context of the particular type of society with which we are dealing.

All societies which wish to maintain their basic structure must, and do, socialise their young according to the desired values of social relations. This socialisation process takes place consciously through child-rearing and teaching methods, through the direct influence of people and institutions upon the young, and unconsciously through the absorption by the young of the values inherent in the organisation and structures of society.

In a static society, socialisation presents few problems in that the conditions to be experienced by the young will be little different from those experienced by their forefathers. However, in the dynamic industrial society of late twentieth century capitalism, the question of socialisation is more complex; while maintaining the social relations and values which are necessary for the reproduction of capitalist productive relations it is also necessary to allow for the full exploitation of talent (and therefore for the possibility of social mobility) and to prepare the rising generation for conditions of production which will almost inevitably differ from that experienced by their parents. The young must be prepared to be both conservative and dynamic.

'The technologies underpinning capitalist class domination in Europe and the United States have so sharply shifted in the last 50 years as to significantly alter the nature of class relations and the bases for class consciousness on the part of the workers. Indeed, so fundamental are these changes that we may speak of a new emergent sector of the proletariat alongside the 'classical' industrial, blue collar proletariat. This emergent class is, like its predecessor — the industrial proletariat — a working class (ie it bears the same 'relationship to the means of production'), but it differs in that the central instrument through which its attributes are tailored to the needs of capital is the set of educational institutions, primary, secondary and college, and the set of issues around which its consciousness might be built differ widely from simple biological preservation and material security'[12].

Industry in the more advanced areas of capitalism has moved from manufacture requiring a large labouring population to more white-collar professions characterised by an ever-growing bureaucracy and a more highly educated workforce. Such developments have led not only to a decrease in the size of the labouring population — the traditional blue-collar workers — but also to expansion in education, with increasing importance given to educational achievement and the ability to adjust to new conditions of production. The system of education has thus become the major arena of socialisation.

'The real key to the importance of youth lies . . . in the question of the reproduction of the social conditions of production. Central among these conditions is that of ensuring the stable reproduction of the labour force over time — the guaranteed recruitment of the young to their role as the next generation of the proletariat. As the growth of the state educational system . . . indicates, the task of ensuring this continuity is too complex and vital a task to be left to the traditional institutions of socialisation, especially that extremely unreliable institution, the working class family'[13].

Whereas the intentions of nineteenth century education, ie to teach according to class and to reproduce the social hierarchy while ensuring the acquisition of skills necessary in production, were evident both in the arguments proposing the provision of state education and in the actual organisation of the three-tiered system, today state education claims to be egalitarian in its provision. However, as numerous studies have shown, it continues to socialise and select, dividing the young population into its future work roles, and class background is an important factor in its selective processes. Through an ideology of equality which provides for social mobility and the exploitation of talent, the educational system is attempting to maintain and reproduce the social hierarchy while at the same time demanding an ever-higher level of expertise and knowledge.

While increasing numbers of young people are being prepared, through higher education, for the professions, a large proportion leave at the age of 16. It is at this point that the issue of the class composition of young people becomes most complex and the contradictions of school socialisation most apparent. It would appear that those who continue in education are being prepared for middle class roles while those who leave must become working class. However, polarisation of the classes in an era of monopoly capitalism, in the traditional Marxist sense, is ensuring the proletarianisation of those in occupations which previously granted power and privilege. Increasing numbers of young people are being educated for what they consider to be middle class jobs only to find that these jobs require the attitudes and ethics of a working class. Nevertheless, the social division at the age of 16 is real. Longer time spent in educational institutions is causing the consciousness of growing numbers of young people to form around issues raised in those institutions rather than in the traditional arena of the work-place, and many students are developing a highly critical awareness of their social situation and of their future prospects. For those who leave school at 16 the labour market provides little promise. Without educational qualifications it is very seldom possible, if at all, to seek success in the world of work, and most young school leavers, even if they can find a job, face a future of menial, low status work. It is this group of young people who provide the greatest threat to stability. Unable to gain satisfaction in their work, sometimes educated above the demands of the work, they seek status and opportunity among their peers and in their leisure time. This often involves delinquency — rejection of the adult norms and social values which have denied them either success or status — and adherence to an alternative culture.

Thus, while those young people who continue in education are developing their consciousness through abstract understanding and through awareness of their prospects in the labour market, they are creating a youth culture or 'student movement' within the confines of a state institution, continuing to be socialised under the auspices of the state. Those who leave school at 16 are developing an awareness and culture outside the direct influence of the state. It is under such conditions that the state has developed alternative institutions within the framework of education and welfare, in an attempt to maintain its influence and continue the complex process of socialisation begun in the schools.

While recognising the development of a critical consciousness among students illustrated by student unrest in recent years, and the importance of the fact that their future prospects in terms of finance, power or status are no longer secure, this essay proposes that the differential benefits granted to students, provision for whom is much greater than for young workers, and the extended period of socialisation they undergo in state educational institutions, makes for easier containment of their rebellion. Conversely, rebellion of the young worker, which occurs as a result of direct experience rather than abstract understanding, is at present likely to be repressed rather than contained. However, there is evidence to suggest that the institutions of repression, such as DHSS homes for young offenders, are, largely through overcrowding, increasingly unable to perform the task of resocialising the individual. Moreover, it is often the case that repressive measures which involve punishment of the individual only serve to heighten discontent. The rebellious young worker is thus particularly problematic for society and it is becoming increasingly necessary for the state to develop means of containing the discontent of this section of the youth population through ideological rather than repressive measures.

Part Two — Formal Education

It is a fairly common proposition that the educational system is designed to transmit skills and knowledge which will enable the future labour force to cope with the increasingly technical demands of the productive process. This is most adequately illustrated by the arguments for the introduction of state education in Britain in the nineteenth century. Introducing his Education Act into the House of Commons in 1870, W. E. Forster said:

'Upon the speedy provision of elementary education depends our industrial prosperity. . . . It is no use trying to give technical education to our artisans without elementary education; uneducated labourers

are for the most part, unskilled labourers, and if we leave our work-folk any longer unskilled . . . they will become overmatched in the competition of the world'.

Thus any adequate explanation of the relationship between the educational system and the outside world must begin with the fact that the schools produce workers and that the level and quality of schooling bears direct reference to the technical needs of the labour market.

However, the productive processes of capitalism not only require a certain degree of technical competence, they also require an increasingly reduced, though more productive, labour force. More advanced levels of technology help increase output, but as the consumer market cannot expand indefinitely, technological development implies reduced labour. But profit depends upon labour, not upon output. Profits are made through living workers and the organisation of production in such a way that the price paid for the worker's time is less than the exchange value of the goods produced by labour.

Education has developed as a major response to these contradictions, both absorbing a reserve army of labour and, as an industry unto itself, aiding economic expansion by utilising resources and relieving some of the pressures on industry. The increasing length of schooling reflects the shrinking size of the labour market and young people, as the Rowntrees observe, are often channelled through further education as an alternative to unemployment.

As education has developed as an industry it has created its own secondary industries, eg the mass production of books and educational 'aids', while expanding the teaching and academic labour force. Moreover, it has aided manufacturing industry by absorbing, for example, the training functions which industry would otherwise be called upon to provide. As such, education is peculiar in that it has, apparently legitimately, expanded while other industries have declined.

Although in the late '60s education did seem to have an unlimited capacity for expansion, the recent cuts in educational expenditure have shown that, under certain conditions, investment in this industry does have a limit, and may even be counterproductive as far as capital is concerned. In a period of recession, when public investment in education exceeds profits gained, when education trains a large proportion of students for unproductive labour, when a workforce is being produced which is possibly academically more sophisticated than industry demands and is therefore likely to be discontented, it is no longer feasible for the state to continue to direct scarce resources into the educational system on an ever-increasing basis. The extent to which schooling can be increased for those who are destined for low-status manual work is particularly limited, and it is here that the greatest contradictions are manifest.

At the time of raising the school-leaving age in Britain to 16, it was argued that this would improve the opportunities for low-achievers. Liberal theories regarding the benefits of more education for the individual abounded and it was suggested that particular benefit would be gained by those who would otherwise be forced to leave school through family or financial pressures. Such arguments failed to perceive either the relationship between education and the reproduction of the relations of production or that the basic motive for the move was to absorb surplus labour cheaply at a time of rising unemployment. The raising of the school-leaving age is otherwise unnecessary and offers no intrinsic advantage, eg in terms of job prospects, for those who do not do well at school. Moreover, it has probably been influential in increasing the resentment and dissatisfaction of those for whom schooling has only implied failure, as witnessed by the growing problems of truancy and classroom disruption and violence particularly prevalent among those in their final school years. Any further extension of the school-leaving age would serve to compound these problems as well as those arising from general contradictions inherent in being young in present society, eg physical maturity contrasted with social powerlessness. Schooling (especially when it is compulsory) implies childhood, and childhood cannot be extended indefinitely. Thus the only real advantage of extending the school-leaving age has been to temporarily mask the extent of the unemployment situation, reduce the costs to the state of unemployment and extend the state's control over young people. It is this latter advantage to the state which is the most important in the context of this essay.

Education must be seen in its dual role in the social process whereby surplus value is created and appropriated. On the one hand it increases the productive capacities of workers by imparting technical and social skills and appropriate motivations. On the other hand, it is intended to defuse and depoliticise the potentially explosive class relations of the productive process, and thus *serves to perpetuate the social, political and economic conditions through which a portion of the product of labour is appropriated in the form of profits*[14].

The educational system can be understood as an institution serving the needs of capital by repressing personal freedom and development and perpetuating social relations of inequality. It not only facilitates the smooth integration of youth into varying strata in the labour force but also reinforces patterns of social class, of racial and sexual identification among young people which enable them to relate to their eventual standing in the hierarchy of authority and status in the production process. As Althusser points out, education is the major state apparatus for the reproduction of ideology necessary for the reproduction of the relations of production. Under an ideology of equal opportunity the school shifts the responsibility for success or failure onto individual children; while speaking of the inherent values of education for individual development it represses that development through a compulsory system which, in its content and organisation, mirrors the requirements of the economy — individual fulfillment is more an accidental side-effect (if it occurs at all) than a real aim of state education. However, it is becoming increasingly difficult for this ideology to hide both the real relations and the major functions of education.

Contradictions in the productive process are becoming ever more acute in advanced capitalism and as these contradictions are reflected in the educational system, which at the same time attempts to function according to its ideology of equality and neutrality, the organisation of education becomes ever more confused and unable to appear apolitical. The liberal ideology can no longer adequately explain away conflicts and contradictions.

Liberal reforms in the schools, while both reflecting the ideology of the school and certain economic requirements, are at the same time serving to heighten the fundamental contradiction of socialising for changing economic conditions while containing the extent of change. This can be well illustrated with reference to new teaching methods. True to the ideology of the individual, these methods seek to allow the free development of the individual child in an unstructured learning environment which, it is hoped, will produce a more dynamic and self-directing labour force prepared for the professional and bureaucratic posts now characterising the major part of production. However, this conflicts both with notions of repression and authority which are necessary for hierarchical relations and with the necessity of preparing a certain section of the population for the manual work which is still required. As Tony Green and Rachel Sharp[15] point out, these new methods are inherently contradictory within a school system which is necessarily structured both to produce a certain type of knowledge and to reproduce the social relations of the wider society. The implementation of these methods within the schools tends to create a confusion of aims and requirements. Moreover, carried to their logical conclusion in an ideal setting, they speak of a socialisation process which would fundamentally undermine notions of discipline and personal repression necessary for a docile and stable labour force.

The schools have thus been given the unenviable task of de-politicising a situation which is becoming increasingly and more openly political. Their failure to perform this task adequately, as shown by the examples of the development of a National Union of School Students, by the increasing militancy of teachers and by the general breakdown in discipline and standards, all of which are giving cause for concern in society, is indicative of the contradictions from which state education is suffering. This failure to adjust adequately to the new conditions of capitalism has influenced the cuts in educational expenditure, affecting particularly the supply of teachers and thus reducing their political power.

The economic pressures of the current situation, particularly with regard to the employment prospects of school and college leavers, is thus allowing the state to reduce its investment while hoping to increase educational standards, of the type required by industry, through more severe competition within and without the schools. However, such fierce competition will serve to further alienate low achievers from a school system which can no longer afford to engage their interest through experimental and non-academic projects. It is also likely that these same young people will face unemployment when they leave school. At the same time, developing political awareness in the schools and their failure to further adequately mask their real functions are giving rise to a situation where, in rejecting the values offered by the schools, finding that such values have little to offer them, such low-achievers are also rejecting the values of the wider society and thus threatening the stable reproduction of the relations of production.

It is in this situation that, we argue, the state will find it necessary to turn to nonformal education as an alternative (and cheaper) means of influencing young people who do not respond to the socialisation of the schools.

Part Three — Nonformal Education

The sociology of nonformal education is developing within the context of a financial and methodological crisis in the formal educational structure. As has been argued, the organisation of compulsory schooling is such that, while in its traditional form it is adequate for the purposes of conservative socialisation and the preservation of the social hierarchy (functions which are still essential), in its attempt to respond to new conditions of production and to transfer notions of constrained dynamism, it radically threatens its own structure and begins to reveal its political nature.

The assumption that formal education is capable of producing nearly all of the wide range of behaviours which modern society requires to reproduce itself leads to the demanding of educational reforms in response to failure. Brembeck suggests that such reforms are *'exercises in futility'*[16], that education in its traditional form has been doing what it is good at and therefore it ought to be allowed to continue. *'The difficulty may now be that we want it to do some things it is not good at. . . . Perhaps it is time to seek other means which are naturally good at doing them better'.*

In the present situation, formal education is both failing to reach the standards demanded by capitalism and failing to provide a creative and satisfying environment for young people — particularly those of non-academic inclinations — or to contain their discontent. This has led a number of theorists to suggest the implementation of nonformal educational methods as a complement to formal education. Brembeck believes that the learning environments of formal and nonformal education shape and maintain different kinds of behaviour. The goal of educational strategy should therefore be to determine the kind of behaviour sought and to create the educational environments which most clearly support and encourage the behaviour.

He maintains that the critical differences between the structural environments of education lie in their proximity to work, immediate action and the opportunity to put to use what is learned. Nonformal education is characteristically carried on in a context of action, work and use. Formal education takes place outside this context. Thus Brembeck concludes that nonformal education is the better mode where the object is to change immediate action or create new action, and that formal education is superior where immediate action is subordinated to abstract learning or concept building, looking toward longer-range change.

Here we find, in structural terms, the argument that formal education is not suited to cope with the social dynamics which constantly require change and adjustment, particularly in the lower sections of the population wherein the contradictions of capitalism reveal themselves most sharply, and which the vicissitudes of the economy affect most deeply.

Nonformal education is particularly suited to the needs of young people who reject formal schooling and the values it preaches, for its structure is such that state control and socialisation can be maintained while dispensing with the compulsion, abstract thinking, authoritarianism and rigidity against which such young people rebel. As Kleis defines it:

'Nonformal education is any intentional and systematic educational enterprise (usually outside of traditional schooling) in which content, media, time units, admission criteria, staff, facilities and other systems components are selected and/or adapted for particular students, populations or situations in order to maximise attainment of the learning mission and minimise maintenance constraints on the system'[17].

It is distinguished from **informal** education in that it is intentional and systematic, and from **formal** education, not by the absence but by the noncentrality of form, by the persistent subordination of form to ends. Thus any institution which claims educational intentions or lies within the educational framework, but which is neither compulsory nor academically formal in its approach can be classed as nonformal.

It is apparent that such institutions, though they may not be overtly described as nonformal, exist in great numbers in Britain, and it is possible to show that those specifically designed for young people are gathered under the auspices of the state via their connection with the Youth Service.

The Youth Service was created to meet, and continues to respond to particularly pressing needs among working class youth. Furthermore, major developments in its growth can be seen in relation to periods of stress[18]. Within the educational system the Service is generally treated as the 'poor relation', particularly in terms of financial provision, and this perhaps reflects the low status of those it is designed to serve. A census carried out in 1968 among 80 statutory youth clubs revealed that almost 70% of working boys attending the clubs were in manual jobs and there is evidence to suggest that statutory clubs are, in the main, frequented by working class youngsters, although this is not true of the uniformed, voluntary and activities clubs whose clear philosophy and purpose are often relevant to, and attract those from 'professional' backgrounds.

During recent years, local authorities have remained statutorily obligated (under sections 41 and 53 of the 1944 Education Act) to provide for youth, yet since the middle '60s they have been completely deprived of guidance on policy for development. *'Victims of the pernicious 'Administration by Afterthought', they have resorted to their own ideas with the consequence that during the last decade, youth service development has been patchy, ad hoc and confined to localised initiatives'*[19]. This has been reflected in youth work practice which is often pragmatic and individualistic in approach, tending to relate to overt problems rather than anticipating potential problems through a consistent philosophical or political awareness of aims other than those of transmitting the generally accepted cultural characteristics of society which provide for personal satisfaction and individual fulfilment.

Such a situation has left the Youth Service a vulnerable target for cuts in educational expenditure without exciting too much public disagreement. This is partly possible because, although a social-educational function is claimed for youth work, it is seen by many, including a large percentage of workers within the Service, as primarily recreational in character and therefore an expendable luxury. However, the increasing professionalisation of the youth worker and the recent pressures on the Service are causing many of those directly involved with young people to reassess their position and aims and to begin to organise arguments about the need for statutory institutions to provide for the social education of working class youth.

It is suggested that such social education will not only help young people adjust to their future life situations but will also serve as an alternative to the formal system which many young people have rejected. Thus a radical reorganisation of the Youth Service, making it more coherent and purposive and giving it more direct educational legitimation, is being sought. Eggleston advises a reorganisation wherein school facilities are used and the links between schools and clubs become stronger:

'Our evidence . . . suggests that young people . . . keenly wish to use the service. . . . It could well be that attendance at the club, like attendance at the link course in the college of further education, could be seen as appropriate 'school attendance' by the 15 year old 'ROSLA' children providing an acceptable alternative to the full scale contribution of formal schooling and an alleviation of the problems often associated with this group in the schools[20].

Arguments are pointing to the discontent of working class youth in the context of school failure, unemployment, financial hardship and lack of social facilities other than those offered by the Youth Service. This leads to an awareness of the direct political manifestation of discontent and the role the Youth Service can play in containing it. Indeed, most of the recent evidence brought to light by those who support and wish to extend the influence of the Youth Service is concerned with its positive educational functions and its potential for giving young people the possibility of using their creative energies in satisfying and fulfilling ways without the restrictions of curricula, examinations or authoritarian direction.

It is in this manner that a new image of the Youth Service is slowly beginning to emerge and, despite the spending cuts, there is evidence of the development of a new awareness of the potential of the Youth Service as an institution of nonformal education catering particularly for the needs of working class youth. This awareness is witnessed by the recent creation of a youth service forum, the aim of which is to establish clear guidelines for the future role of the Service and to represent it in discussion with the DES; by the national conference on youth — 'Youth Charter towards 2000', held in February 1977 as the opening conference for Wembley Conference Centre, which included among its speakers such notable public figures as Wilson, Heath, Hart and Weinstock; by statements such as that of ex-minister for education Gerry Fowler who, in a recent 'Times Educational Supplement' article, claimed that the Youth and Community Service would have a 'significant' role in any pattern of continuing education, with community-based youth provision 'an essential element in future educational structures'.

This developing recognition of the possibilities of the Youth Service is reflected in the recent publication of what must be seen as the first sociological study of the Youth Service, Eggleston's 'Adolescence and Community'. One of Eggleston's indications for the future is 'that, increasingly, the main thrust of the Youth Service would lie in the development of the participative identity through which the young may achieve meaningful adult roles in the sort of society in which they are likely to live; a society of which most of them are well aware and willing to accept if the community will accept them'[21].

Despite the many valid insights which Eggleston gives into the present situation and future potential of the Youth Service, he fails to notice the contradiction inherent in the suggestion that the function of the Youth Service will in future 'lie in the development of a participative identity'. The wider society is unable to accept the equal participation of youth because of the ideological separation of youth from the rest of society, according young people an inferior status, an ever extending childhood which implies a power-lessness reinforced by the real position of youth in the productive process. The development of consciousness regarding their capabilities and potential power within the environment of a nonformal structure will serve to increase the conflicts between young people and the community, denying the realisation of this power. It is also necessary to observe that the developments of capitalism are causing breakdown in the cohesion of communities and, as such, leaving the community in no position to receive the contribution of young people. Moreover, Eggleston fails to assess the functions of state-controlled educational services as structures of ideological transmission. Seen in the context of analyses of nonformal education, it is apparent that major innovation in the Youth Service would not come about through philanthropic concern for the welfare of adolescents, but would be implemented as a structure for the transmission of values which cannot be presented through formal education, and would provide the state with a further means of control over young people. In a hierarchical society all learning is organised to maintain that hierarchical structure and, as Gramsci pointed out, state ideological intervention in the development of consciousness is mediated through the instruments of state institutions. Young working class people do not learn about themselves or their environment directly through their own experiences of their world; their understanding is mediated by the structures of thought and understanding learned through institutions.

However, the possibility of the Youth Service being used as a major institution of nonformal education by the state, and its promise for containment and social control, must not be allowed to hide its real benefits for young people and its potential for influencing both their development as confident and self-directing individuals with a sense of worth, and the development of a consciousness of the social nature of their oppression which the former implies. These benefits for young people and the contradictory nature of the benefits for the state are particularly apparent in the new experimental approaches being developed in the Youth Service[22], which tend to be highly unstructured, emphasising the self-direction of participants, the value of group solidarity and the active means of achieving desired ends.

Despite its nonformality, which tends to obscure the relationship with the state, such education as the Youth Service offers must eventually face similar problems of contradiction with which the formal educational system is now contending. As Eggleston accurately points out:

'There is a . . . general problem for the adult worker in the new approaches. If he is to help his members to achieve an effective decision-making role in the community he will find himself involved with members in action that is essentially political in nature. Indeed, he must act as their political advocate. . . . But if he is to do this he is likely to find himself 'confronting' the existing power structure of which he himself is a part'[23].

Thus we find that the institution of nonformal educational structures in partnership with, or as alternatives to formal education, is a two-edged sword. While it may prove vital for the government to develop it as a means of containing the discontent of working class youth and continuing its influence in the socialisation process, it may also provide the tools for the development of that very political consciousness among young people which the state wishes to prevent. This is an inevitable result of the contradictions flowing from the organisation and development of the productive processes, particularly as they affect the complex socialisation of young people.

References

1 Crowther Report, '15 to 18': the Report of the Central Advisory Council for Education, HMSO, 1957; Albemarle Report, The Youth Service in England and Wales, Ministry of Education, HMSO, 1960.
2 Talcott Parsons, Social Structure and Personality, Free Press, 1965.
3 John Rowntree and Margaret Rowntree, Youth as Class: the Political Economy of Youth in our Generation, Vol. 6, Nos. 1-2, 1968.
4 Ibid.
5 Samuel Bowles and Herbert Gintis, Schooling in Capitalist America, RKP, 1976.
6 Philippe Aries, Centuries of Childhood, Penguin, 1962.
7 Frank Musgrove, Youth and the Social Order, RKP, 1964.
8 Ibid.
9 Ibid.
10 Ibid.
11 Peter K Manning and Marcello Truzzi, Youth and Sociology, Prentice-Hall, 1972.
12 Martin Carnoy, Schooling in a Corporate Society, David MacKay, 1975.
13 John Clarke, The Three Rs — Repression, Rescue and Rehabilitation: Ideologies of Control for Working-Class Youth, Centre for Contemporary Cultural Studies, 1975.
14 Bowles and Gintis, op cit.
15 Rachel Sharp and Anthony Green, Education and Social Control, RKP, 1975.
16 Cole S Brembeck and Timothy J Thompson, New Strategies for Educational Development, Lexington Books, 1973.
17 Russell J Kleis et al, Non-formal Education: the Definitional Problem, Program of Studies in Non-formal Education, Michigan State University, 1974.
18 Youth Service Tomorrow: a Report of a Meeting arranged by King George Jubilee Trust, Oldham's Press, 1951.
19 Frank Booton, 'Administration by Afterthought: Thoughts on the DES document 'Review of the Youth Service' in Youth in Society No. 16, November 1975.
20 John Eggleston, Adolescence and Community, Edward Arnold, 1976.
21 Ibid.
22 Margaret Gardner, Developmental Work with Young People, National Youth Bureau, 1974.
23 Eggleston, op cit.

Chapter 10

Detached Youth Work in the Late 1960s and the 1970s: a Review of Work in Inner London

DON MACDONALD

Don Macdonald, 32, is a
graduate of Kent University.
After various jobs in youth
clubs, schools and play
projects, he became a qualified
youth and community worker
after completing the course at
Goldsmith's College. He
worked as a detached worker in
West Hampstead, London,
between 1972 and 1977, and is
now an intermediate treatment
officer at Islington.

Detached youth work has a longer history than is often thought. In this country and the United States, churches, missions and youth 'movements' such as Boys' Clubs and Scouts had strong elements in their activities of outreach work to difficult and unserved young people. Many of today's 'traditional' youth activities originated as efforts to meet young people's needs in their own areas (as did some of today's professional football clubs!). But getting out onto the streets to work with young people on their own ground did not become an explicit method of work until the 1920s in the United States, and the late 1950s in this country. In the United States, the impetus for this development came from a concern to contact and work with delinquent gangs, and to this day delinquency prevention features highly in American detached work practice. In this country, however, delinquency prevention and 'gang control' have been much less to the fore.

In discussions of detached youth work, there has been a lack of clarity as to whether it was the worker or the young people who were detached or unattached. In the 1950s and '60s, concern was expressed that conventional youth clubs, with a membership of 20-30% of the relevant age groups at any one time, were not making contact with or working among the so-called 'unclubbable' young people, who were also described as 'unattached' or 'unreached' young people. As a consequence, experimental projects were started, some of which were detached youth work projects, whilst others were coffee bar projects aimed at reaching the same clientele.

In a survey of Inner-London youth projects (done by project workers themselves, and updated by me), it appears that a majority of projects still do detached or outreach work with young people. Those projects not currently doing detached work have done some in the past: this has provided contacts with young people who, in turn, have encouraged other young people, via the grapevine, to use the project. Other projects do outreach work with local adults. Yet undoubtedly some projects spend a great deal of time on work without an outreach element.

The Problems Facing Underprivileged Youth Today

The '60s and '70s have seen a growth in detached work — both projects and workers, nationally and in London. Probably the biggest growth area in the Youth Service has been the provision of school-based youth centres and, in the recreation sector, the provision of adventure playgrounds, neither of which cater for older teenagers, who are not interested in those types of activity. These must be seen in the context of significant influences at work on young people during these years. Such influences as:

1 The enormous growth in unemployment, particularly among young people (in spite of recent indications in some Inner-London boroughs that jobs are not as scarce as is commonly believed). Those who are hit hardest by the economic crisis are those with the lowest educ ional attainment and without qualifications, both of which have recently become necessary for more and more jobs: 75% of those registered as unemployed with one careers office had no educational qualifications.

2 The raising of the school leaving age to 16 in 1972. In spite of various schemes to cope with this extra year at school, pupils in the lower streams are often alienated from the schools, which, in general, value academic success most highly and which, consequently, direct most resources to the sixth forms.

3 The increase, rather than decrease, in the crime rate, in spite of an increasingly affluent economy in which young people and children are being seen as consumers.

4 Increasing racial tension due to the growth of the National Front and the refusal of the young black British to put up with the hostility and prejudice which feed their resentment at lack of educational and job opportunities. Afro-Caribbean children and young people under-achieve at school and suffer more from unemployment than white youngsters.

Thus, in the last ten years, the situation of underprivileged young people in this country has worsened, at least relatively if not absolutely.

Detached workers are therefore presented with a dilemma as to which of these problems to tackle; whether to approach the problems directly or work with the young people to enable them to cope with these problems. Choosing from so many problems and points of intervention, it is often difficult to arrive at a set of priorities, particularly so for inexperienced workers.

Detached Work Methods

In spite of claims that detached work is no longer experimental, there is still widespread ignorance about detached work in youth work circles, particularly in contrast to the almost universal experience of youth club work. Out of 16 detached (or outreach) posts in one London borough advertised over nine years, 13 were filled by people who had neither held a full-time youth work post before nor had experience of detached work. This widespread ignorance among workers and management about detached work ensures that there is confusion about the role, a 'postponement of self-definition'[1], which leads to a great deal of questioning of what one is up to, from oneself, from others, from management. This scrutiny may impose a strain on workers who do not have the right support, but, with the right support, it encourages a more rigorous approach to the work.

A Model of Detached Work Methods

Below I have outlined a model of detached work methods, making a distinction between primary methods, which involve outreach work, and secondary methods, developed from the basis of the outreach work. I will illustrate these methods by extracts from detached project reports.

Primary Methods of Work: Outreach Work

Detached/contact work with young people where they are (the only method exclusive to the detached work approach)
Community/development work with local adults

Secondary Methods: developing from the basis of information gained in the Outreach Work

Information/advice-giving/counselling from a centre
Inter-agency work with local workers
Pressuring and informing agencies about the needs of young people
Setting up and sometimes running alternative provision
An increase in structured-work with small groups of young people

In all these different methods of work it is vital that detached workers see their task as that of an enabler, except where the exigencies of the situation require occasional action as a provider or advocate. As Marchant and Farrant point out: *'It is often easier and quicker to take the provider/advocate role and do it for the adolescent rather than the slower and more difficult task of encouraging self-reliance'*[2].

There is a danger too of a worker with a reputation for 'getting things done', by virtue of some 'pull with the authorities', becoming placed in the role of 'fixer' by the young person. This can limit the worker *'to the role of a high powered go-between'*[3]. Taking on an enabling role should not just be an act of faith, but should involve some understanding of what skills are needed. Different elements of the enabling role are covered more fully in the sections below on detached work and work with local adults.

'It's a slow and lonely business building up detached youth work! But you gradually start to see that you are getting somehere — at least you hope you are'

If detached work is reaching young people where they are, then this implies that the young people themselves, the neighbourhood they live in and the needs they express will help define the aims and objectives of the work. There may be a job description, but it is likely to be quite vague. This *'postponement of thinking about goals'*[4] is one of the strengths of detached work. In order to clarify the objectives, there needs to be a reconnaissance of the area; *'time spent getting to know about the possible areas for working, and later a more detailed study of the area chosen can . . . provide a sound basis for making informed choices'*[5]. One detached worker spent his first month *'generally feeling out the area . . . by walking around the streets, shopping and* eating locally. It was also important to begin to contact the other agencies . . . ' After the first month, the worker began to 'concentrate on the various groups of young people in the . . . areas'[6]. This reconnaissance work in the neighbourhood is similar to, and overlaps with the detached role of making contact with young people.

Detached/Contact work with Young People

'That very first time when Trevor couldn't stop talking because he was pilled up, I asked him if that was why, and they all laughed. The dark, suspicious one became convinced I was a copper. Demanded to see my card. Handed them all round and some of them still have them. But incredible development for the first meeting. And too fast, both of us telling each other too much too soon. No time for trust and confidence to build up. Then the reaction. Running from me, hiding from me, ignoring me — the hard stare treatment, daring me to open my mouth. Throwing mud and stones as they ran along hidden behind the balconies. Then rides in the car. All over it. Up top, hanging out, on the back, up the bonnet. But slowly the beginning of a pattern. Up to the transport cafe, inching warily round the 'grease' (motor bike lads), drinking tea and jamming up the juke box with metal discs. And finally permitted to see their hide-out'[7].

That worker was working with a typical group of teenage lads going through an anti-social phase, whereas some workers spend far more time with individuals, often girls, sometimes single parents. Another detached worker describes how, after visiting various cafes, shops and youth clubs, the worker 'dropped into the local pub to buy some tobacco to be greeted by three of the older girls, two of whom I have been trying to contact for the past few weeks. We talked endlessly about relationships and their involvement on the fringe of the drug scene. I arranged to meet one the next day to write a letter to Social Security and agreed to take another to the hospital where her baby was still being looked after'[8]. The worker still visits weekly two of the girls, both with babies, living isolated in their flats.

'Most of the time I'm saying 'no'. 'Can you find me a job?' — 'No'. 'Can you find me somewhere to live?' — 'Probably not'. At least you can take them through the process whereby they can see why they're not getting what they're not getting'

When detached workers have made contact with unattached youth, what do they do then? It is still necessary to assess the needs of the young people and to decide **which** groups of young people to work with. Detached workers can then offer 'a relationship which the young people (can) understand and accept, and which (can) in part compensate for the absence of understanding adults in their social environment'[9]. As Marchant and Farrant point out, the very nature of the relationship is one of 'self-determination and freedom of choice'. There is some criticism that detached workers see 'the development of the relationship as an end in itself'[10]. I would dispute that this is

147

generally true, although there is a danger of this happening if workers do not analyse their work enough nor isolate the different elements that help a young person develop and change, since merely caring for young people is not enough.

Listed below are the elements which I feel the worker uses to enable the young person to grow and develop; the list is derived from Goetschius and Tash.

1 Acceptance and support; if the detached worker relates with the young person over time *'and if, in addition, one learns to accept certain behaviour (eg verbal abuse) or knowledge about behaviour (eg criminal activity) then the resultant relationship is likely to be in some depth'*[11]. The acceptance by the worker of young people involved in anti-social or criminal behaviour should not be taken to mean that the worker condones such activities; it is accepting the young person and not the act, and there is a very thin line between the two, especially when the worker becomes justifiably angry. For example, a detached worker talking with some white lads about racial prejudice wrote: *'They meet my strongest disapproval directly on this. But then if I get really angry with them they won't talk to me about it'*[12].

2 Information-giving, which also involves telling young people where and how to obtain information.

3 Acting as a bridge to family and agencies, but always with the knowledge and consent of the young person.

4 Passing on simple social skills; eg how to argue with the police and still stay out of the 'nick', how to stay on friendly terms with swimming pool attendants, neighbours, boy/girlfriends and parents, how to present yourself for a job interview.

5 Advice and guidance, oriented towards enabling the young person to make decisions him/herself. In fact, I think the phrase *'insight giving'* is more illuminating a description of this process.

Further to these is the dimension of working with groups. This may involve *'introducing isolated individuals to friendship groups'*[13], enabling individuals to leave groups which restrict their development, or an even more group-oriented approach: *'the worker, accepted by the group, demonstrates a wider social acceptance, attempts to link the group more positively with the community, acts as interpreter and assists the group to move further afield'*[14]. This movement is into not just youth clubs, as some would have us believe, but also different activities and experiences, the process of planning these for themselves, and working as a group in this process.

Community/Development Work with local Adults

Some projects work with local adults on a conventional community development model. Others see their role as working with local adults to increase the youth facilities, such as the following example, from the Bishop Creighton House Youth Project.

'The project worker's job has been to find and encourage local adults who care about young people in their area (five housing estates) and are prepared to help with a club. On one estate, the project started through making contact with two residents who had been involved in a previous attempt at a club there . . . another . . . through members of a church wishing to develop non-evangelical youth work as an aspect of their ministry. On another estate the project responded to a request for help from a tenants' association'. The project made it clear 'to those who wanted to use the project's services that there was a need to form a club management committee separate from, but not necessarily unrelated to, any parent body, such as a church or a tenants' association', which gave the worker a 'clearly defined body of adults with whom to work and with whom to develop the human relations and administrative skills necessary to run a club.

'In the early stages, the worker helped the management committee with preliminary planning, such as the use of a suitable hall, thinking about a programme. When the club actually opened, the worker and one of the project's part-time workers helped at the club alongside the local adults. Continually, the worker has been concerned with 'passing on simple administrative skills, eg writing to confirm verbal agreements, keeping minutes. Some of these skills have been passed on directly . . . others have been 'learnt from experience'. The worker also attempted to 'pass on simple human relation skills, such as encouraging people to say what needs saying to an appropriate person or at an appropriate place'[15].

The worker had also been encouraging people to see the link between administrative and human-relation skills: 'The development of the clubs that the project has been involved with has not been smooth and many setbacks have occurred including 'key people' packing it in, a badly leaking roof, and spates of 'trouble' on club nights. What has emerged from this project, however, is that with interest and support, local adults are prepared to weather such setbacks . . .'[16]. Thus, the clubs set up have been successful in meeting the needs of the young people, with certain qualifications.

Information/Advice-giving/Counselling from a Centre

One girl who was very troubled and needing help said: 'Of all the places I've been to, Hearsay was the only one where I felt they were really interested and cared about me'.

Information, advice-giving and counselling are the primary methods of work for some projects. Some information and advice-giving goes on in the detached work role, but centres provide a more constant focal point for information/advice provision; it is easier to recruit and support part-timers and volunteers to work in a centre, there are no wasted attempts at contacting young people, as in using street work, and the workers can work in the centre while waiting for 'custom'. In 1976, the Portobello Project set up its information service in order 'to have a more immediate impact' than the detached work of contacting young people, which 'can often take many months'[17].

Some centres, such as the Hearsay Centre (Youth Aid, Lewisham) maintain a 'high commitment to various forms of **outreach work** where the workers meet young people on their own territory, eg pubs, cafes, streets, parks etc'[18]. In fact, in 1976/77 a majority of contacts, 964, were made by one project through outreach work, while 656 were made by phone or through young people calling at the centre. A contact is defined as a 'meeting between a worker and the individual where some piece of information is exchanged'[19]; an example of one case being 'a 16 year old girl who was pregnant. She came to us worried and desperate. It took some weeks talking with her and supporting her while she decided in the light of reliable information and worker support about what she was to do'[20]

Overlapping Methods of Work

There is considerable overlap in the three roles of pressuring and informing conventional agencies about the needs of 'unreached' young people, working with local professionals and setting up alternative provision. The last may be set up as a result of a detached worker cooperating with other workers in the coordination of information; information which shows up certain of young people's needs which a group may be best able to tackle (as with the Harbour Project, below).

Inter-agency Work with local Workers

Detached workers should have an overall view of the neighbourhood they work in, based on their detached role, their reconnaissance and outreach work. This should enable them to see the need for the coordination of the efforts of workers in different agencies. Some detached workers pass on relevant information to workers and offer support when appropriate; for example, the group of skinheads mentioned earlier eventually started going to a youth club; the detached worker then felt that he would have to work closely at interpretation and support with the club worker.

One of the more interesting attempts at coordinating the work going on in a certain area is the West End Coordinated Voluntary Services. This was set up by the Soho Project, and several other projects working with young people, with the aims of ensuring that referrals are channelled to the right project, coordinating and increasing fund-raising, and campaigning for the single homeless. In no way was the Soho Project solely responsible for setting up this coordinating body, yet it does seem to be true that, in general, detached projects see the usefulness of, and need for, coordination.

Pressuring and Informing Agencies about the needs of Young People, particularly the 'Unreached'

Large bureaucracies have certain procedures and regulations which militate against a flexible or informal approach, an approach which is most likely to be successful with 'unreached' young people. Because of their size and their ability to carry on a service for the majority, bureaucracies may ignore or be unaware of the needs of certain client-groups; for example, in a large school pupils can register their attendance and then disappear for the rest of the day without being noticed. Such bureaucracies need prodding to recognise the unmet needs of young people. Detached workers perform this role, both in cases of individuals and groups.

The issue of youth unemployment is now well to the fore in the mass media and politicians' speeches. Yet for a long time, detached youth projects were discouraged from getting involved in this issue, the edict was that the Youth Service in Inner-London was concerned with young people 'in their leisure time'. Projects continually pressed to be involved in the issue, and with the young unemployed. The Youth Service bureaucracy felt that unemployment was the concern of the careers service (also part of the education authority, like the Youth Service), and should remain so. Yet large numbers of unemployed young people were not registering with the careers service; truants, who were not reached by the schools or education welfare service, were in consequence not being reached by the careers service. One project, the Central Lambeth Project, was allowed eventually to employ an 'unemployment' worker in 1973, partly because central Lambeth (Brixton) has a very high proportion of young West Indians, who have suffered most of all from the employment crisis. In the late 1970s unemployment became an 'OK' issue for Inner-London projects to be involved in; leisure time was defined as being 'out of work' and the careers offices took more notice of youth workers' information about young people. More detached youth workers were appointed to work with the unemployed; partly because of the economic situation and the funds being pumped into job creation programmes, but also due, in some part, to the lobbying and pressure by projects, in this case primarily on their own initiatives.

Setting up and sometimes running Alternative Provision

This may cover a wide range of provision, from temporary play-schemes to projects to tackle unemployment, truancy or, as in the example below, homelessness. Often the authorities responsible for the provision of services in these different areas will not recognise the problem, let alone a solution. Setting up alternative provision involves researching both the problem and possible solutions.

'In response to the constant crisis of homelessness and lack of accommodation among young people, the North Islington Workers' Group (a collection of youth and community workers in North Islington) invited a sub-group to form and to look at what was being done for single, homeless young people and what plans there were for young people in North Islington in particular. . . . It became apparent that other agencies, whilst recognising the plight of these *young people, were not in a position to help them'.* So an accommodation project, Harbour, was set up *'as a practical demonstration to illustrate the problems the young people face and one possible way to overcome them. Both housing and social services departments have expressed their backing and support for the project, in both practical and financial terms, and in its implications for their own policy development*[21].

Yet, hopefully, detached workers still retain their enabling role and do not slip into becoming indispensable to any project, such as the detached worker running a playscheme who said, *'I just became the boss, the guy who paid part-timers'.* Another detached worker wrote about a project he had set up: *'It is useless to set up a project that collapses when the original worker withdraws'.* This worker had set a time-scale for withdrawing from the workshop, but *'there was a danger that if I had stuck rigidly to my timetable, the workshop teachers would not have been able to cope. My role in the last year has been to play a secondary role to the other workers, supporting them and helping them to take over and run the group without me. It was worth staying that extra time in order that the workshop should get on a sound footing, as it is now'*[22].

An Increase in Structured-work with Small Groups

Often detached work projects see the need to mount more structured-work with small groups of young people. This may be based on needs thrown up by work with young people, for instance, education-oriented work based on referrals from school, detached or intermediate treatment work based on referrals from social workers, or work experience-oriented tasks through contacts with local agencies. It may be leisure-oriented, as in the case of a small group of young people who came into the Hearsay office to find out what the project was about: *'They then frequently popped in to have a chat. . . .'* This group grew and was encouraged to form a committee, become registered as a youth group and meet in a local church.

In the case of the group not becoming so self-reliant, the worker has to play a more directive role and structure the group: this is likely to be true of groups of younger teenagers and those involved in anti-social behaviour, or where there needs to be an element of training.

One detached worker's objectives were *'to contact a small group . . . with a terrible reputation with the social workers, youth workers, police and local people'.* They were involved in delinquency or truanting, were often suspended from school or were without school places. The worker made contact over a period of months, by hanging around their haunts in the neighbourhood, and was non-directive in this role. After nine months a small educational project was set up by the worker in a short-life shop, which meant that there would be greater structure: *'a greater commitment, less aimlessness, a greater scope for activities, and for getting them to make decisions and work together as a group'.* This effected a change in the worker's role. *'I had to become more directive as to their behaviour and also to their activities and work, with more pressure for regular attendance and work on the building, on basic education and on the group's domestic chores'*[23]. This work was very different from the original unstructured, non-directive street work, and the group responded very well to this increase in structure and demands, a response which would probably not have been as positive without the nine months of contact work, since they were a very alienated group, had been expelled from certain projects, and other projects with which they had been involved had closed.

Reaching those Young People other Agencies do not Reach

Goetschius and Tash classify the young people with whom their project was working into categories, ranging from those who can cope and make use of existing services, through the temporarily disorganised, to the seriously disorganised *'who need the most intensive guidance and support on a long-term basis'*[24]. Marchant and Farrant stated that *'there is a strong case for not attempting work with those young people who are coping adequately with the exigencies of life'*, although, as Goetschius and Tash point out, those who can cope often provide a stabilising influence on those who cannot and give more than they take in group-work (thus the Portobello Project makes use of young people to work in their information service).

Detached work should be aimed at the more disorganised categories of young people, those young people other agencies do not reach. I am not sure that the different methods used by detached workers actually reach young people. Thus, the community development model of 'indirectly serving young people' has various limitations; the Bishop Creighton House Youth Project stated that their locally-run clubs did not cater for the older adolescents, nor those who wanted to break away from the locality. The National Children's Bureau study of locally-based schemes for youth stated that these could not cater for the more difficult adolescents. Similarly, building-based projects, without outreach elements, rely on working with those who walk in the door, which removes any choice the detached worker might wish to exercise — since those in greatest need may not come in. Buildings too can be taken over and dominated by a single group of youngsters who may attempt to exclude other young people — as in the Hoxton Cafe Project[25].

The enormity of the problems facing underprivileged young people today is not being fully recognised by the bureaucracies, whose function it is to serve their needs, and who do not always realise that they are failing in this. The bureaucracies need to be prodded in the right direction, and detached workers have a part to play in this. Yet there is a danger that detached workers may abandon face-to-face work with young people, and the detached work method of contacting them, for a less strenuous method of work that may not actually reach the young people at whom the work should be aimed. In fact, in Inner-London several projects do not do detached work — the workers are called 'project workers', not 'detached workers'.

This work must continue for two reasons: firstly, the detached work method can reach, and work successfully with, those young people neglected by other agencies. If this work enables the young people to develop, then there will be an effect long after the worker has moved on. Secondly, to attempt the secondary methods of work, there is a need for up-to-date information. The best way of getting that information is straight from the horse's mouth, from the young people themselves. The needs of these young people change from generation to generation and from locality to locality, thus in the main, the young people with whom the Goetschius and Tash project were in contact were employed. Similarly, certain phenomena, such as glue-sniffing, appear to be confined to certain localities of Inner-London (and other parts of the country) and is unknown to others. If detached workers are not up-to-date with the problems affecting young people they cannot hope to be of service to them.

If detached workers give up detached work, confine themselves to less strenuous work, become more building-based, and do not reach the unserved young people, there is a danger that detached work projects will get as out of touch as the traditional youth organisations, and history will have repeated itself. If the authorities still see the need for detached work they must provide the right support for it — few projects are given funds for either mini-buses or consultants. Such funding would still leave detached work as a cheaper way of working than more expensive building-based projects, and as the most effective way of reaching those young people that other agencies do not or cannot reach.

References

1 **Michael Farrant** and **Harold J Marchant**, *Choosing Objectives: a Stage in the Detached Work Process,* Youth Aid, 1977.
2 Ibid.
3 **Josephine Klein**. Address to CYSA conference on detached work, May 1976.
4 **Farrant** and **Marchant**, op cit.
5 **Klein**, op cit.
6 *Worker's Report, 1978,* Kentish Town Project, 1978.
7 *Annual Report, 1976,* Islington Project, 1976.
8 Ibid.

9 **George W Goetschius** and **M Joan Tash**, *Working with Unattached Youth*, RKP, 1967.

10 **Terry Powley**, *'Neighbourhood Youth Work'* in *Concern*, No. 12, Summer 1973.

11 **Farrant** and **Marchant**, op cit.

12 *Annual Report, 1969* and *Information Service, 1976*, The Portobello Project, 1969, 1976.

13 *Annual Report, 1976*, Islington Project, op cit.

14 *Annual Report, 1969*, The Portobello Project, op cit.

15 **Rod Moore** and **Chris Stratton**, *'Neighbourhood Youth Work'* in *Youth in Society*, December 1978.

16 Ibid.

17 *Annual Report, 1969*, The Portobello Project, op cit.

18 *Annual Report, 1975/6* and *Annual Report 1976/7*, Lewisham Youth Aid, 1976, 1977.

19 Ibid.

20 Ibid.

21 Harbour Project, *History of a Housing Project*, Islington Project, 1976.

22 **Don Macdonald**, *West Hampstead Youth and Community Project Report, 1972-75*, Camden Council of Social Service, 1975.

23 **Areyh Leissner**, **Terry Powley** and **Dave Evans**, *Intermediate Treatment: a Community-based Action-research Study*, National Children's Bureau, 1977.

24 **Goetschius** and **Tash**, op cit.

25 **H M Holden**, *The Hoxton Coffee Bar Project*, National Youth Bureau, 1972.

Chapter 11

Youth Social Work: a Move Towards... What?

TIMOTHY PICKLES

Timothy Pickles became active in the informal education aspects of youth work as a volunteer, whilst studying in Bristol for his teaching certificate. During this period he was involved in the design of a community-based youth social work project, of which he is currently the organiser. In addition, he has university commitments to teaching and research in the field of Intermediate Treatment.

A decade ago the phrase 'youth social work' was unknown. Some would have said it was unnecessary, since youth work and the welfare services were both well-established. Today, the concept is either dismissed as being a fancy name for something which has always been done, or is lauded as a major step towards realistic provision for young people with difficulties. This paper explores what we mean by youth social work, and whether it has any distinctive characteristics. An examination of various issues points to some of the main trends of the present day. It is suggested that these may only be transitory and that the future promises a rather different form of work.

What's so New?

To date I have come across no definition of youth social work, despite the fact that there have been at least two publications — one a regular bulletin and the other a bibliography[1] — incorporating the term in their titles. Youth work and social work both readily conjure a mental picture. The youth work image is of club members and scout groups engaged in five-a-side football, table tennis, camping holidays and voluntary service. A closer examination reveals youth work as an open pursuit, attracting youngsters to its facilities; the degree of participation, loyalty and authority varying between units. Some attempts have been made to move out to youngsters not attracted by clubs through detached and coffee-bar projects. Youth work is, however, still primarily concerned with the voluntary social education and development of interested young people, through their leisure.

Social work, on the other hand, is less concerned with social education than with social care. Whilst, in principle, its provisions are as open as those in the youth work field, in practice it restricts accessibility on a 'needs' criterion, by the use of referral systems and statutory obligations. It has become an intervention service aimed at providing change and improvement for a series of categorised client-groups. The traditional method of intervention has been casework, but in dealing with younger clients, many social workers have seen the interview technique as being too formal, structured and unrealistic. It is detached from the reality of activity and peer group pressure surrounding most adolescents; it demands a skill in verbal communication and analytical reasoning which may not be adequately developed. Instead, some social workers have experimented with other forms of contact, involving an activity-medium such as the camp, small group-work or community work.

These two fields overlap; young people can be identified who have various welfare or social needs and who may also be engaged with youth provision. The question is whether this creates duplicity in services. The common ground is characterised as a service for young people, engaging them in leisure pursuits, constructive activities and social education, but restricting the availability of such facilities to those kids who show some identified or special need (as determined by the provider). A definition of youth social work might then be: 'social intervention through youth provision for a restricted section of young people, defined by reference to social criteria'. This may be illustrated by way of examples. The last decade has witnessed the emergence of PHAB Clubs (physically handicapped and able-bodied), to meet the needs of handicapped people for social activities and enjoyable leisure. In some schools a recognition that educational progress will not be made by some pupils until they have achieved an emotional and physical stability within the school, has led to the growth of special units. But the most common example is that of special provision for disadvantaged or delinquent kids, aimed not only at providing enjoyable (and legal) leisure, but also at encouraging maturity and self-confidence. It is this latter illustration which is commonly associated with youth social work and identified with the idea of intermediate treatment.

If youth social work has a shortage of definitions, intermediate treatment (IT) has a surfeit[2]. Without entering into the debate, we can conceive of IT as a wide range of community-based facilities designed to help individual youngsters who may be in trouble with the law or at risk of being so[3]. Having received official recognition in the Children and Young Persons Act, 1969, a variety of youth facilities have co-operated, been adapted or been initiated to work with difficult kids to keep them 'out of trouble' and 'out of care'.

Here lies the nub of the duplicity argument. Many personnel in the Youth Service (both statutory and voluntary) claim that they have been running a preventive service for potentially disruptive kids for years — and so they have. However, a central idea in youth work philosophy is that youngsters attend of their own volition. Clubs attract members by maintaining a good programme; those who choose to attend may be suspended for poor behaviour. Both youngsters and club workers exercise choice. The social worker allocated a child on a supervision order has a statutory responsibility to provide that supervision — niether he, nor the child, has any real choice. With or without an IT clause, a child may be encouraged by his social worker to participate in the community youth provisions, but there has been disillusionment with the ability of the traditional Youth Service facilities to hold and retain many of these kids. The Youth Service has made efforts to accommodate these demands, but the youth worker is often unable to devote sufficient time to individual kids, unwilling to damage his club's image or to co-erce a child to attend.

For those kids for whom the open clubs and other leisure groups do not, in practice, cater, the social worker has had to turn elsewhere. The result has been a rapid, if uneven, growth in specialist, and often innovatory, facilities: small closed groups meeting frequently; activity centres; neighbourhood community projects; work experience schemes; short-stay residential provisions; and outdoor-pursuits groups. They operate generally on a referral basis, and restrict membership to youngsters with identified problems. Staffing is mainly by social workers, probation officers or volunteers, with only occasional youth work personnel. The child-adult ratio may vary from ten-to-one down to one-to-one. This ensures a closer contact than is possible in the classroom or club, but removes the unreality of a casework interview by providing both a group- and activity-medium.

This changing emphasis towards a specialist youth provision may be charted by examining any of the regional intermediate treatment handbooks. For the south-west region, over 85% of the entries in the original handbook were of facilities that did not discriminate (except by age or sex restrictions), and were therefore open to everyone. In the last two amendments to the handbook, half of the entries have been specialist resources operating on a referral or selective basis[4].

There is an interesting dilemma here, in that most youth social work programmes have, as a primary objective, the integration of the child and the facility into the community — yet to do this they create a specialist and separate provision. It seems characteristic of many school special units, IT groups and community homes, that they should initially create abstraction before attempting integration. If subsequent 're-integration' is to occur (and often the child never perceives himself as being non-integrated in the first place), then youth social work agencies cannot operate independently. They need the traditional open services if the aim of making such intervention redundant by integration is to be achieved.

Issues

How much can youth work offer? If the present growth of youth social work has occurred one-step-removed from youth work, it is not to deny the influence and potential contribution of the youth and community work field. It is widely accepted that, for some kids, the leisure provision of clubs and centres has provided a valuable preventive service which has helped, diverted and educated innumerable young people.

There are many physical contributions which the Youth Service can make to specialist provision[5]. There are buildings which serve as clubs during the evening, but which are relatively under-utilised during the day and at weekends. There is an increasing use of premises as day-centres for unemployed teenagers and for neighbourhood projects, such as play-groups and old people's clubs. The timetabling of other specialist uses for children at risk is but a small addition. Such premises provide space and facilities for small activity groups, and have access to the more specialised resources, like outdoor pursuits and video equipment. Indeed, it is interesting to note that many of the established intermediate treatment centres are physically no more than expanded youth centres, with perhaps an educational or residential wing grafted on.

The youth and community worker has much to contribute him/herself. S/he is experienced and trained in working with young people — in activity and communications skills. If s/he has an interest in disadvantaged youth then these skills can be used to either promote self-designed specialised programmes or work with other professionals offering complementary skills. There have been various projects employing both social worker and youth worker to run small group-work exercises, and the Scottish Association of Boys' Clubs now has a full-time project promoting this sort of co-operation[6].

The involvement of the youth worker is one step towards the integration of alienated or isolated young people. The worker's presence in a smaller, more protective group opens the way for a later transition to the open and permanent facilities. Similar advantages may be gained by using the premises of widely-available organisations to encourage youngsters to know and use them at other times.

If the concept of specialist work with disadvantaged or difficult young people does spread within the Youth Service, we may see the appointment of specialist officers. In other services this has already occurred, with intermediate treatment officers and group-work specialists in both social services and probation service, but so far only the two national boys' clubs associations have taken any initiatives towards new appointments, though qualified youth work personnel are now employed by other services.

The problem for the Youth Service, in making new posts or provision, is the long-standing question of its image. Statutory court orders imply co-ercion (or the threat of it), but youth work has always relied on voluntary participation and openness. It does not want its facilities regarded as 'places to which difficult kids go', nor does it wish to be seen as an agent of social control exercising authority on behalf of other parties.

Is positive discrimination a self-cancelling argument? The separate development of youth social work, and its selective nature for those involved in its schemes, mean that a large element of discrimination is being exercised. This is justified on the grounds of positive discrimination — those who have less shall deliberately be given more. The argument suggests that difficult or disadvantaged kids are emotionally or socially deprived, for which they should be compensated by activities and interests aimed solely at them.

The compensation argument has been widely attacked. In the education field, Jencks[7] has attempted to demonstrate that large changes in schools, to create greater equality by favouring the disadvantaged, have only very small consequences in terms of subsequent attainment, occupational status or income. Attempts in schools to create discrimination, by providing more resources and reducing class sizes in deprived areas, have tended to lead to a demand by other (more affluent) sections of the community for similar treatment by the public authorities. Without widespread education of the general public, it is likely that positive discrimination will become self-cancelling — because of these demands for parity. Thus, in youth social work, we see arguments against discriminatory policies, along the lines that *'holidays for hooligans are wrong'* and *'clubs are for ordinary kids, why encourage the bad ones'*[8]. On a wider scale, discrimination between communities in locating public facilities, such as swimming pools, skateboard parks and libraries, often leads to similar resentment.

In this climate it seems unlikely that community-based (and therefore publicly-seen) provision for delinquent or difficult youngsters, for whom there is little public sympathy, will be tolerated unless the rest of the community either receives its own 'compensation' or is persuaded to accept such policies by their results.

Will liaison ever occur? The overlap between youth work and social work suggests that the different professionals have much to contribute to each other in their knowledge of individual kids. All too often, probation officers, teachers and others in the community come up against the same needy individual in different contexts.

If intervention programmes are to stand much chance of succeeding, it would seem beneficial for the principal agents to collate this diverse knowledge. However, it has proved so much easier to write about liaison in job descriptions and project reports than it ever has been to communicate between different professional workers, in practice. The hindering mechanisms are varied. Some services place a great emphasis upon confidentiality, and will not disclose case notes and assessment reports. Trust becomes a necessary pre-requisite for the exchange of information, but a rapid staff turnover inhibits the growth of personal-trust relationships. Some people wish to retain their own professional image, fearing attack if they are seen to share the work, whilst others are happy to refer kids to other agencies to lighten their caseload, and then take no follow-up action.

Experience varies widely, but the future of youth social work as a joint approch is bound to the development of effective and regular liaison channels between agencies at field level. Because these are so often inefficient and frustrated, there may be some demise in co-operative approaches involving people from different agencies and the replacement of such models by different professions working for the one agency.

Models

During the past decade there has been an almost continuous evolution in the models of youth social work practice. Initially, specific support would be provided to individuals placed in existing organisations; more personal attention within the larger unit, be it school, club or family. This was thought by many to be impractical: there were too many pressures within the larger unit and insufficient time to allocate to each individual, so the new model was of abstracted smaller units, based upon a semi-closed group with a high staff-child ratio. This model was adopted by the schools special units, the family group homes and IT groups. Despite the very limited attempts to evaluate these smaller units[9], they have achieved widespread approval from both the practitioner and the policy-maker searching for ways of coping with the problems of some kids.

The small group model is not without its critics or its problems. Its growing popularity undoubtedly reflects the greater success and relevance which social workers and others feel that they are achieving in using group methods to work with and influence young people, but it cannot be expected to operate as a panacea. There are unresolved questions, as outlined earlier, and, in order to break away from such restrictions, various organisations and agencies are trying to develop different models.

More intensive programmes The non-residential programmes outlined so far have generally been of a low intensity, involving perhaps one or two contact sessions a week. This compares very favourably with the social services casework model of supervision, in which contact may only be an hour a month, but it contrasts poorly with the scope of residential programmes for maladjusted children or those in care. Consequently, efforts have been made to provide a more intensive programme, whilst still using the group-work method. Northorpe Hall, in West Yorkshire, invites groups for a residential weekend each month and maintains contact with the children at home during the week. In Edinburgh, Panmure House operates a day-care programme in the week, which includes an educational provision instead of normal schooling. Other groups arrange for up to five evenings a week of contact. Residential periods on camp will achieve the same effect of developing personal relationships and trust as a basis for future work, and are included in the programmes of most groups.

The concept of intensive work has been given a greater stimulus by the Personal Social Services Council's suggestions for intensive intermediate treatment as a direct alternative to care orders for persistently delinquent young people. It envisages both residential and community components in a programme lasting up to 90 days. Within this relatively short period, a concentrated attention on educational, social and work needs would be directed at helping the child without removing him from home for more than an initial week or two[10].

Integrated centres or 'non-centres' The problems of inter-professional liaison, the possibilities of more intensive programmes, the development of new centres designed to accommodate youth social work approaches — they have all tended to lead to the growth of 'integrated centres'. Such centres combine some of the component parts of youth clubs, community centres and counselling services, and in some of the more developed examples, the emergence of a new approach towards caring for young people may be seen.

The origin of such centres can be traced in other directions too. Our administrative system provides services for young people by imposing divisions — education, leisure, welfare, judiciary, health — and the boundaries between these services are clearly marked. Liaison may be poor or ineffective: corporate management is too far removed from the level of personal problems, and inter-professional communication is often erratic. From the child's perspective, a personal problem does not naturally fall into any of these imposed divisions (though its symptoms may) and it is confusing to be confronted by so many 'care-workers'; teacher, tutor, head of house; social worker, educational welfare officer, IT worker; doctor, health visitor; youth worker, club leader, community worker; educational psychologist and pscyhiatrist. To the child, problems are rooted in boredom, self-status, peer pressures and family relationships, and the different behaviour patterns we attempt to 'treat' — truancy, delinquency, introversion, aggression — are only indicators of such problems in different contexts.

The integrated centre attempts to reduce this plethora of roles by concentrating the different aspects of work with the child into one centre. To some extent it builds upon the assessment centre model, where different professionals have managed to work together under one roof. The provision of one centre with a limited number of professional staff, and perhaps volunteer aid, can provide for the educational, leisure, counselling and, at times, residential needs of young people. The staff become 'key-workers', capable of seeing, and being seen with, the child in each of the different areas of his life. Such intensive personal contact, if it is accepted by the child, leads to trust and mutual respect, from which the child can be expected to grow in self-discipline, maturity and stability.

Multi-disciplinary centres require considerable co-operation to be established. Much of the initiative has been from voluntary agencies, such as 870 House in Birmingham, operating at the community level in responding to the needs of young people in the surrounding neighbourhood. The Markhouse Centre in Waltham Forest is a joint education and social services venture which also serves a community restricted by the local schools' catchment areas. Within the co-ordinated management of this project a variety of different professional staff are employed.

Such centres have the potential to demonstrate the irrelevance of our service divisions in helping kids at risk. By blurring worker roles and not defining work areas, they become more open and responsive to the problems being presented. The centre, which can then integrate itself into the local community, has the exciting potential of becoming a genuine caring unit, responsive and relevant to the many needs of the kids it serves. If these can be accomplished, then the unit ceases to be specialised and abstracted, and become a 'non-centre' — a community response to diverse human needs.

Radical (non-) intervention The models which have evolved so far have provided a service or facility for younger people. Whilst recognising that the root causes of deprivation, disability or delinquency may be multi-factoral, the intervention programmes designed to cope with these problems have been based on 'treatment' for the individual or group. An alternative radical approach makes a more structural analysis, concluding that deprivation is a relative term created by inequality within society, and that the delinquency problem is caused by a society which has wronged some of its members.

Approaches based on the idea of radical intervention contain an overtly political message in trying to persuade society to accommodate all its members. Many youth social work organisations would not dispute the social or structural causes of the problems with which they are coping, but the radical argument suggests a different approach, aimed at changing society and not an individual's behaviour. Adams has suggested various component elements for a radical approach to delinquency: 'offenders' would be maintained in the community and not removed; the courts would evaluate as well as enforce the law; the criminal law might subsequently de-criminalise various acts; and the police would concentrate more on preventing than arresting offenders[11]. The argument is taken further by Schur, who expounds the idea of non-intervention — that kids should be left alone wherever possible — implying that our policies should aim to encourage society to accommodate *the widest possible diversity of behaviour and attitudes, rather than forcing as many individuals as possible to 'adjust' to supposedly common societal standards'*[12].

As yet, youth social work practice is still working at the level of the individual, but practitioners are concerned by the structural causes of disadvantage. Community action and awareness are playing an increasing role in the programmes of some such groups.

A Transition Stage towards. . . . ?

The field of youth social work has been characterised by many initiatives during a brief ten year period. New methods of work have evolved and been tried, but today we are faced by issues which question and threaten the continued existence of these initiatives. There are three directions in which youth social work may move.

Since the methods have drawn upon and extended both youth work and social work approaches, there will be some attempt to re-integrate youth social work into one or other service, by making minor adjustments to the scope of that service. In this event, the social services are more likely to absorb the initiatives, partly because of their statutory responsibilities and partly because of their greater diversity. Already social services departments are employing other professionals and establishing multi-disciplinary units. Such developments are piecemeal and any absorption will be a compromise in which the innovatory ideas are likely to be lost in the relatively static structure of a large department.

If youth social work can 'prove' its effectiveness, in terms of more realistic intervention techniques, then the second option may be a reforming and broadening of the fields of the present services. This implies a recognition by management that a significant new contribution is being made which should be willingly encompassed by redefining and extending the scope of present provision. This, too, may ultimately lead to absorption within an existing service, but it may also lead to joint-funding exercises and grant-aiding of semi-independent agencies which would continue to explore the contribution of a youth social work field.

Thirdly, we may envisage a time when the value of more integrated and localised approaches to young people in need results in the establishment of a different service structure; a co-ordinated and responsive model dispensing with the existing service divisions and providing a genuine alternative in integrated community care for kids. If this option replaces youth work and social work with a 'community care for all youth' model, then youth social work will have made a significant change in our present provision.

During the coming decade there will be more evaluation of the impact of youth social work programmes. So far, the results have been limited and confused, and more data will be required before reliable assessments can be published. One problem in measuring effectiveness has been to determine the principal objectives of each programme. Aims have often been two-fold: an adjustment of children to the demands of the society in which they live; and a reduction in delinquent behaviour. Different schemes have varied in their emphasis. It is difficult to measure social adjustment and personal maturity criteria, though most projects would argue that 'improvements' have occurred (though the extent to which this can be attributed to the project's intervention is often debatable). The Wincroft Youth Project measured statistically changes in social adjustment, attitudes, use of leisure facilities and other indices, to demonstrate a *'dynamic adjustment'* as a consequence of the project's work[13]. Measures of delinquent activity, though more objective, give fewer grounds for optimism. Paley, in reviewing a number of studies, suggests that there has been little impact on re-offending rates. Furthermore, he argues that there is no direct reason why programmes which tackle the disadvantage and deprivation problems should influence delinquency — the two may be interrelated, but one cannot expect to stop delinquency by reducing disadvantage[14].

A clearer distinction between the problems of delinquency and of disadvantage will clarify the issue of effectiveness in youth social work. In doing so, more accurate assessments of target groups for intervention and the outcomes which may be expected from different programmes can be made. The Children and Young Persons Act, 1969, emphasised the interests and needs of the child as the prime consideration; by concentrating on the problems of social disadvantage and deprivation, the 'delinquency problem' may come to be disregarded by youth social work programmes as a rather unreliable indicator of more fundamental problems. This debate will continue into the '80s, but these recent developments have contributed to the innovation of new methods which, as they are diffused, may lead to a re-appraisal of our care and support services for kids in need.

References

1 *Youth Social Work Bulletin,* National Youth Bureau, 1973-1977, and **Maria Johnstone**, *A Bibliography of Youth Social Work,* National Youth Bureau, 1974.
2 Compare the definitions in *Intermediate Treatment Project,* HMSO, 1973, with **Leissner, Powley** and **Evans**, *Intermediate Treatment: a Community-based Action-research Study,* National Children's Bureau, 1977, and *A Future for Intermediate Treatment,* Personal Social Services Council, 1977.
3 For a general introduction to IT see Personal Social Services Council, op cit., and **Jim Thomas** and **Trevor Locke**, *A Bibliography of Intermediate Treatment 1968-1976,* National Youth Bureau, 1977.
4 *Schemes of Intermediate Treatment Facilities for Planning Area No. 11,* South West Children's Regional Planning Committee.
5 See *Summit,* No.5, National Association of Boys' Clubs, February 1977.
6 *Intermediate Treatment, Social Work and the Youth Service,* Scottish Association of Boys' Clubs, 1976.
7 **Christopher Jencks**, *Inequality,* Allen Lane, 1973.
8 Quoted in **Aryeh Leissner** et al., op cit., and **Ray Jones,** *Fun and Therapy: Consumer and Social Worker Perceptions of Intermediate Treatment,* National Youth Bureau, 1979.
10 Personal Social Services Council, op cit.
11 **Robert Adams**, 'The Development of Policies for Social Work with Delinquents' in *National Intermediate Treatment Forum Conference Papers 1977,* National Youth Bureau, 1978.
12 **Edwin M Schur**, *Radical Non-intervention,* Prentice Hall, 1973.
13 **C S Smith, M R Farrant** and **H J Marchant**, *The Wincroft Youth Project,* Tavistock Publications, 1972.
14 **John Paley**, 'The Implications of Research for IT' in *National Intermediate Treatment Forum Conference Papers 1977,* National Youth Bureau, 1978.

Chapter 12

Street Aid: another type of Voluntary Agency

ALAN DEARLING

Alan Dearling was born in Sussex and first worked in a youth club there. During university days in Kent, Alan continued helping in youth work projects, and in 1972 'went full time' in Essex. Since then he has worked in youth and community service in West Sussex and London, and is now Training and Publications Officer at the Intermediate Treatment Resource Centre in Edinburgh. He has been a regular contributor of articles on youth work in *'Rapport'*, *'Youth in Society'*, *'Times Educational Supplement'* and the radical education journals.

Firstly, I must, as they say in all the best council chambers, 'declare an interest'. I worked at Street Aid from October 1975 through until the end of July 1976. In point of fact, I was dismissed from my position as youth work research and development worker on 20th May 1976 and given two months' notice. But this is not going to be the story of my actions at Street Aid, although they will be touched on; rather it is an attempt to chronicle, with some objectivity, the origins and history of one of the more bizarre voluntary youth organisations to have originated in recent years. To set the scene, I will use my own knowledge of the buildings and the feel of the many and varied meetings which took place, but most of the information has been gleaned from the mountain of reports and papers which was created throughout the period from December 1969, when Street Aid was born.

Street Aid circa 1972

This is a convenient time to start familiarising ourselves with Street Aid and its earliest developments. It is a far cry from the Street Aid of the mid-70s, and 1972 provided a 'watershed' all of its own. The *'Street Aid News Bulletin 7'*,1975/76, doesn't even mention the earliest part of this period, instead of describing 1971/72 as the period when:
'Street Aid supplies evidence to Covent Garden public inquiry.
We carry out a survey of children's facilities in Covent Garden.
First outdoor events — fireworks carnival and Covent Garden cup.
We make proposals to ILEA youth service department for youth club with educational workshops'.

From 1970 to 1972 Street Aid had been operating a West End welfare centre. Phil Cohen was the originator, and it was styled in his view of the world, combining aspects of BIT, Release and the Soho Project. When the lengthy reports of 1975 and after started to appear, this early period of the organisation's development was glossed over. The pedigrees of many voluntary youth organisations which grew out of the alternativism of the late 1960s are forgotten, or at least played down by the 'respectable' successors, who find themselves running very different types of facility, even if the original name is retained. In the first 18 months, Street Aid ran on a shoe-string budget of £700, and employed four 'staff' on an unpaid basis. Phil himself was slightly 'infamous' as the legendary Dr. John, of London Street commune, which had held the famous squat in Piccadilly. The original idea was to provide a place which would attract groups of young people whose *'values or behaviour are outlawed by the dominant class and/or by their respective parent cultures'*[1].

The approach was novel. The workers were part of the West End scene. They were in as much need of a roof over their heads as the clients, and they shared many of the values of the 'drop-outs', the runaways and the violent teenagers. Phil Cohen said, at the time, that many social workers operating in the area pushed the young offenders back into 'the maximum security prison called society'. While drugs were the single, most obvious symbol of 'belonging' to the alternative society, the Street Aid team tried to get away from the official agency style, a style which viewed the youngster in the 'West End scene' as 'socially inadequate' and 'at risk'. Instead, the team understood all about getting an immediacy of response, and operated what Cohen calls 'intervention into the prevailing value orientations, patterns of recruitment and career structures of the West End scene'.

With John Hartnell, Toni Guttman and Maria Bevilacqua, Street Aid was providing 'a clearing-house for those lawyers who . . . (were) . . . willing to take on work with working class youngsters, and sub-cultural groups[2]. They were also busily producing pamphlets on coping with the dole, 'Street Selling', 'Thefts and Eviction'; and together with other concerned agencies, they produced the 'Mental Health Bust Book'. Those first months were primarily used as a mobilising period; the seven workers recruited off the street gave as much advice as they could, but in essence were almost as much on the 'receiving end' of help. It was one of those very exciting, intoxicating periods when the workers could feel that they were at the forefront of the new wave of community action programmes. The housing aid and crash pad service was central to the work undertaken, and, through another housing association, the workers were able to extend their housing welfare work, using two houses as a base. These were of the near-derelict type, and most of the young people who were referred there only stayed for a couple of months. It was a very positive answer to the official hostels, which refused to take couples and which often saw the young people who Street Aid took on as hopeless cases. In that first year, 7,000 informal visits were made to the Street Aid premises — two rooms in Southampton Street. By 1972, they had moved operations to King Street in Covent Garden. None of the original seven workers were now with Street Aid, as Street Aid looked for a new form of labour. Instead, Street Aid turned to the student population, who were well-used to catching the 'volunteerism' bug. Gone now was the early collection of charismatic street-personalities, and in their place the student workers offered more skill in dealing with the office work and advice-giving. The street culture of Piccadilly met with the student culture of 1972, and the result was that the 'collective hangout' rooms in the new premises were more strictly separated from the office facilities.

Even in these early, halcyon days of heady idealism and radical street-work, all was not the bed of roses one might suppose. The character of the revolutionary left and the disorganisation of the alternative society militated against stability. Often the effectiveness of the work was undermined from within: But at this time Street Aid was still able to adopt this air of healthy self-criticism, which became submerged as the organisation entered its next phase of development. This era was heralded by the evidence which Street Aid supplied at the Covent Garden public inquiry. Originally it was only expected to make a short presentation, but in the event the collective evidence lasted the best part of two weeks. David Bieda had, at this point, joined Street Aid after a writing career working with the underground press in the late '60s. It was David who co-ordinated the evidence which was submitted.

This submission put forward *'objections on political grounds, couched in sociological language'*; and David notes that '(throughout) *the inquiry we made contact with a number of local people, and in October we decided to extend these contacts and make our presence better felt in the area by holding a two-day festival'*[3]. Phil Cohen supports this view of Street Aid's intervention in the area, and at the time said that they were intending to adopt *'a policy of conciliation, both vis-a-vis the local community and the local authorities, and consequently changing elements in our original policy which would have antagonised them'*.

The new workers were more professional in their outlook (relatively), and more accurately reflected the views of the politicised middle-class alternative society, than the street culture of the West End scene. Again, using Phil as the spokesman, *'the middle-class domination (of Street Aid) is not, of course, the result of any conspiracy, it is inherent in the logic of the new situation and corresponds to the change in our basic objectives'*.

King Street became the haven for two groups, each at opposing ends of the social spectrum. One was the 'hopeless' cases that no other agency wanted; the other group comprised the young people who were opting out for various ideological reasons, and who were assured and eloquent. It was still a welfare agency at this time, but there was an immediate recognition that Covent Garden was an unusual area, with a particular history which made interlopers, like Street Aid, the subject of much suspicion. So, whilst the organisation continued with its welfare-advice service, new areas of work were investigated; notably those involved with off-site education. Some of these pilot schemes were involved in getting a coffee-bar project off the ground; others were offering day-release classes for secondary schools in the inner-London area. The premises in King Street were not really ideal for this expansionist plan, and there were difficulties during this period of frenetic fund-raising. John Ewen described Street Aid's approach to work as *'closer to Joan Littlewood's fun palace concept'*[4]. Add to this that he recognised that ad hoc, spontaneous voluntary organisations have *'a political irritant function'*, and that they require funds without strings attached, and you have something of the picture of the earliest beginnings of Street Aid.

Street Aid was not alone in what it was trying to achieve; other organisations, especially those with links in the cultural world of the arts and theatre, were developing in the early 1970s. Inter-Action grew from Ed Berman's theatrical experiments with group experiences; New Horizon provided a philanthropic helping hand to young and drifting sections of the central-London community; and Action Space, Islington Bus Company and Centaur Project each offered alternative 'modus operandi' and 'modus vivendi' for tasks/facilities normally provided in the capitalist economy. If it was photocopying, second-hand records or a theatre group, the radical voluntary organisations were meeting needs in an off-beat manner. Street Aid was allied with different groupings of these other 'radical organisations' at various points in its development. The early self-help, welfare agency phase brought it close to Release and characters like Alan Beam (one of his pseudonyms), who was instrumental in the banned 'Project London Free' booklet which espoused the legend:

'Take what you need
Make what you want
There is plenty to go round
Everything is free'.

Later, with the development of an education ethos, the Winchester Project in Swiss Cottage, the world of playschemes and events, and the ideological base of of educational de-schooling provided the links with the other radical organisations in London. With expansion, these links stretched outside London, and the Young Volunteer Foundation project in Watford became interested in similarities of pedagogy. The development of links with the Youth Service led Street Aid to using some of the theories underlying 'detached work', as was being organised in Kilburn and at the Caversham Road/Kentish Town Project. These were all parts of the whole, which became known as the 'radical departures' in youth work.

To end this section, it is interesting to give a hint of things to come. John Ewan was a shrewd crystal-ball gazer, and he understood the mechanics of radical voluntary organisations. He realised that these agencies would be far more likely to operate within the working class confines of the inner-urban youth, and that they could offer the vitality of approach which was often sadly lacking in the statutory service. But, and it is a big 'but', the movement from being young and angry to being 'middle-aged and just a little better off' often doesn't take all that long. This will inevitably cloud the ideals and the aims of the founding organisation, as views are moderated by the demands of running an expanding institution and raising cash. John ended by saying: 'middle-age spread is a notoriously universal disease'. Phil Cohen, in 'Five Cent's Worth', talks about this same period of early development in political terms:

'Alternative or progressive agencies all start out life as more or less explicit attempts to escape the exigencies of class mediation. Yet, the fact is that the more successful they are in pragmatic terms, the *longer they survive, the bigger they grow, the more they fail to do so*[5].

The Middle Period 1973-1975

This was the period when Street Aid began to expand quickly. It was situated in the decaying area of Covent Garden, and there was a conscious move away from the method of acquiring equipment by the 'beg, borrow or steal' technique. In *'Street Aid News'*, 1972, the organisation asked for about £15,000 to enable the work to continue and develop. The specific aims were to obtain charitable status; to obtain better premises for the office and the welfare work; to provide more accommodation units for therapeutic use and for low-income young people; to provide a warehouse for weekday local activities and weekend alternative city-centre functions; to run arts/social activities jointly with the Covent Garden Community Association and the Inns of Court Mission; to obtain a double-decker bus to provide information/coffee bar facilities in the West End for summer visitors; and finally, to organise the five-a-side football Covent Garden Cup competition in the spring and autumn of each year alongside a carnival. Not a bad shopping list!

Perhaps such a programme was grandiose, but its eclecticism fired the imagination of a large number of staff who came through the portals of Street Aid's premises. It was an amazing period of activity, as David Bieda took over the reins of the organisation from Phil Cohen. Very quickly the style of the work began to shift in emphasis. The ideas concerning mental health work and drug-information work were dropped from the official vocabulary. They were replaced by 'experimental work' and 'community involvement'. David Bieda was charismatic, at times nearly brilliant in his world-view of developing Street Aid, but, like so many leaders, he proved difficult to work with. Not all the schemes mentioned in the fund-raising pamphlets were ever followed through. Some graduated to 'pilot-project' status, others were allowed by successful funding to blossom immediately.

Dominating the whole period was the spectre of the Lepard and Smith project, ie the warehouse scheme which aimed to put all the workshops, social facilities, sports provision and information and recreation areas into one super-facility. The 1972 version was revised and re-revised through time, and bundles of paper later it reared its head again as the Market Project (see below) in 1975. The Lepard and Smith warehouse project never happened, but it sowed the seeds of the idea and developed into the even more ambitious Market Project. These schemes, perhaps because of their scale, perhaps because of Street Aid's loose community-base, caused a considerable degree of suspicion and animosity within the Covent Garden community. As I try to point out later, this community was itself often fractitious and politically divided. No-one, except Phil Cohen, stayed with David Bieda throughout Street Aid's history. In 1974, Phil Cohen moved out from the parent organisation with a Leverhulme sub-cultural research grant. From then on, with Dave Robins, Phil Cohen opted-out from the main Street Aid organisation and their unit was then only dependent on the 'parent' for making the umbrella applications for the funds in order to continue to produce *'Aspects of the Youth Question'*. These occasional papers were of a loosely-sociological style, dealing with the political nature of youthful behaviour and its relationship with the labour movement. So the 'sub-humans', as Phil, Dave and their entourage were affectionately known, never again played a fully active role in the life of Street Aid after the end of 1974.

The ensuing period in the life of Street Aid took on various faces. The main one was what is known as 'the unacceptable face of capitalism'. Street Aid was at that stage of economic growth whereby it could, in W. W. Rostow's terms,'take-off'. The political climate was 'right' to respond to the 'needs of youth'; the Covent Garden base was 'right' as operations-headquarters; the staff were energetic enough to concede a year or two of low income in the pursuit of the ideals they had perfected in their three years at university; and to crown the scene, David Bieda was the right person to spin-off ideas and, what is more important, to organise the fund-raising. This exercise required the presentation of an 'image' and doing the 'hard sell'. David was very able, the only trouble being that he held onto the reins so tightly that the staff teams tended to feel frustrated. During this period, the truancy project was commenced with Dave Bennet, the youth leader in charge, working with four kids referred from the social services and from schools. However, the project was never really a 'saleable product' for the leadership of Street Aid to merchandise, so after six months of fairly successful operation the scheme of 'alternative' education was dropped and replaced with the more fashionable 'supplementary' education, where the young pupils came from the schools on a half-day release basis, learning pottery, photography, music and women's studies.

Alongside these developments, Street Aid kept its contacts with the youth tourism scene through the newspaper *'Use It'*, which published information in English, French and German, in the format of *International Times'* and with much of the layout style of *'Time Out'*. This was one of the more successful Street Aid ventures, and was funded for four years, up until 1976, by the London Tourist Board. The print run in 1975 was 120,000, and the newspaper represented what was probably the only youth-related service which was provided to young tourists. The proposal for the double-decker bus was turned down by the GLC after lengthy discussions, ostensibly because of parking problems. In 1976, it was heard that the London Tourist Board was facing cut-backs and had given *'Use It'* the axe.

The holiday projects and the adventure playground, together with the performance activities at the Basement and the bonfire night extravaganza in the Japanese water-garden, were some of the project activities attempted at this time. They were very much geared to local involvement, and therefore had spin-off value — in terms of creating goodwill towards the organisation in the local area. The work at these times really only involved local youngsters from the Garden itself, and so numbers were fairly low — in the region of 50 to 80 per day. In 1974 the site for the adventure playground was at the Seven-Dials, while in 1975 the water-garden and the Basement were used. Much emphasis was placed on community arts-type activities, with dressing up, video-work and puppet-making. Drama and music were subsidiary activities, but it is always difficult to decide whether these were separate workshops or part of the events and projects as a whole. November the Fifth always produced a happy event, and in 1975 this climaxed with 400 people enjoying the food, steel band, fireworks, a kids' play and ignoring the rather wet weather in the Japanese water-garden. The plan was that the 1974 experiment should be used as a means to pressurise the local councils to provide a permanent site for an adventure playground, under the auspices of Street Aid. Other applications, like the one to Wimpey for a kiosk for distributing 'Use It' were backed with the information that the hut would be put into operation on the adventure playground, after use in the Jubilee Market.

The 1972-74 pilot educational workshops, which preceded the list of educational day-release classes mentioned previously, were paid for through ILEA tutor sessions and were of the 'community arts' type, particularly silkscreen and drama. Some of these early classes were run in the daytime, but most operated as the prototype for the youth club, which was acquired in the beginning of 1974. One of the other main projects of the early years was the video-workshop, which was a very short-lived experiment. Equipment was obtained and, for a short summer, two workers operated 'video' as a workshop. After a conflict with the leadership over work methods and project objectives, the two workers left Street Aid and the video equipment left too! So much for the video workshop!

The King Street coffee bar had folded in a brief, sharp flash of publicity as the owner locked Street Aid out. At this time, Street Aid was operating more closely with the Covent Garden Community Association, and the coffee bar and the CGCA's playgroup shared premises. The King Street premises were lost forever, but the new initiatives paid dividends and the outfit moved in two directions. In 1974, the organisation acquired the Basement in Shelton Street, which was fitted out as a youth club and opened on a limited scale at the end of the year. Simultaneously, 36 Earlham Street was obtained as the headquarters for the 'sub-humans', and the offices, the print room, the meeting room and the music room cum social area cum kitchen were established. This building, with its four floors, was a tall thin inner-city house, with lots of character but in poor condition. Appeals for renovation monies were heeded, and the top floor was turned into an office, with dividing beams left intact and all the wood varnished a deep brown. The 'sub-humans' lived on the next floor down, and the print room and the meeting room were established on the first floor. At ground-level, kitchen, social and limited teaching areas were set up, and this was the situation until late in 1975. Two doors down the road at 40 Earlham Street, the other 'workshop' activities were sited. Again, the building and renovation work took a fair time, but money was gradually forthcoming and the pottery was equipped with a kiln in the latter part of 1975. Women's studies occupied the two rooms at the top of the building and silk-screen and photographic darkroom filled the second floor. The building was very similar to No. 36, but it was not so well decorated and there was no ground floor because of an entry to the yard. Again, it was, as a whole, not fully operational until the end of 1975.

Intermittent building work, linked to the fluctuating availability of funds, makes the smooth operation of any such voluntary agency difficult. A voluntary agency such as Street Aid, without a clear goal, or perhaps with too many purported goals, naturally inclined towards chaos in the organisation and confusion outside. By this I mean that there were internalised problems developing at two levels. The first level was in the recruitment of staff. Workers were attracted from various fields; some, like David Bieda and Dave Robins, came from the underground press; others moved from formal education to the world of Street Aid on the premise that it would offer them the freedom to operate 'outside the system'. The possibilities of the organisation were real for all the workers, but for varying lengths of time. Regrettably, there was a sense of fantasy, existing as a construct of the staff, which was then supported by the endless reams of reports, grants applications and meetings. It was always, even in the developmental stage, a catch 22 situation; Street Aid could not operate without enlightened, visionary leadership; at the same time Street Aid was in the throes of transition. From 1973 to 1974, the old welfare work was phased out, David Bieda became the pivot of the new organisation, and took on the role of visionary and fund-raiser. The problem for the organisation was the clash between working as a collective or as a one-man enterprise. Many of the staff were politically motivated, most were keen to experiment with alternative ideas and modes of operation. The organisation structure was such that, whilst meetings took place, real power was located in the traditional management post of co-ordinator. Differences between the theory of group management, and an hierarchical structure in practice, created a large proportion of the resultant tensions. It is necessary to point out that whatever the staff involved felt at the time about David Bieda, it is important to depersonalise the problem, at least to some extent, and realise that he was merely playing a role which could have been filled by a number of protagonists. Ideologies were changing, as was the 'free enterprise' between the extremes of capitalist and socialist organisation. Strong leadership, successful fund-raising and internal dissension are, in this context, seemingly inextricably linked.

The expenditure for the year 1974-75 was £37,513. Street Aid had 'arrived', and amid this self-perpetuating helter-skelter, David sat producing visions of youth projects for the future and new gambits for raising funds for these projects. Staff came and left, many were broken by the tension and hyper-tension on which 'Street Aid' survived, and those who got away were pretty embittered by the whole experience.

Street Aid Funding

Explaining how the funding changed is difficult to communicate. From a 'very' alternative agency of the early 1970s, with £700 a year income, David Bieda had done the impossible and transformed Phil Cohen's Frankenstein monster into a Topsy which just *grewed and grewed'*. The projected income for 1976-77 was in excess of £140,000, and most of that had already been granted by the time the seventh news bulletin was produced, early in 1976. And how was this feat achieved? By, as I said before, real flair on the part of Street Aid for raising funds, and a self-fulfilling prophesy. Once the local authorities see their neighbours funding a project, they tend to assume that the said organisation is OK; and from then on the task is comparatively easy, playing off funding organisations as 'competitors'. Every voluntary agency does this — the Scouts are possibly the most successful of all!

The private trust funds were, and are, easily impressed with documentation and the mention of prestigious backers. Like the 'Jones's', they are sombody to keep up with, and since the first grants of money for Street Aid came largely from Camden Council, the Inner-London Education Authority and the London Tourist Board, there seemed to be no question about 'respectability'. This is the world of the patronage system. One grant begets another. The early money was used for the holiday projects, the salaries of the staff (at about £1,000 per year) and the production of *'Use It'*. The money raised from the trust funds was used to aid the building programmes from 1973 to 1974 and to put in the accumulated fund. 1974-75 saw the move into more extensive funding from the ILEA, adding the education department to the Youth Service. Westminster council started to match the money given by Camden, and the Arts Council began to back the concept of the Street Aid 'community arts' programme. The sub-cultural research unit was established under a £5,000+ grant from the Leverhulme Trust; the Chase Charity, Allen Lane Foundation, City Parochial Foundation and the Pilgrim Trust became the main subscribers amongst over 20 sources of income.

In some ways this is only the tip of the iceberg, for much of the Street Aid work was carried on through donations of equipment and services. In the news bulletin these are set out under four headings: building materials, labour etc; fixtures, fittings and furnishings; discounts; and ongoing assistance. In this way, tons of cement and sand, pipes, toilets, fire doors, carpet, lino, elaborate lighting, equipment, chairs, tables, records, hi-fi equipment, a golf-ball typewriter, cookers, alongside free typing, car parking, legal assistance and architectural advice, were all obtained. This was how the Basement youth club and the Earlham Street premises were equipped.

It was a mammoth task to compile bulk and individual letters to trusts and authorities. It included many personal meetings and much production work on appeal documents and reports. The leadership excelled itself in marketing the product. However, all the staff tended to get involved in being one huge publicity machine, and for part of their stay they would also be competing for the next share of the cake.

In the 1973-75 period, there were plenty of reasons for breathing enthusiasm and optimism out of the nostrils. Premises, albeit on a short-lease basis at that time, were forthcoming. The project work, with all its shifts of emphasis down into the Covent Garden area, and with the preoccupation with supplementary and 'linked' education/youth service provision, seemed an absolute hit. With the acquisition of one part of the Market Project in 1975, and the Jubilee hall upstairs area as a sports hall, the Sports Council donated £9,750 for 1976-77. The other grants were all increasing in size as the project became established, thus consolidating its credibility. The ILEA youth service department was expected to give £15,308 for the year 1976-77 and the schools' department had been asked for £17,400. The other big 'coup' of 1975 was grant-aid obtained from the Leverhulme Trust to pay for three workers, two on research and one secretary, for three years. This application provided a good example of how the grant system operated.

The application was couched in 'academic' language, talking about the development of pedagogic style in the youth and education programmes, with research into such diverse topics as European city centre provision and individual school syllabi. Referees for the scheme included Michael Marland, the famous head of Woodberry Down school, and Alderman Ruth Howe of Camden Council. The application also listed other grant-aiding bodies who had already 'coughed up'; ILEA schools, Sir Halley Stewart Trust, Rowntree Social Services Trust and the John S. Cohen Fund were among those itemised. In fact, Street Aid was a very amorphous body, and it might be questioned whether the grantors ever contributed to the particular scheme to which the Leverhulme application referred. The Market Project umbrella was enough to hide all other applications which could be easily encompassed.

A problem which concerns many workers, who are paid for through trust or research grants, is the lack of accountability the organisation which is in receipt of the grant has to the funding trust. This means that once the money is awarded it is regarded as 'allocated', and most trusts do not have the machinery for keeping tabs on the manner in which their money has been used. There is also a feeling that, say, a Leverhulme research grant paid to Street Aid should provide 'a Leverhulme researcher' at the other end of the sausage machine. This is not the case; to quote Leverhulme, 'Street Aid . . . becomes *completely responsible for planning the project, engaging such staff as are needed for it, controlling the grant during that period, and also administering the funds paid to it by the trust'.*

This method of allocating grants totally depersonalises the researcher and obviates any relationship between him and the trust making the award. it also lays the trust open to malpractice, through their funds being re-allocated for projects and items not originally intended. This is especially true when the application is of a diverse and somewhat vague nature. What they were doing was to use the flexibility of the grant awards system to the full.

To end the section on funding, it is interesting to mention, if only in passing, that the changes in policy direction and the internal conflicts which recurred between members of the staff often led to two forms of wastage. One occurred when there were arguments between David Bieda and individual members of staff over the value of their work. Tension can be either creative or negative, and in these cases it usually led to the abandonment of a project area and the resignation of staff members. Out of this frustration, quite a lot of equipment and fittings went 'missing' — keeping an inventory was never one of Street Aid's strong points. The second area of wastage arose when staff left and there was a resultant change in use for an area of the premises. This happened fairly frequently, and there were quite often changes in policy regarding room use, which would also lead to the re-equipping of areas and the buying of new fittings. The Basement was the most susceptible to these winds of change — it served as the focus for pressure arising from a change of policy, because it was the frontispiece of the organisation's activities. With at least five different full-time youth leaders operating in the Basement at different periods of its development, the result was an untidy synthesis of disco facility and coffee bar, small rooms and a table tennis and dancing area. Walls, light fittings and hi-fi systems came and went with alarming regularity.

Covent Garden and Street Aid Policy

This is one of the most difficult areas of this study. It does seem that everyone agrees that Covent Garden constituted, in the early '70s, a 'geographical and social island' marooned in the middle of the West End. There is also no question that the area was at a very low ebb, following on from the exodus of the famous market. Population and trade had fallen off drastically, and the issue under discussion at the Covent Garden inquiry had been whether to ditch the area and redevelop it as a new centre for flats and offices (mainly offices), or whether to allow a new population and a new set of trades to develop in the old trading centre. Even today, the answer to the question has not been resolved. Subsequent inquiries have failed to find an answer which is satisfactory to all sections in the community. 'Sections' in this case implies 'factions', because, as with many political groupings, the internecine warfare within Covent Garden is often more hostile than the war which originally raged between Covent Garden and the GLC planners. The GLC, by setting up the area as a 'development area' and establishing the planning team in their posh offices with smoked glass windows on the corner of King Street, successfully guaranteed a number of more or less permanent jobs. Reports and plans were drawn up and shot down with almost yawn-worthy regularity, and simultaneously the forum was set up as the body for local residents and trades-people to air their views — membership was by election. Similarly, both the Covent Garden Community Association, with its office over the pet shop in Shelton Street, and the Covent Garden Community Centre, which was the ground floor level of the old warehouse underneath which the Basement youth club operated, also in Shelton Street, were set up. Both the CGCA and the CGCC had their groups of 'new'- and 'old'-wave members, and the scandal and vibrant excitement of the area was almost daily transmitted in something approaching a speeded-up version of Coronation Street. The community newspaper added coals to the rumours, charges and counter-charges, and many amateur political careers were thus smashed.

The area is dominated by theatre-land, yet turns an ambiguous face back into its Victorian past, with its high, narrow streets of greying warehouses and the market complex, which in 1975 was still empty with the exception of the ground-level of the Jubilee market, used as a rather poor quality street market. The prospective use of the other old market buildings was still at the discussion stage at this time, but already rumours abounded that the main buildings were to be revamped into arts and crafts boutiques and shops. This now seems to be the future for the Garden, a future which will cause the old residents to wince, for it is the intrusion of swarms of trendy intellectuals into their home that they hate most. New theatres have opened in the Covent Garden and there are large numbers of clothes and craft shops there now. This was the setting in which Street Aid wanted to run its community arts activities, its off-site education workshops and the interrelated youth programme.

The rationale behind the Street Aid policy runs something like this: there are no secondary schools in Central London, therefore the local kids go to schools like Starcross, Islington Green, St Marylebone, Sir William Collins, Pimlico and Barnsbury. These were to be the schools with whom the education team at Street Aid was to operate, which, it was thought, would help to give the organisation a local base in the community. Similarly, it was hoped that those young people who came to Street Aid for daytime classes would come back to the Basement, and later the Jubilee hall, for their leisure and sports recreation. Again, to appease the local community, and thus gain support for the extension of premises, Street Aid adopted the unusual policy of restrictive membership for the Basement club. Only young people living in the 'catchment area' of the four central wards of Camden and Westminster could use the club; that is, those living in

181

Holborn, Bloomsbury, Regent Street and Charing Cross wards. This was an oddly artificial boundary to adopt and, although it made some sense when asking for funds from both Camden and Westminster councils, it made no sense to either the local population, the youth workers at Street Aid, the youth organisations outside or the kids; and it was the kids' 'voting with their feet' that finally led to the philosophy of the project being called into question.

Kids will not travel very far to a youth club; it is a local facility almost by definition, and unless something very specialised is offered which is also very attractive to the kids, they would be unlikely to travel across the centre of London just because Street Aid had given the four central wards as **their** catchment. This indeed proved to be the case, and whatever figures are gleaned from the publicity 'blurbs' of the Basement, the numbers were extremely low, with often as few as three kids attending during a whole youth club session. The reasons for this were evident in two directions. There were 29 youth organisations (excluding the uniformed bodies) operating within the catchment area, and this did not include any school-based provision which may have existed at the schools outside the area — to which all the children went. The population in the smaller, Covent Garden comprehensive development area was very small and unlikely to increase very much before the late 1980s. In the whole of the catchment area there were 4,033 in the 5-19 age range, but in the Covent Garden area there were only 239 in the 5-15 age group and 138 in the 16-19 range. This number was very small, when you consider that it would be divided amongst a large number of competitors in the youth provision market. Also, it was more or less accepted that only about 30% of the youth club age-range (normally referred to as the 14-21 range) would be using the youth facilities at any one time. In the end, the Street Aid catchment policy exacerbated a case in which too many clubs were chasing too few kids. This state of affairs led David Bieda into asking the research and development workers to go out on the street and do some 'detached' work with kids and community groups, so as to more adequately fill the Basement club.

Perhaps this all sounds rather harsh comment, or against the kids in the area. I hope it's not too cynical, but I feel that although Street Aid operated a misguided policy in foreclosing against kids from outside the area, the local community was greatly to blame in being so militant, asking for extra resources for an area which, despite the very poor housing conditions of the Peabody flats, was already relatively over-provided. The over-provision was at the expense of other areas in Inner-London, which were not so well organised and which had not been able to get that political 'clout' together — the 'clout' which was so successfully wielded by both Street Aid and the Covent Garden Forum.

To end this section, it is amusing to note that much of the dynamism comes not from the old population of Covent Garden, people like Jim Francombe and Maria Gibbons, but from the 'new' organisations and groups, who have no more right to influence local affairs than Street Aid. This group of community agitators included Maggie Pinhorn, who worked through the CGCA to operate the Basement film-makers group, and Janet Robertson, who ran the CGCA itself. Together with political groups such as the Workers' Revolutionary Party, they helped to inject just the correct amount of hysteria into a community which had already almost lost it head. However, when talking about a community, it is hard to separate what 'was' from what 'is', and it is all too easy to fall into the trap of becoming fanciful and nostalgic about the 'old days' and what might have been. Covent Garden is a vital and changing area, and the new professionals and artistic communities moving there will give the Garden a new colour and flavour in years to come. With the development of the main market building and the ever-increasing influx of tourists, the character of life in the area is due for more metamorphoses than even the departure of the old fruit and veg' market created.

Street Aid circa Late 1975
Some general information

It was in the early purge of 1972 that Street Aid changed both its staff team and its direction; in 1975, the changes were less dramatic, but were of more import to the destiny of the organisation. The early changes were the product of the need to 'professionalise' the approach, so as to gain patronage through the funding systems. This was also the underlying aim of the 1975 changes which Street Aid set into action. Street Aid was trying to establish the Market Project, and they felt (at that time) that the way to do this was to take on two professionals to head the youth work and education teams. Street Aid needed respectable representatives who could be used to present its case to the ILEA and the local councils. It was becoming clear that these were where the future funds were going to have to come from. The trusts were very useful for supplying 'starter' grants, but it then proved difficult to find supplementary money to continue whatever project had been established. On paper the research and development team was supposed to comprise the two new research workers appointed through the Leverhulme money, plus the co-ordinator and the general administrator. Together these posts made up the planning team, who would '(aid) *continuous discussion of our theory and practice*'. These new workers were also members of their respective youth work and education teams, in order to be able to monitor the workings of these two main areas of Street Aid's operations.

This phase of Street Aid's development was the 'youth and community projects' stage, which resulted ultimately in a crisis for the entire organisation. In effect, it was an attempt to get the work of Street Aid talked about in the national education arena, and the use of the R & D team was an attempt to increase Street Aid's influence; an issue which is different from 'patronage', but in an organisation expanding at about 100% per annum in terms of income, the work of the organisation was thus likely to come in for closer inspection.

On paper the agency was thriving. Everything seemed to point to a straight line of growth, but at the headquarters in Earlham Street all was not well. When Barbara Portwin took up post as education team leader alongside myself, we spent a couple of weeks finding out that the staff, apart from David Bieda and Graham Keen, the general administrator, did not want us to be appointed. There were various reasons for this, many of them very well founded.

The education team was not so much a team as a set of individuals getting on and doing their own thing. These 'things' were a thriving 'music workshop', run by John Russell; a women's studies workshop, which was heavily into the women's movement approach to education; and then there were pottery and photography workshops which were not being used at all. For the youth club, attendance was about 25 per evening, with the majority of these youngsters coming from Stockwell. The full-time youth leader was Jo Green, and she was in sympathy with Anita and Jo who were running the women's workshop. Her style of working was non-directive in the extreme and was, apparently, a legacy of the old full-time worker, Dave Bennett. Add to this group a full-time worker, Ian McNicol, who was appointed as recreation organiser to run the sports provision at the Jubilee hall, and you have the measure of the full-time workers. Most were skilled in some form of alternative education and had taken a conscious choice to come to an agency working as an alternative to the statutory provision in either education or youth work. There were also about ten part-time workers who ran the various drama, silkscreen, dance, cookery and general youth club sessions throughout the week at the Basement and the workshops at 40 Earlham Street.

As well as depositing the 'new regime' of teams and team leaders on the staff, Street Aid continued to put out reports of the work of the teams, often based on future plans rather than present capacity. For instance, the 'Youth work team — general brief', which was used as a publicity 'blurb', stated that the Basement ran 'sports: five-a-side football, basketball and other recreation facilities at the Jubilee hall'. This was not true, ie the Jubilee hall never opened under Street Aid's management. Equally untrue were some of the figures for attendance and frequency of activities held in the club. The performance activities were always stressed as a major feature of the Street Aid approach to youth work. In 'Street Aid News Bulletin 7' it states 'it is even more important for the children themselves to be able to present publicly the results of their work'.

'Bright Lights hit the Basement' was the title of two shows which featured work by youth club members and members of the day-release guitar class. These activities were a lot of fun and those involved got a lot from them, but there was a big question mark hanging over the reason for these shows. Identifying why some action was taken was always something of a chicken and egg problem. With this case in point, 'Bright Lights' had the spin-off value of giving a few kids the chance to perform in what was a very well-equipped 'club atmosphere' in the Basement. Perhaps the primary reason for the event goes back to the need to impress the outside world. Here was a 'product' which could be marketed; so it wasn't young people and their parents who witnessed these spectacles, it was members of the council, trust fund representatives and those with influence. Hundreds of pounds were spent providing wine and food, in the hope that more money could be raised. Some of the pitifully small youth club membership were turned out for the occasion, and the photographic workshop, in the form of the tutor, took lots of snaps which were later turned into publicity material for the organisation. I think that the method **should** be emulated by more youth agencies to get their work publicised, but there are dangers inherent in the competitiveness of free-enterprise youth work.

What it was like to work there

I'm quickly owning up to the fact that this is going to be the most personalised piece in what will sometimes be a subjective account. Here goes, anyway. The building at No 36 was instantly charismatic, if you can say that of a place. You either hated it or loved it. I fell into the latter category. It was the informality of the staff and the exciting possibilities of working in a large complex of buildings, all with massive potential, that spurred me on to accepting the appointment in the first place. There was also the prevailing sense of being in at the 'beginning', even when the organisation was six years old. In fact, it was six years young, because it could afford to create a new project spontaneously. The inhabitants all became part of a kind of fantasy as they negotiated their roles to either try to work as part of the staff team, or to opt out and get on with their own 'corner' of the whole programme. The youth club, lurching in different directions at different points in time, and the women's studies teachers — Jo, and Onya who came back from abroad to take over from her — never allowed any real interference from David, Barbara or myself. In the youth club, the workers didn't want anything to do with me unless I was willing to become a fully participating member of their team. In retrospect, I would have fared slightly better if I had opted that way, but instead I took the research side of the job-brief as the major component. I was also increasingly hesitant in being used to publicise the Street Aid set-up to the formal education and youth work authorities. This created even more heartache for Barbara, who had come from a deputy head and senior lecturer's post to work for Street Aid. This indicates the professional dilemma that can be a part of life in the radical voluntary organisation.

This different approach led to very early clashes with David, as the co-ordinator. We never really did the job which he required, since both of us said that, in essence, the 'Street Aid' which was to be displayed to the local authorities was, in part, a mythical creation, and never had existed. The whole edifice was like something from

Alice's adventures, where reality is a construct of those who are 'out there'. Phil Cohen pinpointed the problem when he said of radical youth organisations, *'there comes a point when the contrast between public affluence and private squalor of an agency becomes an official scandal . . . all money, buildings etc and no kids'*[6]. David Bieda was one of the great entrepreneurs, but there was never any real hope that he would allow sufficient autonomy to any of his staff for them to really make his projects bear fruit. The creation of the public image was almost total, but that was inversely proportional, at almost all times, to the 'togetherness' of the staff team internally. There was most certainly a lack of sensitivity in the staff relations within Street Aid.

On a day-to-day basis, Barbara and myself, coming from the most formalised jobs of anyone on the staff, found the life at No 36 rather chaotic. Firstly, it would only be the two of us who would crawl into work at 10am. There was an understanding that David, Graham (the general administrator), Barbara, the secretary (a post that changed hands pretty frequently) and myself, were to be the administrative backbone of the organisation. But even on monday mornings, when there was meant to be a regular, all morning R and D meeting, Graham would invariably be late and David would often not come at all. The Street Aid and the expansion programmes that existed couldn't be implemented without his knowledge of funding, thus the hierarchy was reified. David was not above reminding members of staff that, although they were technically employed by the trustees, it was he who had raised the money for their jobs and signed their pay cheques.

A reasonable grouse which many of the staff had at the inception of the R and D team was the anomaly in salaries which the appointment of two more bosses brought with it. David himself only received £2,800 per annum and the general administrator £2,200, while the youth leader was paid over £4,000; likewise Barbara and myself. This acceptance of low pay was partly a hearkening back to alternative days of the '60s, when it had been seen as grossly unfair to accept payment beyond the minimum needs of the individual. But there was also the element that a 'private income' helps to keep the creditors at bay. There was a general feeling that the operation of Street Aid had not been satisfactory up to the end of 1975, and that the provision of teams and team meetings might be the answer. The problem was that each member of the staff, as an individual, had a very personalised interpretation of how the teams should function. David and Graham each had the idea that bringing in 'professionals' would be like calling for the fairy-godmother — all interpersonal squabbles would vanish overnight. The other full-time workers were suspicious of David and they really only wanted to be able to get on and run their respective sections of the organisation without outside interference **and** without having to be part of the Street Aid world. On balance, you were safe if you could remain separate from the meetings of the whole staff. The trouble was that this was not at all easy, with panics occurring almost daily, for example, everyone having to work together to organise the fund-raising aspects of 'Bright Lights', or paint or clean a building because an HMI was coming. Another day it might be a member of the council, or the secretary of an important trust, or the press. It was in this twilight world of fears, distrust and near-hysteria that the work went on — only in a lot of cases it didn't! During the end of 1975, and in the early part of 1976, the education classes were poorly attended, and in the cases of pottery and photography they often failed to occur at all. David was annoyed with Barbara because she couldn't organise more secondary schools' usage of the workshops. But, as she rightly said, we had to be sure that our teachers would turn up and be able to offer a valid lesson before selling the courses to the schools. For David, what went on was subservient to the all-engulfing motivation for expansion. He wanted greater stability, so as to produce more applications to establish more workshops and, hopefully, sell the 'Market Project' idea.

Within all of the bedlam there was one oasis of creative insanity; that was the music workshop which John Russell organised for pupils from Sir William Collins school in the daytime, and anyone else who wanted to use it in the evenings. At the end of 1975, John was still having to use the downstairs room (staff social area) as his teaching area in the daytime, and in the evening was trying to operate at the end of the youth club open space. Even with these drawbacks, he was attracting about 50 young people per week. His methods were off-beat, his style was distinctly odd — acting like an intellectual Keith Moon. But despite, or because of, his dress and his generalised lunacy, the kids loved him and, being only 21, he could relate to them in a real and non-patronising way. He was also a very nifty guitarist, with a well-grounded knowledge of rock, jazz and classical forms. He had graduated as a performer from the world of rock to improvisation, performing at the ICA and other experimental venues. A natural teacher, he was perhaps the only one who could turn to a heavy-looking 15 year old, thumping out a Status Quo riff through the Street Aid, ex-Cream amplification gear and say: *I was reading Becket this morning. It's right on'*. Elsewhere things were stagnating. The potential for growth in numbers was limited by the state of the internal dialectics. Staff would get so heated that they wouldn't talk to members of the opposing 'camp' and, rather than settling differences, the 'all staff' meetings served to produce widening rifts. In all, there existed a silkscreen workshop, which was lucky to be used once in two weeks; a photographic darkroom with four enlargers, which was used (for kids) once or twice per week; a pottery room with a large kiln that was used intermittently, perhaps twice a week, then not at all when the teacher, Jill Donald, walked out. The Jubilee hall, the Street Aid sports area, had its recreation organiser but no money, and a policy on usage which was split between Street Aid's use of it for kids, and a local community who wanted it for themselves — a firm did the stone cleaning, and the staff used it with some local adults for occasional five-a-side football, but that was all it was used for through until the summer of 1976. Because of the frequent coming and going of staff, the ILEA youth service department at Camden had some idea of the internal problems, but they were caught in the dilemma of not having the hard evidence to recommend 'un-funding'. Remember that many of the allies of Street Aid were the councillors and big names of the education world, who had been wined and dined and shown round the splendidly-equipped Street Aid buildings. They were rightly impressed by what were ideal surroundings and a fine set of ideals, but the poor use of resources and the siting in Covent Garden all militated against much being achieved.

The meetings which were held during this period were interesting, especially those which concerned the Basement youth club and its catchment area. They serve to show how dissension was widespread on fundamental issues. 'Bright Lights' occupied many of the agenda in late 1975. The budget for food, drink and the staging of this event was £250, and then there was a lot of gear donated. The issue of contracts to staff also caused consternation when it was found that they contravened the government regulations. The catchment area question, which was originally raised by David under pressure from the local community to exclude all but the local kids, resulted in the establishment of the four-wards scheme as a compromise. Jo Green moved from the youth club and was replaced by David Lamont as the full-time youth leader and, at the same time, a salary for a second youth worker was obtained from the ILEA — Peter Mitchelson was appointed. David Bieda used this change of staff personnel to implement the catchment area scheme, and although David Lamont said, on 28th March, that *a clear policy should be defined as to why there should be provision for youth in the catchment area'*, and that it would be useful to have someone providing the team with information on the great variety of projects and schemes being operated around the country in the youth and community field, he also stressed that this should occur *'without being encumbered by the daily trivia of organisation and face-to-face work'*. This was his idea for the youth work R and D worker, but by this time my position had virtually disappeared.

Returning to the catchment debate, the minutes of the youth team meeting of 11th May 1976, prove interesting. At this time the Basement youth club was closed, both for a policy to be worked out and because the offices had been broken into and David Bieda wanted the Stockwell kids banned because of it. Since they were the main users of the club, the Basement had been closed.

David L.: *Limit the membership to the catchment area and localise the base of the provision. Also have provision for those outside the area who are 'activity based', to be given associate membership, controlled through a members' committee.*

John R.: *Wants the music to be independent, with no restriction on the catchment.*

Mary (part-time worker): *Have a non-restricted membership, but stress the recruitment aspect of the work on the local area.*

David Bieda: *When the club is closed engage in contact work throughout the catchment area. Try to implement the original policy. Must be strict at first and only work with local kids, perhaps later building on a firm local base.*

Jo G. (then a part-time worker): *Restriction means a large proportionate drop in seniors especially. The membership question raises the whole question of 'what is youth work?' The decision should be a majority one, then stick by it.*

Mc (recreation organiser): *Try to lay the ghost of whether locally-based club work is viable or not. Must meet the needs of the kids who have been using the club as well. If we show that we can handle the 'outside' kids to the parents, then we can work with both groups.*

Alan: *Why not link up with the social centre space and run two clubs, (1) to meet the needs of the local kids, as defined by the community adults and (2) to utilise the central London resource we occupy. In relation to the wider catchment area, leafleting and recruiting is over-competitive against other clubs.*

Mitch (second full-timer): *Agreed to try out the catchment area but would like a compromise to include the existing kids.*

As a general policy, it was agreed to attempt further development of activities for day-release students in the Basement.

There was no decision reached on the catchment issue. This was a pretty typical meeting in that David Bieda was able to push his implementation of the catchment area policy through David Lamont, despite the obvious dissension of the staff. The Basement remained closed for about seven weeks following this meeting. A new office for the youth work staff was built in the youth club itself, thus freeing them from the Street Aid life at No 36. David Lamont stayed on with Street Aid until about March 1977, and Peter Mitchelson left at about the same time. David Lamont was to return to the Central London Youth Project in the autumn of 1977. It was at the end of 1977 that 36 Earlham Street suffered a serious fire and was closed down by order of the local council because it was dangerous.

The Trustees, the Management Committee and Chaos

If the normal daily life of Street Aid was hard to stomach, then somebody somewhere must have said, 'You ain't seen nothing yet'. David Bieda's main schemes for that period included the establishment of, with as many staff as possible, an urban studies workshop and to obtain the house between 36 and 40 for both this workshop and the guitar workshop. If you read the seventh news bulletin, you might be forgiven for thinking that Street Aid had already acquired No 38. In this bulletin, it is drawn in on the plan of buildings, along with the Jubilee hall (plus a whole list of sports activities) as *'coming into full operation 1976/77'.* The only problem was that, in 1976, the 'Women's Aid' centre was in residence. This group hadn't been paying rent to the landlords, and, therefore, much effort was made to negotiate with them to gain this tenancy for Street Aid. The result was both confused and confusing; one minute the staff were told that the building was 'theirs', the next minute that there were problems. Street Aid was split within, and the strength of feeling from both female staff and some of the male staff against helping to get the Women's Aiders thrown out thwarted the plan. Street Aid did try to find the women alternative premises, but in the end they were out-manoeuvred. The rather 'heavy' women moved out and a more moderate bunch moved in; the result was that Street Aid definitely obtained No 38. However, when the news bulletin went to press, David Bieda knew that No 38 did not belong to Street Aid.

Other things were going wrong as well; secretaries kept leaving and the London Tourist Board refused Street Aid a grant to continue *'Use It'*. There was also the problem of what to do with a recalcitrant R and D team. Since they wouldn't back the policy, then the removal of myself, the pressure on Graham Keen to resign and Barbara's resignation in August 1977 all followed a time-honoured pattern. Frustration was at the root of most disaffection with the organisation. How could you beat the particular system when your own jobs were, in many senses, a fiction? This phenomenon often occurs in ordinary youth club jobs; the local authority would prefer to see the club operating at a very low level, rather than creating problems by developing expansive programmes. Some of the trustees were in their positions through friendship with David Bieda, so they were hardly likely to question his ultimate authority.

The original briefs for the R and D teams were so wide as to be all things to all people. They also made the assumption that Street Aid was an actual living organism. Barbara and myself could have spent three years researching comprehensively any one of about 20 areas of work listed on the 'brief', quite apart from becoming involved in the day-to-day organisation of telephone calls, letters and public relations work. But it was on the issue of not selling Street Aid to the local community that I was dismissed, although it was true that I had not wanted to engage in this section of the work.

The dismissal went to an Industrial Tribunal, which I lost. To throw some further light on the subject, I quote Barbara Portwin who asked of Street Aid at the tribunal:

'Why did an organisation receiving grants of between £80,000 and £100,000 per annum, do so very little work with children — often no more than a handful in the youth club at night and tiny groups with two teachers in the daytime school programme?'

'Why did they entice two well-qualified people out of the statutory sector with promise of 'respectable' research fellowships, only to attempt to use them as a public relations front for the money-gathering activities of Street Aid?'

190

Further to this, Barbara stated that *'to act as a PR man for Street Aid would* (have been) *to commit professional suicide'*.

Graham Keen and I left just before Barbara, leaving, on the full-time staff, only Mac, David Bieda, John Russell, Anita, Onya in the women's studies and the 'sub-humans' (by now in separate accommodation), from the full-time staff of nine months previous. About six part-time staff had also left, plus the seemingly endless succession of secretaries. It was like the aftermath of some recurrent explosion.

The aftermath continued. The wind-up of the original R and D team did little to settle the rifts in the structure. The trustees were becoming worried and the whole super-structure began to wobble. According to the constitution there was a body of trustees who looked after the management of the estate — they had the usual posts of chairman, honorary general secretary and honorary treasurer. Then there was a body called the council, who *'(were) established to assist the trustees in achieving the organisation's objectives'*, and the steering committee, who *'(were to) be an advisory committee to the trustees and staff at Street Aid'*. This, then, was the structure which was ratified at the trustees' meeting on 14th January 1976. It was the trustees who had met and, on the co-ordinator's advice, hired/fired and discussed the expansion of Street Aid over the years. But, as 1976 wore on, the trustees began to worry about their degree of responsibility if the structure crumbled, and they made investigations regarding their mandate to operate, through Bircham and Co., a solicitors' firm. Chris Webb had resigned from the post of chairman of the trustees, and in December 1976 he left Frank Dobson, the new chairman, to pick up the pieces.

Mr Smith of Bircham and Co. wrote to Frank Dobson on the 3rd December 1976, saying *'I understand that the administrative structure of Street Aid is currently in a state of some confusion, partly because the management committee has fallen into abeyance and the trustees have taken over, so far as possible, the day-to-day management of the charity. Furthermore, I understand that there is no record of who are 'ordinary members' of the charity'*.

The letter went on to say that the trustees, under the 1972 constitution, which was still binding, were merely *'custodian trustees'* and *'have no management powers'*, ie merely holding the legal estate of any properties. The management committee was meant to consist of the honorary officers, plus not less than three nor more than six ordinary members. Mr Smith then pointed out that the trustees had been changing their personnel too often, and that there was no limited liability, so that the trustees/management committee were likely to be liable. He added: *'The present constitution has not been implemented, so that it is quite unclear who are the ordinary members of Street Aid, and there is some doubt as to which persons actually comprise the management committee'*.

The letter was a lengthy one, and he said that prior to incorporating a new company, which was necessary, the old management committee would have to be reconstituted; this could then set-up the mechanism to bring about the necessary changes in the constitution. In the meantime, he said, *'the legality of the acts of the trustees or anyone else is in doubt . . . (and) . . . the existing management committee must be prepared to meet and act. If some of the existing members are unwilling to act, the constitution permits the committee to co-opt any persons whatsoever as members of the committee'*.

There then followed one of the stranger episodes in this affair. A document was drawn up listing the new co-options of the committee. This was meant to be discussed at a meeting which took place in David Bieda's flat at the Peabody Estate on the 12th December. The document also ratified David Bieda and Maria Gibbins or Ruth Howe as signatories of the new Street Aid, and Frank Dobson as acting chairman of the new committee. The whole document appeared as minutes of the meeting, and was complete with signatures and a note that David Bieda, Maria Black (nee Bevilacqua), Jean Gardner, John Hartnell and Chris Webb were all in attendance. To end, it said: *'The above resolutions were proposed by Mr Bieda, and seconded by Mr Webb and agreed unanimously by those present'*. Attached to these minutes, by the time the document arrived for public consumption by the staff at Street Aid, were two sheets of typewritten decisions taken by all the trustees who met on 17th May 1976. The papers were headed: 'Street Aid Trustees' Decisions — ratified by the committee meeting dated 12th December 1976'.

Chronologically, the next piece of documentation concerning the management structure of Street Aid was a letter from David Bieda to Mr Smith at Bircham and Co. Things at Street Aid were 'hotting up'. The staff were worried, and the honorary secretary, Alan Spence, had backed them to stop a new management committee being formed without reference to the staff. Alan was very upset with the way staff contacts, and indeed the staff were being treated. The letter of 15th December 1976 to Mr Smith says, *'The document co-opting new members onto the management committee, Mr Webb, Alderman Mrs Howe and Mrs Gibbins, who I have consulted, feel that you should write at once informing the staff of Street Aid of these changes and their implications, with a copy to Mr Spence pointing out that he no longer has action on behalf of the organisation'*. David Bieda then suggested an inclusion for the circular to the staff: *'A clear statement concerning the question of action on behalf of Street Aid, which leaves no room for misapprehension about the consequences of disregarding this resolution'*.

A memo from David Bieda to all Street Aid staff was next on the agenda. Dated the 19th December, this memo appealed to the staff that he was the only person who was trying to get Street Aid operating within the law. He went on to say that the defunct management committee had met and decided: (presented in abridged form)

1 *Action on behalf of the organisation . . . shall be restricted to the acting chairman, or in his absence another member of the committee* *at the absolute discretion of the committee, and the co-ordinator.*

2 *Bircham and Co. to act for Street Aid on matters of constitutional change.*

3 *Mrs M Gibbins or Alderman Mrs R Howe and Mr D Bieda to act as signatories for cheques.*

4 *The decision sheets of the trustees' meetings were ratified. The members of the committee include myself (as original signatory of the constitution), Mr T Hoskyns, Mrs M Gibbins, Alderman Mrs R Howe, Mr D Birdsall.*

The pre-Christmas presents that the staff received were letters from Maria Black, Jean Gardner and John Hartnell, who were on the old management committee, constituted in 1972. You will also remember that David Bieda's management meeting, which passed such a lot of material, took place as minuted on the 12th December. Maria Black said in her letter to Street Aid:

'This letter is a record of my meeting with David Bieda on Tuesday, 17th December 1976. The meeting was arranged so that I could sign two sets of documents . . . I was told that a new constitution was being drafted: Street Aid trust to be reconstituted as a limited company. My signature was required to dissolve the old committee . . . As far as I was concerned, the signing of the documents was a mere formality. Therefore, I had no reason to ask any questions about the documents involved, nor did I examine them in any detail. I was told that the other members of the committee had also signed, or were going to sign, these documents'.

Jean Gardner wrote: 'I was shown a document which bears my signature which purports to be a record of a meeting held on 12th December . . . (at David Bieda's flat) . . . I would like to state that there was no meeting and that my signature was obtained on 14th December at the above address (her home), at the time of signing the only people present were David Bieda and myself . . . I was informed that the document that I was signing was releasing me from any interest in Street Aid, and have since found that this was not the case. Consequently, I feel that my signature is now void as it was obtained under false pretext'. John Hartnell added: 'I was asked by Mr Bieda to sign two documents relating to Street Aid on 12th December 1976. Mr Bieda called at my home at about 9 pm. He told me that the documents released me from my interest in Street Aid. Without reading them carefully, I signed them. I now understand that these documents were in the form of resolutions to a Street Aid management committee. No such meeting ever took place to my knowledge. As a result I regard the signature as being executed unproperly, and therefore not effective'.

What of the background to the hole the co-ordinator had dug for himself? In the summer of 1976, the staff, with one exception, asked for David Bieda's resignation. However, he avoided this by offering his resignation to the trustees, who granted him four months' holiday.

It was when he returned in December, and found the staff still opposed to his 'generalship' that David made his plans to turn Street Aid into a limited company. Christmas passed, and in January he was sacked. Alan Spence took over the reins, and by the middle of 1977 had become the full-time co-ordinator of the project; but problems in all shapes and sizes continued to beset Street Aid.

The major problem was the fight for the name, Street Aid. David Bieda, after being sacked, tried to register 'Street Aid Ltd' as a company, but at the threat of an injunction from the staff at Street Aid, he withdrew his application. Meanwhile, the Street Aid bank account was frozen and David Bieda had the mail re-directed from 36 Earlham Street to his home address. Understandably, feelings ran high. David was chased by two staff members across Piccadilly, and later a brick was thrown through the window of his house. There was also the question of the money due to come from the trust funds, and David is believed to have notified many of the Street Aid trusts that his organisation had changed its name to the 'Central London Youth Project'. Hence the article in *Time Out* on 10th April 1977, entitled: *'From Street Aid to a CLYP Joint'*.

CLYP then, at the end of February 1977, approached the owners of the Basement Club and had the lease transferred from Street Aid to CLYP. The Basement was duly padlocked up and Peter Mitchelson and the kids were unable to use the premises. ILEA's other youth worker, David Lamont, continued to work with David Bieda while the Youth Service tried to make out what was going on in Covent Garden. David Lamont was later withdrawn under the terms of secondment by ILEA, only to return again at the end of the summer after CLYP made a successful application for staffing to ILEA. Whether this placement was permanent or not, I'm unsure. Certainly, CLYP has re-opened the youth club and is pursuing a local policy of use, with 'events' scheduled at weekends.

Street Aid, after considerable hassles in trying to disentangle the management committee constitution, appointed new members in about May 1977. David Robins and Phil Cohen once again got involved in a new Street Aid, under the guiding hand of Alan Spence. Without the youth club, the loss of some of the funds and with a frozen bank account, they had considerable problems. Amid it all, Peter Mitchelson left and John Russell quit from the music workshop, which was a bitter blow. Other staff changes followed in the established pattern of constant change. One of the constructive projects to arise from the new Street Aid was a job creation project, which employed two young architects to work with unemployed youths to build a garden by the floral market. This was opened in mid-October 1977, amid real-ale supping and a rainstorm. Apart from this, the question of whether it was really worth trying to rejuvenate the dying remains of Street Aid came to be uppermost in the thoughts of the newly-formed management committee. Already this has caused dissension and members of the committee have resigned, perhaps fearing a repetition of earlier disasters. Among the resignations was that of Phil Cohen, who would perhaps rather see the ghost laid quietly to rest.

Alan Spence now carries on with the limited premises of 40 Earlham Street. But even now, David Bieda is suing Alan for defamation of character. David Bieda, likewise, continues to run the Central London Youth Project. Mac is still involved in the recreation sports project at the Jubilee hall, but not under the auspices of either Street Aid or CLYP. In all, it is a sad story of under-use and over-capitalisation. The 1960s produced what could have been a really powerful and creative life force in British youth and community work. In some instances, it has succeeded. Street Aid stood as an example of many remarkable visions, including a far-sighted funding policy and a set of interesting, imaginative workers. It is a great shame that it never really fulfilled the promise of things to come.

A Beautiful Dream

The reality and the dream of Street Aid, David Bieda and the Market Project are so closely inter-linked that to extricate the good from the bad is an impossibility. The dream of the Market Project was beautiful; this sort of resource has worked to great effect on the continent, particularly in Holland. But the reality of Street Aid, its history of power politics and its habit of placing entrepreneurial gain before people are not so pretty. The size of the agency got out of control, and eventually the nature of the hierarchy led to insurmountable dispute.

Appendix — The Market Project

Oft quoted through the Street Aid story is the Market Project. It was a magnificent programme, and its implementation would have led to the establishment of an *alternative to commercial leisure facilities* (in the West End)'. The building, which the proposal was geared for, was the Jubilee Market, and the idea was to put all Street Aid's eggs in this one basket. In the basement of the building there were to be general teaching areas; between four and eight specialist workshop areas; the administrative offices and kitchen; upstairs, the large hall was to be used for performance activities; and there were also to be refreshment areas, two shops for use by the local community and what was called a 'library and circulation area'. The plans for its feasibility had been drawn up by architects, quantity surveyors and structural engineers.

In these plans there was no mention of the large hall being used for 'sports-style recreation'. This was an 'about-face', displaying Street Aid's flexibility for 'occupying' any space that was allocated to it. When the Market Project, in toto, was turned down by the GLC, the Jubilee sports hall (to be opened in Jubilee Year — how's that for fortuitous opportunism?) was the compromise. The lease was only on a short-term basis, and it was awarded on the understanding that the area would be jointly administered by Street Aid and the Covent Garden Community Centre. This agreement was also linked to the undertaking of repairs to the fabric of the building, and the necessary conversions and additions. It had been planned to have the building re-wired, painted and equipped for limited opening in the latter part of 1975. This did not transpire.

References
1 **Phil Cohen**, *'Squaring the Circle'* in *Street Aid News*, Street Aid, 1972.
2 **John Hartnell**, *'Towards Alternatives'* in *Street Aid News*, Street Aid, 1972.
3 **David Bieda**, *'Work in Covent Garden'* in *Street Aid News*, Street Aid, 1972.
4 **John Ewan**, *'False Teeth'* in *Street Aid News*, Street Aid, 1972.
5 **Phil Cohen**, *Five Cent's Worth: a Study of an Alternative Youth Organisation in Crisis* in *Aspects of the Youth Question, Working Paper 7*, Street Aid Sub-cultural Research Unit, September 1976.
6 **Phil Cohen**, ibid.

Chapter 13

Crisps and Coca-Cola or Agents of Change?

JOHN EWEN

John Ewen, one of the first detached youth workers in the early 1960s, was subsequently warden of a county youth centre in Essex, training officer for Berkshire and Reading youth service, head of the Youth Service Information Centre and director of the National Youth Bureau. He has recently returned from setting up a new Ministry of Youth Affairs in the Sultanate of Oman, and is currently co-ordinator of youth employment programmes for Community Service Volunteers. His major written contribution has been 'Towards a Youth Policy', published in 1972.

13

Why do we believe a Youth Service is a good thing? Why does the government, and the local authority, support it financially? Why do we as adults work in it? In short, what youth policy underlies our Youth Service?

The United Kingdom has never really had a youth policy. The Youth Service 'growed' like Topsy, and now everybody (or at least some ¼ million of us) is doing it. We could answer the question why in personal terms, and that is the way it is usually answered; for example, because we like being with young people, because we want to help them broaden their experiences, or perhaps because we want to share with them our particular concerns and interests, whether it be in terms of hobbies, pursuits or moral values.

What we rarely do is ask the question in broader social terms — what role has the Youth Service in our society? Perhaps we can only answer that question when we have asked which roles young people can play constructively in our society.

Do we want the young to be replicas of ourselves, and do we want their society to be a replica of ours? If so, then the sort of Youth Service we operate will reflect those desires. It will be a 'beer and skittles' service, filling in the time, keeping them out of mischief; a form of occupational therapy which will contain them until they become like us. It will be a holding operation, distracting them from evolution, let alone revolution, until they accept their status in our quo.

It is a big temptation, in a country which has come through a rapid period of change with the maximum preservation of stability, for the elders to rest on their laurels. Those of us who have seen the enormous expansion and development of the education system, and who have seen the modern welfare state established during our lifetimes; who have witnessed great progress in standards of general affluence, improvements in housing, in working conditions and in many other areas of life, are tempted to become self-satisfied at what has been achieved. The adults who have experienced and witnessed such strides forward have inevitably vested interest in preserving that which they believe they have a right to be proud of.

In such a situation, it is perhaps inevitable that the Youth Service which they offer should be about conformity, a kindly device to contain the young until they have the good sense to recognise the value of 'that which is', It must, therefore, be largely about play, like the bread and circuses of ancient Rome. It must, above all things, avoid such issues as politics, as race, as poverty, for as long as the young are happy with their five-a-side and their discotheques, they are nice young people; not like those hairy students breathing revolution around every cloister corner. So we devise a Youth Service which reflects the beer and bingo conformity of our safe society. Even when the kids are unemployed (as so many of them are now), we offer the daytime opening of the youth club, so that they can play snooker or ping-pong, in case they get into mischief or vent their anger at the odd lamppost.

Another World

It may seem a far jump to another country, on the other side of the under-developed world. But, perhaps by making such a sudden contrast, the point may be made more vividly. Bazimi is an imaginary country, struggling to find the resources to meet vast development needs. She sees the young of her country as her greatest potential force for making the changes which she believes to be right for her people, and so she invests a considerable share of her budget in their education. Bazimi sets out to encourage a developmental role for her young people, confronting them with the challenge of what is possible; deliberately involving them in the processes of change, whether it be in the housing programme, or whatever. The young become the weapon of change. They have a high status in the society of Bazimi, and they have a clear role in that society. But they are not alone in fulfilling it; numbers of volunteers from the developed countries go out to join them. This was the advice of Herr Eppler, the German Minister of Economic Co-operation, to such a group of young people going out from his country:

'Developmental work is a highly political task. The volunteer should know the reasons for the backwardness of his environment; he must be aware of the political, social, cultural and economic consequences of his work. He cannot act alone; he needs the backing of a political and conscious organisation which regards volunteer work as a peace service . . . The volunteer is a peaceful revolutionary, who, by doing practical work, brings about political and social progress without the use of force'.

Bazimi, of course, doesn't exist, but many other nations like Bazimi do. The youth policy of those countries is very different from ours — it advocates not beer and skittles (or perhaps, more aptly, crisps and coca-cola) to the young, but the role of agents of change in the creation of a better society.

Back to the UK and Us

Is it too unrealistic to suggest that our youth policy might have something to learn from those of the Third World? Are we so sure that our achievements of the last 40 years leave nothing for the next generation to improve upon? Are we so complacent as to believe that ours is such a wonderful world, that it is worth hanging onto and preserving at all costs? Or do we see the need to involve the young as a regenerative influence in our society; not as a destructive force, nor as a generation of bored, frustrated or apathetic cabbages, but as a real force for change for the better?

There are moments (often when we need funds for the new football strip from a recalcitrant local authority) when we can lyricise about the value of youth in society, when we embue them with an idealism with which, perhaps, we would ourselves like to be identified. We expect that idealism to be turned on like a tap, for example when we think it would be a good thing for them to make up parcels for the elderly at Christmas, or take the handicapped on an outing. We are often surprised and hurt when that idealism fails to appear, yet we have no right to expect the young to have any more monopoly of idealism than any other age group, so long as it is prescribed by our own definition of the route it should take and the expression it should be couched in. So long as we treat them like junior trainee consumers, to be palmed off with pastimes and potato crisps, it is unlikely that any wish to be involved in regenerative processes in society will emerge.

This is what the Youth Service Development Council was talking about in postulating, as a philosophy for the Youth Service, 'education for active membership of a participative democracy'. Is that really what the Youth Service, by and large, is about at the moment? Is it really what that wednesday evening in the church hall is for? Is it really what the learning of semaphore and tracking is all about? Are we involved in anything more than fun and games? What are we doing which is relevant to life, in what the YSDC described as an urban mobile technological society?

A Transition

Even if we wanted to, we could not make such a massive change of policy overnight. The young are not suddenly going to take on new and dynamic roles because we think it is a good thing to do so. Many of them are themselves so trapped in the day-to-day grind of just about coping with life that they have little steam left for outward-going concern. There is no fear that we should, by the adoption of this policy, release a violent and bloody revolution. It is not revolution we have to fear; it is ultra-conservatism, narrow and frustrated existencies and downright apathy; for those adjectives form a far more representative picture of the state of the young in our society. Read the YSDC publication 'Contact' on the Liverpool detached project; or better still talk with the young people of St. Anne's in Nottingham or Highfields in Leicester. Their lives are confined and limited. We need not worry about making them conform; we should be worrying far more about how we liberate them from their situations.

With these young people, there will be an ongoing need to offer means by which their horizons are widened, their interests broadened, their narrowness of view extended. For many of them we shall need to provide much support — personal, moral and social. But such provision should not remain the only aspect of a two-headed penny. The other side of the coin is to turn them onto society; to help them find solutions to their own problems which, in the process and in due time, will enable them to find constructive and dynamic roles in their relations with others, with their neighbourhood and with society at large. Such a Youth Service needs to be more than just a palliative, a time-out before the realities of life catch up, an escapist fantasy world of popcorn and milk-shakes — it needs to be rooted in the reality of young people's lives. If their school is inadequate or limiting, it needs to help them change it; if their housing conditions are miserable it needs to help them change them; if their jobs are monotonous, repetitive and soul-destroying, it needs to help them to ask why this need be so; if their relationships at home, with their mates, with their boy-or girl-friends are sticky, it needs to help them sort out the reasons — do they lie in me or in others? For, in looking at me and my problem, and in being enabled to resolve it, it may be that I can look at the other man and his problem, and help him to resolve that. Service of youth and service by youth are thus only different faces of the same coin.

A youth policy needs two aims: to protect a vulnerable age group, and to prepare them for an immediate and future contribution to the modernisation of their society. In the UK, we have been too protective, and may be guilty of the charge that, acting from the best of motives, our protection has become an insidious form of paternalistic control. We have done very little constructive work towards realising the second of those aims; in the process we may well have dammed up the potential of youth, and been responsible for the growth of apathy. By denying youth a developmental role in our society, we have left them with no role.

Worse than that perhaps, the very existence of the Youth Service has been a major distraction. The very fact that such a service exists implies that the UK has a youth policy. Yet that service's aims have been so limited, its resources so narrow, that it has had only a peripheral impact, both on the young and on society. It may well be that the Youth Service, as we have known it develop, has served its limited purpose for long enough. It should now be the precursor of a range of co-ordinated and cohesive youth services, which together could offer a valid youth policy; one which offers protection and a role in future development.

Why then are we involved in services with young people? It is not enough to answer purely in terms of personal motivation; rather it is about roles in society. Are you, am I, an agent of conformity or an agent for change — not change for change's sake, but change towards a better, fairer, more caring society? Do we want to reproduce ourselves and our society in the next generation, or are we in the business of enabling the young to share a developmental role in the society in which they will be living longer than we will?

Recommended Reading

The following are not a systematic or comprehensive bibliography (references are given at the end of each chapter), but instead have been compiled jointly by the contributors to this collection as a list of significant titles, published during the 1970s, within the subject areas covered by this volume. Titles are given here alphabetically by author. Paperback editions are quoted where possible, and the place of publication is England except where stated.

N Armistead(Ed.), *Reconstructing Social Psychology,* Penguin, 1974.

R Bailey and **R Brake**(Eds.), *Radical Social Work,* Arnold, 1975.

J Benington, *Local Government becomes Big Business,* CDP Information and Intelligence Unit, 1974.

H Bowles and **H Gintis,** *Schooling in Capitalist America,* RKP, 1976.

C Cockburn, *The Local State,* Pluto Press, 1977.

P Cohen and **D Robbins,** *Knuckle Sandwich,* Penguin, 1978.

Consultative Group on Youth and Community Work Training, *Realities of Training,* National Youth Bureau, 1978.

D Collyer, *Double Zero,* Fontana, 1973.

A Cox and **G Cox,** *Borderlines: a Partial View of Detached Work with Young People,* National Youth Bureau, 1977.

R Dale, G Esland and **M Macdonald** (Eds.), *Schooling and Capitalism,* RKP/OUP, 1976.

B Davies and **A Gibson,** *The Social Education of the Adolescent,* University of London Press, 1967.

DHSS Social Work Service Development Group, *Intermediate Treatment: Planning for Action,* DHSS, 1977.

J D Douglas(Ed.), *Understanding Everyday Life,* RKP, 1974.

M Dungate, P Henderson and **L Smith**(Eds.), *Collective Action,* Association of Community Workers/Community Projects Foundation, 1979.

J Edginton, *Avenues Unlimited,* National Youth Bureau, 1979.

J Eggleston, *Adolescence and Community,* Arnold, 1975.

B Finn, N Grant and **R Johnson,** *Social Democracy, Education and the Crisis* in Centre for Contemporary Cultural Studies, *On Ideology,* Hutchinson, 1978.

R Frankenburg, *Communities in Britain,* Penguin, 1973.

M Green, *Teacher as Stranger,* Wadsworth Press, 1973.

R Grunsell, *Born to be Invisible,* Macmillan, 1978.

J H Gulper, *The Politics of Social Services,* Prentice Hall, 1975.

S Hall et al, *Policing the Crisis,* Macmillan, 1978.

S Hall et al, *Resistance through Ritual,* Working Papers in Cultural Studies Nos. 7 and 8, Centre for Contemporary Cultural Studies, University of Birmingham, 1975.

A Leissner et al, *Advice, Guidance and Assistance,* Longman, 1971.

M Marland, *Pastoral Care,* Heinemann, 1974.

D Marsland, *Sociological Explorations in the Service of Youth,* National Youth Bureau, 1978.

J Matthews, *Working with Youth Groups,* National Youth Bureau, 1978 (Reprint).

I Mildener and **B House,** *The Gates,* Centreprise Press, 1974.

S Millham, R Bullock and **K Hosie,** *Locking Up Children: Secure Provision within the Child-care System,* Saxon, 1978.

Young People and the Police, written evidence to the Royal Commission of Criminal Procedure, National Youth Bureau, 1979.

M North, The Directory of Social Change, *Vol. Two: Community,* Wildwood House, 1977.

J Paley and **D Thorpe,** *Children: Handle with Care,* National Youth Bureau, 1974.

H Parker, *Social Work and the Courts,* Arnold, 1978.

H J Parker, *View from the Boys,* David and Charles, 1974.

A Future for Intermediate Treatment, Personal Social Services Council, 1977.

A Platt, *The Child Savers: the Invention of Delinquency,* University of Chicago Press, 1969.

A Richmond (Ed.), *Readings in Race and Ethnic Relations,* Pergamon Press, 1972.

Teachers and Youth Workers, Schools Council Working Paper No. 32, Evans/Methuen, 1971.

K Robers, *From School to Work,* David and Charles, 1971.

T Rogers, *School for the Community,* RKP, 1971.

C S Smith, M Farrant and **H Marchant,** *The Wincroft Project,* Tavistock, 1972.

J Thomas (Ed.), *National Intermediate Treatment Forum Conference Papers 1977,* National Youth Bureau 1978.

R White and **D Brockington,** *In and Out of School,* RKP, 1978.

G Whitty and **M Young** (Eds.), *Explorations in the Politics of School Knowledge,* Nafferton Books, 1976.

G Whitty and **M Young** (Eds.), *Society, State and Schooling,* Falmer Press, 1977.

P E Willis, *Learning to Labour,* Saxon House, 1977.

P Willock and **J Hayman** et al, 'The School as a Community Centre' in *Youth Service,* Vol. 10, No. 5, 1970.